Make Love Like a Prairie Vole

ANDREW G. MARSHALL is a marital therapist and the author of *I Love You But I'm Not in Love With You: Seven steps to saving your relationship*; *The Single Trap: The two-step guide to escaping it and finding lasting love*; *How Can I Ever Trust You Again?: Infidelity: from discovery to recovery in seven steps* and the *Seven Steps* series of practical relationship self-help titles. His work has been translated into over fifteen different languages. He writes for the *Mail on Sunday*, the *Guardian*, *Psychologies* and women's magazines all over the world.

Andrew trained with RELATE (the UK's leading couples' counselling charity) and has a private practice offering counselling, workshops and inspirational talks.

He has created an app for *Make Love Like a Prairie Vole* with videos explaining each week's activities, to make it easier to introduce your partner to this programme and gain his or her cooperation. More details about Andrew and his work can be found at:

www.andrewgmarshall.com

Make Love Like a Prairie Vole

Six Steps to Passionate, Plentiful and Monogamous Sex

Andrew G. Marshall

BLOOMSBURY

LONDON · NEW DELHI · NEW YORK · SYDNEY

First published in Great Britain 2012
This paperback edition puclished 2013

Copyright © 2012 by Andrew G. Marshall

The quotations on pages 3–4 from *Splendors and Miseries of the Brain* by
Semir Zeki are published by kind permission of Wiley-Blackwell

The moral right of the author has been asserted

Bloomsbury Publishing Plc
50 Bedford Square
London WC1B 3DP

Bloomsbury Publishing, London, New York, New Delhi and Sydney

A CIP catalogue record for this book is available from the British Library

ISBN 9781408830529

10 9 8 7 6 5 4 3 2 1

Typeset by Hewer Text Uk Ltd, Edinburgh
Printed and bound in Great Britain by CPI Group (UK) Ltd, Croydon CR0 4YY

MIX
Paper from
responsible sources
FSC® C020471

www.bloomsbury.com/andrewgmarshall

Contents

Introduction

Sex plays a central role in our lives. It not only makes us feel desirable and loved but also an orgasm is a great physical release and a reducer of stress. Most important of all, sex bonds us to our partner and stops our relationships disintegrating into just being friends or co-parents. It is not surprising that we are fascinated by the subject. Unfortunately, sex is extremely difficult to discuss sensibly, even with our partner – in fact, especially with our partner. First, we don't have the vocabulary without sounding smutty or purely physiological. Second, even an innocent discussion of what we enjoy can be interpreted as criticism by our partner. The whole topic is so full of traps that most couples retreat into silence and hope for the best.

On a national level, the topic is dominated by sex education in schools, avoiding teenage pregnancy and cutting the rate of sexually transmitted diseases. This is seasoned with a prurient interest in the sex lives of celebrities and salacious court trials. To further complicate matters, we are fed unrealistic fantasies and misinformation by the authors of racy romantic fiction and by pornographers. On the subject on which we need the most information – how to keep a loving relationship sexually alive despite the familiarity of day-to-day life, the exhaustion of bringing up children and earning a living – there is a resounding silence.

I am afraid that my world – marital therapy – does not have a distinguished record either. Counsellors have tended to help couples with their emotional issues or referred them to a sex therapist to work on a specific physical problem (such as erectile dysfunction or an inability to orgasm). The first approach hopes that improving communication and helping couples to like each other again will have a positive knock-on effect on their lovemaking. The second concentrates on the physical aspects of sex and downplays the feelings. However, good lovemaking is both an emotional and a physical act.

My ambition in writing this book is to combine my knowledge – gleaned from over twenty-five years of helping couples who have okay but not particularly satisfying love lives – and the structured programmes of sex therapy with the latest research by neurobiologists into our hormones, the pleasure receptors in our brains, and what creates sexual desire.

At the end of each chapter, there is one key task to complete. Although I don't want to be prescriptive – because I believe that deep down you know what's best for your relationship – these tasks encapsulate the main ideas of each chapter and help your partner take on board the underlying philosophy, even if he or she does not read the whole book.

The case histories are based on couples with whom I have worked (their identities have been changed to protect confidentiality and sometimes two or three cases have been merged together) and individuals who have written to my website, filled in a questionnaire or kept a sex diary.

Andrew G. Marshall
www.andrewgmarshall.com

Prairie Voles and Love

Only 5 per cent of mammals are monogamous and form endur-ing pair-bonds, with the male making a significant contribution to raising the offspring. Scientists have long been fascinated to know why some creatures are faithful while others play the field. The breakthrough came entirely by accident. Lowell Getz, professor of ecology, ethnology and evolution at the University of Illinois, was studying why in some years the population of voles would boom and in others it would bust. For twenty-five years, he set wooden traps with cracked corn on the grassy planes of east Central America. In the summer, he covered the traps with vegetation or aluminium shields to stop the voles from getting too hot. His team checked the traps several times a day and tagged the voles by clipping two of their toenails.

The first surprise was not only that he would often find a male and female vole sitting in the traps together but also that he kept catching the same pairs again and again. There was no bedding in the traps, so the voles were not using them as nests for breeding. He concluded that they must spend a high propor-tion of their lives together.

The second surprise was that while Getz frequently found pairs of prairie voles together, their close cousin, the meadow vole, was almost always caught alone. To the untrained eye, these two species of brown rodents – which weigh just thirty grams – are almost indistinguishable, but their lifestyles seemed polar opposites. Getz wanted to study the prairie voles more closely but he was a field biologist rather than a laboratory scientist. Therefore, he recruited a colleague at Illinois University, Sue Carter, who was a neuroendocrinologist and had been studying the effect of hormones on behaviour. Studying monogamy in voles dovetailed nicely with her work.

The prairie vole turned out to be an advert for family values. Getz and Carter discovered that once bonded, only 10 per cent split up, and even more touching – considering that voles are a major food source for foxes, hawks and snakes – after the death of one mate, fewer than 20 per cent of widowed prairie voles acquire a new partner. The male is also a model father and the pups stay in the nest for several weeks after weaning. By contrast, the meadow vole is a real Don Juan. This kind of vole breeds promiscuously. The males make terrible dads and even the mothers abandon their pups soon after birth. These two voles share 99 per cent of the same genes yet have radically different attitudes and lifestyles. So what is it that makes the difference?

Scientists had already been studying oxytocin, a hormone and neurotransmitter (something that relays, amplifies and controls signals around the body) which is made in a mammal's brain. In some species, oxytocin promotes bonding between males and females and between mothers and their offspring. Carter thought that oxytocin might be responsible for making prairie voles settle down and form life-long partnerships. She injected the hormone into females and found they were less picky about choosing a mate and practically glued themselves to their partner. Fascinated by the results, Carter tried the opposite. She injected the females with an oxytocin-blocking chemical and the previously faithful voles deserted their mates.

At first sight, it seems a big leap from prairie voles to humans. Certainly nobody is suggesting there will be a pill anytime soon to make humans faithful. However, the research does show that love has an important biological ingredient – which goes beyond culture and social pressures.

Semir Zeki is a professor of neuroesthetics at University College London, and has conducted research into the primate and human brain: 'Evolution does not proceed by solving problems. This would be too expensive and dangerous a procedure, which might even entail the extinction of a species. Rather, evolution proceeds in such a way that problems are minimised or do not arise in the first place. One way of securing such an outcome is to use a solution that evolution has devised and that has proved to be successful in other domains.' In other words, what works for less socially sophisticated animals will probably still be used in more highly evolved creatures. So maybe the vole brain and the human brain are not so different after all.

In his book *Splendors and Miseries of the Brain* (Wiley-Blackwell, 2009), Zeki combines his physiological knowledge of the brain with a review of art, literature and music over the last millennia to gain a greater understanding of love. The job of the brain is to acquire knowledge which it processes in two different ways: inherited and acquired. We are born with the inherited concepts (which are almost impossible to ignore, disobey or discard) but the acquired comes from a lifetime of experience (and can therefore be continually modified and updated). Zeki's most interesting idea is that our guiding principles about romantic love are inherited: 'There is a universal element dictating these experiences that varies little, if at all, from one culture to the next or with time. According to the evidence that we obtain from reading the literature of love, the fundamental concept behind the emotion of love – that of "unity-in-love" – is also immutable.' It is this inherited understanding of romantic love that compels us towards passionate sexual relationships, as intercourse is the nearest that we can get to merging with another individual. We pursue this union with such a force because it is biologically ingrained in our brains.

However, sex in long-term relationships is seldom simple and straightforward. Although we prize the bliss of an orgasm and every couple is committed to great lovemaking, something is stopping us from reaching our goal. Sixty per cent of the UK population is dissatisfied with their love life (Source: Durex research, 2009). Only 55 per cent have sex on a weekly basis – in comparison with 70 per cent in France, 80 per cent in Russia, 82 per cent in Brazil and a massive 87 per cent in Greece. Fortunately, it is not all bad news. While the frequency of our lovemaking is low (only Americans and Japanese are less likely to have sex), our enjoyment levels are in the middle of the league table and higher than the Italians, the French and the Germans. So why does desire and commitment to our partners not turn into more satisfying and frequent lovemaking?

In other words, how can we make love like a prairie vole?

Step One:
Understanding

We have a very clear picture of what good sex should feel like: exchanging loaded looks, the building desire, the intimate touch, the lingering kisses as two people give up control and surrender to each other. For a few blissful moments, you are not alone but united in giving and receiving pleasure. In your lover's eyes, you have become supremely desirable and that makes you feel powerful and at peace with yourself. At the same time, you're offering the same gift to your lover. All your everyday problems melt away as the feelings build and build into a long and satisfying climax. Afterwards, you lie in each other's arms as your breathing slowly returns to normal . . . But what happens to sex after the lust wears off? At this point, the picture either blurs or gets very depressing.

We have no real sense of how our lovemaking changes over time – beyond myths such as: 'Put a penny in a pot every time you make love over the first twelve months; take a penny out every time after that and you'll never empty the pot.' No wonder, so many people are terrified of settling down (as who would willingly give up the transforming power of an orgasm or the afterglow's gentle balm to the soul) and so many people launch themselves into dangerous, painful and destructive affairs.

However, sex does not have to go from a tidal wave of lust – sweeping all before it – to a gush and then a trickle. It flows through six different stages, each with its own pleasures, problems and rewards.

Six Stages of Lovemaking

Sex means different things and has different jobs in your relationship at different points along your journey together. Understanding your stage and its particular challenges is the key to passionate and plentiful lovemaking.

Lustful – first six months

Lust narrows the distance between us and an attractive stranger, so we have the courage to cross the room and say hello, and provides the impetus to turn an acquaintance or friend into something more. Without lust's power, it is doubtful that we'd have the nerve to get naked, touch each other and fuse our bodies together.

Lust provided the spur for Jeff, twenty-five, to ask out his future wife: 'I used to park my motorbike at a mate's garage. I often went round for a spin to unwind after a hard week. On this occasion my friend wasn't there, but his new female flatmate answered the door. She invited me in for coffee and we sat in the kitchen and talked and talked. All the time, I hoped my friend wouldn't come back because I knew he had designs on her too. My tongue would be talking about the weather or something, but my brain would be thinking: How can I get her? Suddenly, I had this inspiration: "Do you fancy going for a burn-up together?" Having a normal pillion is nice but a sexy girl . . . and when she's your mate's eighteen-year-old flat-mate that just adds to the edginess.'

Women are just as responsive to lust as men, although traditionally they have been the gatekeepers to sex and supposedly less under its spell. 'This fireman dropped by the office where I work, he'd been looking for the building super-visor. He smiled and I literally felt all light-headed and giggly,' explained Samantha, thirty-one. 'He stayed by my desk a moment longer than necessary and I asked his name, so I could tell the supervisor, who'd been looking for him – noth-ing more, honest. When he left, I ran round to the front of the building – which looks over the car park – to see if he'd brought his fire-engine. Disappointingly, he hadn't. At just that moment, he looked up and caught my eye. Perhaps it was the uniform, perhaps it was pure lust, but I sort of waved. Instead of getting into his car, he strode across the car park, came back upstairs and asked me out on Friday night. We spent the whole weekend in bed.'

Although there may be a strong physical connection with the object of our desire, and the possibility of an emotional connection too, lust is actually very inward-looking – more about ourselves and our personal fantasies than the other person. Looking back on her weekend of hot sex, Samantha admitted that it had been more about her desire to be rescued (her divorce had just come through) than laying down the foundations for a relationship.

For Jeff, however, the bike ride was the beginning of a three-year courtship: 'She was completely different from anybody I'd ever met, it was exciting and I was living on pure adrenalin. Her father hated me, thought I was a Jack the Lad. We came from different worlds. Could she love me back?'

Problems: Lust makes us blind to both the weaknesses and the strengths of a budding relationship. At one end of the scale, it can bind two totally unsuitable people together. At the other, when lust wears off, two lovers with a perfectly viable future will start to doubt themselves. This is especially common for people who've had a difficult childhood; although they might allow someone to become physically close, they find it hard to translate this into an emotional intimacy.

Tip: Look back over your past relationships and understand the patterns. Have you had a series of short-term affairs? When the lust wore off, did you worry that you had made the wrong choice and start looking for the right person all over again? If this is the case, talk to your current partner about your feelings – rather than going cold and distant – and look for solutions to your fears and anxieties. If lust has bonded you with a string of unsuitable men or women, try waiting a bit longer and getting to know potential partners before sleeping with them. (There is more about making good relationships in another of my books: *The Single Trap: The two-step guide to escaping it and finding lasting love.*)

Bonding – six months to three years

While lust is all about claiming and possessing – however fleetingly – the other person, this next stage is about building a durable relationship. Instead of your beloved being a walking, breathing, sighing embodiment of your fantasies, he or she is emerging as a real person – with all the complexities this involves. Sex can also become more complicated, as two people's individual sexuality (how someone likes to be touched, what turns him or her on, whether he or she is more sexually responsive at night or in the morning) is fused into a couple sensuality (what a couple enjoy doing together).

Sheena, thirty-two, had been so swept away with the passion of her early lovemaking to Christopher, thirty-one, that she had been carried over some of her personal boundaries. 'I'm not really comfortable about being touched in intimate places,' she explained on her first session. Like many people, Sheena did not have the words to discuss sex and used a variety of euphemisms or dropped hints hoping that Christopher would understand. (For more on talking about sex, see my lexicon of lovemaking in the exercise section.) I asked Sheena a few questions and identified that although she had agreed to oral sex at the beginning of the relationship, she had changed her mind. 'I didn't mind so much to start off – it felt nice and I didn't want to upset Christopher – but when I'd had a chance to think, I wasn't so sure,' she explained. Meanwhile, Christopher was not only unaware of these reservations but also hadn't realised that she had not enjoyed giving him oral sex: 'I was so turned on that one touch with her tongue and I almost came, so I didn't really clock that she wasn't that keen.'

Fortunately, Sheena's feelings about oral sex – 'I think it's dirty, I can't help it, that's just the way I am' – did not prevent the couple from bonding. After all, as Christopher said: 'There're plenty of other things we enjoy in the bedroom.' However, oral sex did remain an issue – especially as it had been a part of their lovemaking, albeit briefly, when they first met.

Problems: Some people find that the closer they get to their beloved, the less they desire them. It is almost as if they have separated love and desire into two separate boxes. Some couples discover that once lust has worn off (along with the physical overwhelming need to possess the other person) it is harder to find a way from their everyday life together into the sensual world of lovemaking.

Tip: Rather than telling your partner what you don't like – which will probably make him or her defensive or clam up – focus on what you do enjoy and try building on that. Start by talking about an occasion or a time when things went well and then look at what you can learn from that experience and how to incorporate those lessons into your lovemaking today.

Settled – three-plus years

While lust is based on surprise, the unknown and novelty, settled sex is about security, comfort and stability. While bonding sex is about spanning the distance between the 'me' of two individuals into the 'we' of an established relationship and discovering the real person behind the fantasy (which can be a source of anxiety), settled sex is both reassuring and safe.

On one hand, it is good to be able to relax and worry less about what our partner thinks. Sheena, for example, started to allow Christopher to leave the bedside light on while they made love: 'I know he loves me and accepts me, so I've started to worry less about how I look.' Christopher was also able to admit to his body issues too: 'I stopped leaving my T-shirt on when we went to the beach – to hide my love handles – and didn't think I had to hold my breath in the whole time I made love.' The previous negotiation and conflict over what will be and what will not be part of your lovemaking is replaced by an acceptance of what you do both enjoy and a greater knowledge of each other's bodies. However, this sense of security and being sure of each other can easily tip over into taking each other for granted. Instead of setting aside time for your erotic needs, it is easy to demote them and prioritise cleaning the kitchen, checking emails or watching a late-night television programme.

At this stage, sex is about making us feel complete human beings. Imagine a spectrum with 'control' at one end and 'surrender' at the other. Modern life stresses the importance of taking charge of our destiny and technological advances offer us the opportunity for more and more 'control' over our environment. Meanwhile, we have downgraded 'surrender' to an afterthought, a luxury, something that can only be enjoyed after the serious job of earning a living, getting a pension and doing our chores is completed. However, control and surrender are equally important and sex is one of the few places where these two different needs can be reconciled.

Strangely enough, the best way to illustrate how control and surrender can coexist is to look at the history of ship-building. Wooden ships had to be regularly taken out of the water and patched to stop them from leaking. When technology improved it became possible to make ships that didn't expand and shrink as much as the wooden ones. In theory, greater control over what happened to the ships in the water and under different weather conditions should have been a huge step forward. Except that these new ships were a disaster. They were too rigid and, under stress, would crack apart. So boat builders went back to ships that didn't quite fit properly; ships that could flex. In effect, the best vessels *surrendered* to their environment and allowed themselves to be moved by circumstances. No wonder, with our current emphasis on control and refusal to surrender, that so many of us have mental breakdowns or are floored by depression and forced to give up our obsession with controlling everything.

Our grandparents' generation had the benefit of being religious, and faith offers many opportunities to surrender – either by giving up control to a higher power or through communal worship (where each member of the congregation is no longer an individual but part of something bigger). Considering that surrender is a basic human need, it is not surprising that our society faces a huge increase in the abuse of alcohol and drugs (which temporarily allows us to let go).

However, there are two other kinds of surrender which can fill the gap in less damaging ways. The first is art – in the broadest sense of the word. We can sing in a choir, join a band or go dancing and submerge ourselves in something greater than ourselves. We can also be carried away and forget our own lives by identifying with the characters in a good book or sit back and enjoy the narrative drive of a blockbuster movie. The second source of surrender, of course, is making love.

That's why my aim in writing this book is to show how to be truly in the moment while having sex, so that you forget your everyday concerns, completely let go, enjoy an orgasm and – having stepped away from the modern mania of being in control (if only for a few minutes) – bask in the joy of feeling complete.

Problems: Settled lovemaking can easily tip from safe into predictable and all the anticipation and passion heads out of the door. There is an added danger that by this stage in your relationship, you imagine that you know everything about your partner (closing your eyes to his or her true complexity and only seeing what reinforces your own picture). Worse still, we can imagine our partner's character and tastes are fixed and therefore believe change is impossible.

Tip: Shake up your lovemaking by surrendering to the creativity of play – tease each other, chase each other round the house or get messy together. Use the whole house and not just the bedroom. Life and sex in particular does not have to be always serious and 'grown-up'. Allow your inner child off the leash, access his or her imagination and return to a time before you started censoring yourself with 'don't be so silly'.

Parenting

Trying for a family can empower your sex life: there's no longer any worry about getting pregnant and the biological drive for a baby can throw up lots of lusty lovemaking. No wonder both men and women often look back at this time with fond memories. Falling pregnant can also provide a boost to a woman's self-confidence, self-esteem and sense of her own femininity. I've counselled many women who have finally made peace with their body, enjoying their new curves and revelling in the miracle of creation – especially if they had teenage eating disorders, self-harmed or were sexually abused. Some men find their partner's bump and the proof of their own fertility a real turn-on. With all the emotions closer to the surface, couples can grow closer and bond more deeply – even if making love happens less frequently than before.

Unfortunately, the opposite can also be true. Infertility issues can transform lovemaking from an adventure into a chore. After conception some couples worry about harming the baby during sex (not a problem unless there is a history of miscarriage, low-lying placenta, bleeding or a cervical weakness). In addition, morning sickness, the problems of finding a comfortable position in bed for lovemaking and the general messiness of pregnancy can take its toll. In a survey of 3,000 mothers-to-be, 40 per cent found it hard to feel sexy and 20 per cent were convinced their partners had lost all desire for them (babywebsite.com, 2008). For some men, watching their partner give birth and breastfeed can have a serious effect on their libido, as her vagina and breasts are transformed from sources of fun to something functional.

Mike, forty-two, and Jenny, thirty-five, found sex went from 'exciting' to 'just get it over with' after their daughter was born. By the time they decided to come for counselling, when their child was three, Mike was feeling so unloved and undesirable that he had threatened to move out. Not surprisingly, Jenny felt under attack: 'I'm trying my best but when Mike comes at me "all hands", it can be a bit overwhelming. You see, my mum never cuddled me as a kid so I can find that sort of intimacy tough.' Mike cut in: 'You should be flattered that I still find you so attractive.' Their sex life had deteriorated after a miscarriage five months ago. Unfortunately, they had not really talked about this experience together and Mike was not aware that Jenny still had feelings of grief. So my first job was to talk about the biology of desire and how women seldom feel spontaneously horny in the first eighteen months after the birth of a child. This is particularly problematic when couples have two children under five, as not only are both parents exhausted, but also the woman's hormones have only just begun to recover before she is pregnant for a second time. Mike had thought that Jenny's lack of interest was personal: 'I'd thought she no longer fancied me, didn't want me and I'd begun thinking: "What's the point of carrying on?"'

Problems: Babies bring out the protective side in everybody. We want to hold them, hug them and bounce them on our knee. We blow on to their bellies and nibble their toes. They smell wonderful. Just handling a baby, changing their nappies and caring for them provides lots of skin on skin contact. No wonder some women say: 'I'm not interested in sex' – the bond with their baby is providing all the validation and human contact that normally comes from sex with a partner.

Tip: Make your bedroom a loving refuge and put a lock on the door – if there is an emergency, your children can knock. This will not only allow you to make love without the fear of being interrupted but will also teach your children an important lesson for when they grow up: parents should never forget that they are lovers too.

Personal reinvention

For most people, personal reinvention happens around forty years old but it can be anywhere between thirty-five and fifty. The increased confidence that comes with getting older, and a better sense of who we are, makes us less likely to do what is expected of us and more likely to do what is right for us. Naturally, this confidence spills into our sex lives and many people find new ways of expressing themselves. Hopefully, these changes are done as a couple but if communication has broken down or someone views their husband or wife as an obstacle rather than a partner for change, this can be a time of affairs and relationship breakdown. Even in the best relationships, there are challenges and worries. The compromises forged during the Bonding stage – where a couple created a joint sexuality of what they enjoyed together – need to be revisited and refreshed. After all, however pleasurable lovemaking might be, if it is performed in the same way, over and over again without any changes, the shine is bound to wear thin.

Paul, forty-two, had always been a gentle and considerate lover and that was perfect for Susie, thirty-nine, when they first met in their early twenties: 'I was just out of university, rather shy. I'd had one or two boyfriends – nothing serious. So it was important that Paul took his time and really wooed me, but I'm no longer that person.' Susie had worked hard, gained promotion and headed up a team of six people. 'They're always coming to me and asking, "Should I do this?" or "What about that?" So when Paul and I are lying in bed and he asks, "What can I do for you?" I want to scream – and not with passion!'

'So what kind of lovemaking would you like?' I asked.

'I want him to be forceful, take charge,' she replied.

I could tell she wanted to say something more, so I nodded my head encouragingly.

'I have this fantasy where this burglar breaks into the house and ravishes me in a hundred different ways.'

'And that makes you feel desired and sexy? A grown-up woman who can not only take care of herself but can also reduce an intruder to a quivering wreck – in the best sense of the word?' I asked.

It was finally Paul's turn to talk: 'Why didn't you tell me?'

Susie looked embarrassed, partly about confessing her secret fantasy and partly at how hard it had been to tell her husband that she fancied mixing things up.

They returned the next week wreathed in smiles.

'It was great to take charge, let myself go,' said Paul, 'none of my normal dropping hints or wheedling for sex. I ordered her to strip. When we started, I was worried that I might be hurting her or being disrespectful but Susie was moaning with pleasure.'

Again, I could tell he wanted to say something more. He looked shyly at Susie.

'In my head, I was that burglar – enjoying myself and not caring what she thought – really pounding away.'

For some people the changes in their middle years are more profound than just mixing up their normal lovemaking or discovering new things to do in bed. For Alastair, thirty-eight, he had to come to terms with his attraction for other men: 'When I was in my late teens and early twenties, I was basically horny all the time so I had no trouble responding to my girlfriend's overtures. Sex wasn't really at the centre of our lives but it was fine. I worked in a very macho environment and my parents were very traditional. My girlfriend and I loved each other and I was able to ignore my feelings about other men, so we decided to get married.'

One of the great advantages of being young is that there are so many opportunities, we have plenty of time to explore the different possibilities and lots of doors are open to us. Unfortunately, this is also the disadvantage of youth: it is easy to be side-tracked into relationships or jobs that other people believe are right for us. 'Not a day goes by when I don't think about her or miss my wife. It wasn't right what I was doing to her but that doesn't change how much I loved her. It really broke me up to see her suffering but I knew I could no longer lie to myself,' said Alastair. Eventually he stopped having affairs with men behind her back, told his wife about his sexuality, and they split up.

Problems: Our fears about ageing and loss of sexual potency often tips the reinvention phase of lovemaking from a difficult bump in the road into a complete block. Many people jump out of a perfectly good relationship terrified that this is their last chance for happiness. Ironically, they end up leaving at the moment when the best lovemaking is just within their reach.

Tip: If your partner is asking for change, it is easy to become frightened and panic. Instead of becoming defensive and 'talking up' your joint sex life, use your partner's honesty to look at your own feelings about sex, what it means to you and how your joint lovemaking can be improved. Next imagine, for a second, that every word your partner is saying is true – at least from where he or she is standing. Ask plenty of questions and check out that you've heard his or her message correctly. Finally start to negotiate about both your visions for a reinvented sex life and what experiments you'd like to try.

Glory days

If you have successfully negotiated your mid-life personal reinvention, you're ready to reap the benefits – especially if you and your partner have been together for twenty-five years or more and have really got to know each other. Contrary to popular belief, sex is not just for the young, beautiful and horny. For truly satisfying lovemaking, you need to bring the whole of your personality – not just your genitals – so the extra self-knowledge that comes with age and experience is a real asset. That's why many of my clients in their fifties and beyond are having the best sex of their lives. The great advantage of being older is that you are less likely to be trying to prove yourself. Sex is simply a source of pleasure rather than a way of bolstering your ego or getting reassurance. While previously the focus has been outward – into career and child rearing – time and energy can now be devoted to each other and sex no longer has to be the last thought of two exhausted people.

James, fifty-one, had been a high-flying lawyer but decided to take a step sideways to a less pressurised job: 'When I was growing up, I had a deep fear of things not going right. I couldn't just pass the exams, I had to come top or at least in the top three of my class. This fear of failure and this desire to impress other people carried over into my career. I'd be away a lot. My marriage suffered because I was always exhausted or working – even on weekends. I missed the first half of my fortieth birthday weekend in Antigua because I was closing a deal in London. I just attached so much importance to everything, because if I didn't get it right, there was this incredible doom looming behind it.'

It took the death of his father – a similarly driven man – for James to stop and take stock. 'I realise I hardly knew him. I was angry because he'd cut himself off from everybody – even my mother and his second wife. Nobody knew him. Then it hit me, sitting by his hospital bed: I was looking at myself twenty years down the line – or maybe less, the way I was working.' So how had this revelation affected James's love life? 'I don't try to live up to the expectations of being the best at work or at play and ironically, when I stopped trying, I had this huge weight lifted off my shoulders, and I started to enjoy sex more. I don't know what my wife thinks but I think it's brought us much closer.'

His wife, Marie, agrees: 'Beforehand, sex was fine but I always felt like it was another thing he had to tick off – like going for a run or catching up with emails. Now he's actually one hundred per cent with me and that makes everything that much deeper, more connected. The other night, after we had made love, he cried and I held him in my arms: "What's the matter?" I asked.'

James took up the story again. 'All these dark feelings came up, all these regrets, why had I put so much energy into pleasing everybody but the very people who really counted?'

'You're here now and that's what counts.' Marie took his hand.

They were truly in the glory days of their relationship.

Growing older for Donna has been liberating and, in her late forties, she is having better sex than ever before: 'In my body, I feel free. It might not be so nice to look at, but I've stopped worrying about what I might look like from this or that angle – and that's wonderful. I would definitely say I'm enjoying myself more today than twenty-something sex, when I felt under pressure to do what was supposed to be exciting (like dressing up) and what my husband expected (like groaning in the all right places) rather than what I wanted.' But, as Donna admitted, at that age, she had no idea what she wanted outside the bedroom, so what chance did she have of expressing her true sexuality? 'In fact, I'd describe my twenties' sex as porn star sex.' So what has brought about the change? 'I feel very safe in my relation-ship – my second husband and I have been together for twenty years and we know each other inside out. The kids are grown-up, life is less of a struggle, and a lot of my friends are reporting the same thing: they're feeling much hornier. Perhaps it's something about approaching the menopause and the change in hormones, but I'm finally into sex. I take it as a gift from mother nature.'

While some people think familiarity breeds boredom, the opposite has been true for Donna: 'I feel able to experiment, push my boundaries and try different things – like playing with toys and anal sex – which my twenty-something self would have thought disgusting and perverted but which I find really exciting.'

Richard, fifty-one, is embarrassed to admit to some of his twenty-something hang-ups. 'I thought men should be in charge in the bedroom, so when my girlfriend started writhing under me during intercourse – thrusting up to meet me –

I thought "Hang-on, that's my job" and would stop until she was still again. How stupid is that? She was really enjoying herself and instead of revelling in how she could lose herself in the pleasure of the moment, I was worrying that she might guess that she was my first lover. In those days, I could ejaculate up to three times in a row – resting for a moment and then starting intercourse again – but I don't think we ever really connected because I was an insecure control-freak.'

'I was brought up to be very goal orientated,' says Philip, fifty-five, 'I spent so much time trying to influence things that couldn't be changed.' Fortunately, he had stopped being so 'outcome focused' and this had revolutionised his sex life. 'I had to give my wife an orgasm and if I didn't come myself – that was a terrible failure. So I'd stay over my side of the bed – unless I was sure of delivering. Nowadays, our lovemaking is more leisurely, more cuddles and less goals. It's so much better.'

Problems: If a couple have not mixed up their lovemaking during the reinvention stage, it is likely that one or both partners will be bored. Often, in counselling, one partner will admit to being afraid of showing their inner lustiness – for fear of being judged or rejected – only to find that their partner has similar inhibitions. They are caught in a double bind as it's hard to let go with someone who is buttoned up.

Tip: Although your current comfort zone feels safe, too much safety can kill desire. So take a small risk and test to see if your fears are correct. Will your partner really be so shocked? You might be turned down, and that's unpleasant, but could you handle a small amount of rejection – especially as you've only taken a small risk? Ultimately, nothing is worse than the helplessness of just lying back and accepting the status quo.

How is Your Relationship Outside the Bedroom?

Whether you've been together a few months or many years; whether your love life is good and you're looking to make it even better, or poor and you're seeking to improve it, you should put sex in the context of the rest of your relationship. If there are unresolved issues, or one partner feels taken for granted, the general unhappiness will slowly seep into the bedroom and however good your technique or overall sexual compatibility, the passion will drain from your lovemaking. This is why I always ask couples coming into counselling about sex – even if they seek my help for other reasons – as boredom and dissatisfaction are key indicators of buried conflict or avoidance of pressing problems.

When your love life is routine or infrequent, it is easy to blame outside factors: 'We're so busy', 'It's the children', 'We never seem to go to bed at the same time' or 'All marriages go through bad patches'. Few couples want to look much deeper and either resign themselves to 'okay' sex or resolve to try harder. Accepting okay sex can take the pressure off and stop couples blaming each other. Trying harder will sometimes improve lovemaking for a while but, before long, everything settles back into the same patterns. So what's really going on?

Glenda and Graham were in their late forties. He had a successful accountancy business, where she worked as office manager, and their daughter had recently left home. Financially secure and with no significant responsibilities, it should have been a great phase of their lives, but they were both unhappy. 'I feel like a spectator in my own life,' explained Glenda, 'all these things are happening but I'm not really involved.' Graham was equally puzzled: 'I always thought that once our daughter was off our hands, we would start putting each other first but somehow it doesn't seem to happen. We're always doing things for other people.' Their sex life had ground to a halt, partly because Glenda had had a hysterectomy three years previously and partly because neither felt comfortable having sex when their daughter was in the house. 'It's stupid because her boyfriend would often stay over and I've no illusions about what they got up to,' explained Glenda, 'but I just can't relax.' If Glenda's health and their daughter had been the real reasons why they made love only two or three times a year, they should have already made significant progress. Instead, they felt despondent and stuck.

So I looked at their general communication. 'I feel Graham undermines me. He's always telling me what to do,' explained Glenda. Naturally, Graham saw things differently: 'I only want what's best for you.' Glenda countered this with an example: 'I have never been a very confident driver and I started driving less and less – letting Graham do the lion's share. However, I told myself "This has got to stop" and so I took advanced lessons and passed. On our first trip out together, he told me to "look out for that car pulling out from the left" and that was it. I've not driven since.' It soon became clear that Graham's interventions were meant to be helpful, but because he found it difficult to express his emotions, he would behave like a professional accountant – detached, cautious and aware of every risk – even at home. For Graham and Glenda to be intimate in the bedroom, I needed to help them dismantle the barriers that they had erected to protect themselves in their day-to-day lives before they could work on their sexual problems.

In my experience couples who are dissatisfied with their love lives fit into one of five patterns.

Friends rather than lovers

The modern trend is for our partner to be our best friend too and therefore supportive, endlessly understanding and prepared to accept us as we are. That's all fine in theory, but being best friends makes it harder for a couple to argue – because friends don't have blazing rows. In the meantime, longer working hours and fewer people playing sports or belonging to clubs means that most of us have a smaller circle of friends and see them less often. These changes have reinforced the central importance of our partner and with all our emotional eggs in one basket, it is doubly difficult for us to argue or fall out with him or her. However, it is impossible for two people to live in close proximity without conflict but to stay friends; these couples 'agree to differ' or suppress their annoyance, irritation or anger.

Unfortunately, we can't pick and choose which feelings we push down and which we express. So there might not be any arguments but there is not much lovemaking either – this is because anger, passion and desire are all part of the same continuum.

Graham and Glenda certainly fitted into this category: instead of letting their anger come to the surface and creating the sense that 'something must be done', they had settled into a superficially friendly relationship but one which hid the issues under the surface and was largely devoid of sexual passion.

Tip: Desire needs space as well as closeness, so make certain that there is time for both of you to pursue separate hobbies and interests. Another way to step back and see your partner as a separate person (rather than as your other half) is to witness him or her in his or her world – for example, picking him up for lunch (and seeing the respect in his colleagues' eyes) or watching her give a conference speech (and listening to the applause). Being aware that other people find your partner interesting, capable and maybe even fancy him or her will rekindle those same feelings in you.

Separate tracks

While some couples are too close and turn into brother and sister, others are too far apart and they become strangers. These partners are on parallel train tracks, aware of each other's movements, waving as they pass in the kitchen, but seldom getting really close to each other. In my experience, there are normally three different scenarios that prompt separate tracks relationships.

First, couples with fundamental differences which cannot be reconciled. For example, Matt, thirty-nine, and Karen, thirty-six, who had been in an on/off relationship for ten years. 'When I look back, I wonder if we're right for each other,' said Karen in their first joint session. 'I want to settle down and have children but Matt has never been ready.' Over their time together, the closest they had come to living together was Matt renting a flat around the corner from Karen.

'But I did spend most of my time round your place,' said Matt.

'Except you never had your mail sent to my place and if we had a row, you'd disappear back to your bolt-hole.'

The couple had split up and come back together several times.

'I'll think I've seen the last of him, and I'll start seeing someone else, but he'll pop up again all sad and missing me,' said Karen. 'We'll have a coffee and agree to try again but nothing really changes.'

'Is it like you can't live with, and you can't live without, each other either?' I asked and they nodded.

Their sex life had been good during the lust stage – and this memory was still keeping them together – but Karen could never really relax and enjoy their lovemaking as she was always expecting him to leave. In effect, they were truly on separate tracks as neither their day-to-day lives nor their futures were intertwined.

In the second kind of separate tracks relationships, the couple does bond and form a lasting relationship, but children, career or circumstances set them on different courses. James and Marie, the glory days couple, are a good example of this scenario.

'I always put my career first. In fact, I was so selfish that when Marie's father was dying – and she was nursing him round the clock – I still went off on a business trip to America,' said James. 'There was nobody to look after the children and in the end my sister took up the slack and they went to live with her for ten days.'

'Why didn't you ask him to stay?' I asked Marie.

'I thought it was obvious that I needed him, we needed him, but I didn't want to beg. In fact, I covered up for him, telling everybody it was a crucial deal when all along I knew it was just a quarterly board meeting.'

'It sounds like you were frightened to ask in case he said no,' I said.

'What sort of marriage is that?' Marie asked herself.

No wonder that their sex life had been perfunctory – just going through the motions – as neither took a risk outside the bedroom and tackled the real issues.

While the second type of separate tracks relationships ignore important issues, the third kind puts them under the spotlight. Unfortunately, although these couples argue a lot, they never find a resolution. At the beginning, high-conflict relationships can produce fireworks in the bedroom – especially when the couple are making-up after a row. However, after a while, the arguments spill into their sex life.

'We were making love but she was just lying there,' said Jake, forty-two.

'I was tired,' replied his partner, Chloe, twenty-eight.

'So I thought, why am I bothering? And stopped.'

'And we argued about it the whole weekend.'

'Exactly. What's the point?' Jake turned away.

Although their sex life had taken the brunt of the row, there were fundamental issues driving the anger which weren't being addressed: Chloe wanted children but Jake had had one family and didn't want another (and if he did, not while they were arguing so much). Until these topics could be talked about sensibly, they were doomed to remain on separate tracks.

Tip: Commit to going through the next few weeks with your eyes fully open, truly mindful of the patterns in your relationship – rather than focusing on the latest row, a scheme to bring the two of you together (like a special holiday) or a time when everything will be better (like when the children leave home). When you strip away the distractions and coping mechanisms, what is your relationship really like? What fundamental issues are not being talked about?

Mismatched levels of desire

It is very easy for one partner to take all the 'blame' for a sexual problem or for a couple to 'blame' each other. For example Mike and Jenny, whose sex life had dwindled since the birth of their daughter and a miscarriage, alternated between labelling themselves and each other as the cause of their unhappiness. 'If I'm not in the mood, he gets the hump,' said Jenny. 'He asks time after time until I'm worn down and say "Just get it over with." Anything to keep the peace.' Unfortunately, Mike felt that pestering was his only way of getting sex: 'I have to keep asking because I'll eventually strike lucky.' When Jenny wasn't angry with Mike, she was angry with herself: 'I wish I could be a normal wife and mother and enjoy sex.'

Although blame was being passed around like a rather toxic parcel, I viewed the problem as how Mike and Jenny communicated about sex, plus how they negotiated about how often and when they made love. Communication is not down to one partner or the other, it is a joint responsibility. What's more, by reframing the problem as different levels of desire – rather than anyone's fault – it is once again a shared problem.

In my experience, once blame has been taken out of the equation (which makes people defensive, unable to see the bigger picture and less likely to change), a couple can start working like a team and the differences in their levels of desire become much more manageable. (There is more on this subject in Step Six.)

Tip: Try this quick quiz with your partner. Don't think about the answers too much, just write the first thing down that comes to mind:

1. When I think of love, I think of . . .

2. When I think of sex, I think of . . .

3. In a typical month, how often would you like to have sex?

4. In a typical month, how often do you think your partner would like to have sex?

When I did this quiz with Mike and Jenny, they came up with very similar answers to questions one and two. Interestingly, they both wanted to have sex *eight* times a month. However, Jenny thought Mike wanted sex 'every day' and he thought she wanted sex 'never'. They were surprised and delighted to discover their fantasy of the other's level of desire was a long way from reality.

Polarised ideas of expressing love

Our culture rates talking as the highest form of intimacy. We want access to our partners' private thoughts and consider it essential to know their feelings. No wonder that we are forever asking: 'Tell us how you feel' or 'A penny for your thoughts'. If somehow our partner does not match our level of self-disclosure or openness, we feel cheated and angry. Julie and Ian, both in their early thirties, started counselling after a row turned nasty and Ian disappeared for twenty-four hours: 'I don't know how to start getting Ian to open up to me and have constructive communication. He cannot see that there is anything we need to discuss. Still, he couldn't be a nicer person; believe it or not, he has always bent over backwards for me.'

I suspected that Ian communicated his feelings in a different way from Julie – especially as male identity has generally been based on self-control and not showing weakness. So I explained about the five 'languages' of love and intimacy: Appreciative Words, Caring Actions, Present Giving, Creating Quality Time Together and Affectionate Physical Contact. It was clear that Julie used 'Appreciative Words' but just because that was her 'love language', it seemed unfair to expect her husband to be fluent too.

'He's an intelligent man but really can't see what troubles me and seems a bit "thick" emotionally,' said Julie.

So I got her to look at whether she had been so keen for him to speak her own language that she had not heard him communicating in his.

The next week, Julie returned with a smile: 'You were spot on about our different ways of showing love. Neither are wrong, but we need to respect each other's language. Previously, when he did stuff for me, I just thought he was practical, not that he was showing his feelings for me. So I told him how thoughtful he was, getting some shopping for me when he went round to see his mum. He couldn't wait to show me what he had bought. I picked up on it. I think it seems he's really saying: "I did this for you." I could also see he was relieved that I appreciated him.'

Although I don't like to make generalisations about men and women, it is true that many men feel more comfortable using 'Affectionate Physical Contact' than 'Affectionate Words'. So I am always saddened when women say, 'He's only after one thing' or 'He's got sex on the brain', as I'm aware that their partner is probably asking to be close – the only way he knows how.

Tip: Instead of stressing the importance of talking, consider the other side of the coin: listening. Next time your partner is telling you something, monitor yourself. Are you giving him or her your full attention? (Don't take a sneaky peak at your phone or carry on preparing supper; turn and look your partner in the eyes.) Whenever you're tempted to inter-rupt – even if it seems your partner is rambling or having trouble expressing themselves – bite the inside of your cheek and stop yourself. (It could be that your partner needs time to warm up before moving on to something meaningful.) Encourage your partner to expand by nodding your head from time to time and repeating back the last sentence he or she said – for example: 'So you hailed a taxi?' (This proves to your partner that you're listening and truly engaged.)

Expecting too much from our partner

In successful and happy relationships, each partner looks after each other. Traditionally, this has been earning enough money to provide for material needs or cooking, cleaning and running a house. More recently, this has expanded to looking out for each other's emotional as well as practical needs. Unfortunately, in some couples, the expectations have grown even greater from caring for our partners – cheering them on and cheering them up – to being responsible for their well-being. With this new mindset, if you're suffering from low self-esteem, are angry or unhappy, it is because your partner has not been supportive enough, has behaved badly or does not properly understand your needs. In the bedroom, if you're not turned on, it is because he or she is not pushing the right buttons or making you feel desired enough.

Emily, thirty-one, has been married for a little over a year but had known her husband for several years previously. 'Our sex life has never been passionate, but I don't think I noticed (or I tried to ignore it), as he often works away, so I put it down to that. However, sex has always been an important part of my previous relationships and I am now feeling unattractive and I miss being desired.' Instead of wondering how she could feel more attractive and desired herself, Emily had passed this responsibility on to her husband. 'He says he does find me attractive, but is quite childish in the ways he shows it (by quickly groping me in an almost comical teenage boy-type way).'

Tip: Take a fresh look at problems both inside and outside the bedroom. First, ask yourself: How could I communicate my needs differently and make it is easier for my partner to take them on board? Next, ask yourself: Am I expecting too much? Especially when you are dealing with long-term health problems (your own or your children's), a bereavement or other stressful events, it is easy to be overwhelmed and makes demands that your partner would need to be a social worker, a trained therapist or a sex worker to fulfil.

Summary

- To improve the overall quality of lovemaking, it is important to identify what undermines passionate, plentiful and monogamous sex. This involves not only a better understanding of how our brains work and the impact of hormones such as oxytocin, but also how lovemaking changes over time and how general relationship issues can spoil sex.

- The ease of sex during the lust phase (claiming and possessing) can blind us to the more complex lovemaking of the bonding (from 'me' to 'we'), the settled phase (finding a balance between security and uncertainty) and parenting stages (bringing up babies and small children).

- During the reinvention phase (taking a fresh look at the compromises made, possibly years earlier, during the previous three stages), it is easy to believe that time is running out and that this is the last chance for sexual happiness – thereby increasing the likelihood of affairs and relationship breakdown.

- Couples who learn from the reinvention phase reap the benefit of glory days sex when each partner brings a greater knowledge of who they are, rather than just their genitals, to lovemaking.

- Good relationships need balance. If a couple gets too close – especially if they never argue – each partner's individual identity can get swallowed up into a bland couple sexuality (based on what each person doesn't mind rather than on what they truly want). Conversely, if a couple are too separate, there is never enough trust to be truly intimate, or for anything beyond fleeting moments of 'make-up' sex.

Exercises

How to Talk About Sex

The better you know someone, the easier it should be to talk about sex. Unfortunately, the opposite is more likely to be true. Time and again, I find couples are left guessing what each other likes and doesn't like – often making false assumptions. So how do you talk about this most sensitive of subjects?

1. **Never talk about sex in the bedroom.** Although your bedroom is a private space, it is too loaded for such an intimate discussion. If the conversation happens after sex, one partner can easily take it as a bad review. If the conversation happens as you're getting undressed, one partner can take it as an invitation to make love – rather than to talk. Better scenarios for talking are long car journeys (it's hard for one person to storm off) or over dinner (eating can cover potentially embarrassing silences or provide thinking time). I've also had clients who've discussed sex in a shared bath – a sensual rather than purely sexual space.

2. **Concentrate on the positive.** Most people have insecurities about sex. We worry about our bodies, our technique and our lack of knowledge. So even the most innocuous statements can be heard as criticism. Therefore 'I need to talk about our sex life' is often heard as 'You're rubbish in bed', or 'I think we need to spice things up' is interpreted as 'I'm going to leave you for someone else.' To get round these problems, start with a positive statement: 'I really enjoy our lovemaking' or 'I was thinking about that wonderful time when we...' Follow up with a

question that invites your partner to think creatively: 'How can we build on that?' If you have any complaints, frame them in a positive way. Instead of 'You're too rough', phrase it as 'I like it when you really take your time'; instead of 'You never seem to relax', try 'I get turned on when I know you're really enjoying yourself.'

3. **Avoid words that up the stakes.** As soon as you say 'never' or 'always' your partner will start to get defensive or remember the exception to the rule and start a row. Own the statements: 'I feel . . .' rather than 'You make me feel'.

4. **Be as specific as possible.** When my clients first talk about sex, they always use such generalities that I have no idea what they mean. So try and be as precise as possible. Instead of saying 'I'd like longer cuddles', give an indication: 'I'd like us to cuddle for at least five minutes', otherwise your partner might be thinking you're asking for hours of foreplay. Instead of 'I wish you'd make more of an effort', which could mean anything, ask for what you really want: 'Can you wear that lingerie I bought you?'

5. **Show rather than tell.** When communicating during lovemaking, a touch is worth a thousand words. So take your partner's hand and put it where you'd like to be caressed, guide his or her hand by pushing it down (if you want a firmer touch) or raising it slightly (if you'd like him or her to gentler). If things go wrong, have a cuddle rather than talk (you can post-mortem another time) and never turn your back in a huff (this will be interpreted as rejection).

Lexicon for lovemaking

One of the biggest barriers to talking about sex is that we don't have a working vocabulary to refer to parts of the body and the various types of lovemaking. So in the first counselling sessions – where there is a sexual focus – I go out of my way to name as many 'forbidden' words as possible, partly to normalise them but mainly to remove any embarrassment. (As recently as 1996, an article I wrote for a magazine aimed at young women created problems because I needed to use the word 'penis' to explain about how to give a man sexual pleasure, and even in 2010 the word 'masturbation' was considered too strong for a broadsheet newspaper.)

Sometimes, to break the ice, I get couples to come up with as many names as possible for the male and female sexual organs. (Here are a few examples to get you started: cock, lunch box, wedding tackle, pussy, mound of Venus, front bottom.)

Personally, I use the medical terms wherever possible:

Vagina
Penis
Foreskin
Testicles
Anus
Buttocks
Breasts
Nipples
Masturbate – to pleasure yourself or your partner using your
    fingers and hand
Oral Sex – to pleasure your partner using your tongue, lips
    and mouth
Intercourse – penetrating the vagina with the penis
Erection – when a man's penis is stiff and ready to penetrate

Flaccid – when a man's penis is in its normal unaroused state

Lubricated – when the woman's vagina is aroused and ready to be penetrated

Orgasm – a pleasurable involuntary reflex action

Semen – thick whitish fluid produced in a man's testicles

Ejaculate – the release of semen when a man climaxes

Premature Ejaculation – a lack of control over ejaculation

Retarded Ejaculation – an inability to ejaculate by intercourse, however long it continues

Inorgasmia – not being able to have an orgasm

Vaginismus – a condition where a woman's vagina cannot be penetrated

How to Diagnose the Problems in Your Relationship

Some of the skills that make for a good relationship outside the bedroom can destroy passion inside. Look at the following myths about relationships and ask yourself if any of them are undermining your sex life?

1. **Intimacy is about being valued and accepted by our partner** – thereby prompting a warm, cosy atmosphere where love can thrive. Except, this is only part of the story. Real intimacy involves sharing the difficult bits of ourselves, too – which are possibly less acceptable to our partner – rather than hiding them away. Unfortunately, many couples are fixated on safety and security. This is fine, but promotes polite rather than passionate or exciting lovemaking.

2. **Relationships are all about compromise.** Certainly, for arguments or deciding how to spend spare time, and many other day-to-day issues, compromise helps. (For example,

he will play golf on Saturday but get back in time for a family lunch.) However, too much compromise in the bedroom can be a disaster. It provides either 'If you do this for me, I'll do that for you' (which is off-putting) or what each partner will put up with rather than truly enjoy (which is not particularly satisfying).

3. **A good partner should make us feel valued and acceptable.** This myth means we get angry and resentful if our partner cannot pull off this difficult trick. Ultimately, we need to be able to validate ourselves too.

Central Task for Understanding:
How I Learned About the Birds and the Bees

At the end of each chapter, I have inserted a key task to share with your partner. This will allow him or her to take on board my underlying philosophy, even if he or she does not read the book.

It is helpful to have some idea of your partner's sexual history, so you know if there are any past events still casting a shadow today. However, it is hard to cover this topic without raising the spectre of jealousy. This is why I recommend you telling your partner how you discovered the facts of life as this story is both safe and revealing. Here is Graham's experience, which I fleshed out by asking questions and probing for more details:

'Towards the end of the Easter term, at my all-boys' school, a rumour went around: We were going to cover sex in biology lessons. I must have been about twelve and I'd already gleaned a basic understanding by watching our pet guinea pigs on the lawn. I'd read the relevant section in my biology book, with its diagram of men's and women's sexual organs sliced in two and the parts labelled, but most of my knowledge came from schoolmates. For example, I'd been told that Henry VIII had caught syphilis from too much masturbation and that men had erections to prevent them from urinating into women's vaginas! So when our biology teacher, Mr Osbourne, finally announced that "yes, next lesson we're doing sex", there was a buzz of anticipation. One boy, who had an elder brother, claimed it would involve measuring willow leaves. When the lesson finally arrived, it was a huge anti-climax. Mr Osbourne went into great detail about how single-cell creatures reproduce by splitting in two. There was also a lesson on how worms were hermaph-rodites. It was not until halfway through lesson three that we graduated on to humans. There was a very biological explanation of how eggs were released from the fallopian tubes, the competition between sperm to fertilise the egg, and the length of human gestation period. There was nothing about pleasure, emotions or relationships. When he'd finished, a red-faced Mr Osbourne asked if we had any questions. We had millions but nobody dared put their hand up. When the bell rang, it was hard to know who was most relieved – him or us.'

When you have shared your stories – and make certain they are as comprehensive as Graham's – discuss your parents' attitude to sex and the influences of any other significant people. What other sources of information did you have? (Books, TV, pornography?) How accurate were they? How informative? What messages did you get about sex? What influence did these formative lessons have? What is the impact on your love life today?

Prairie Voles
and Cuddling

In order to get a better idea of a day in the life of a prairie vole, scientists set up what sounds like a vole cocktail party where a male prairie vole was free to roam but two females were confined to different areas of the testing chamber. The first female was the mate of the prairie vole and the second a complete stranger. Who would the male choose? The scientists sat back, watched and waited. Over three hours, the male prairie vole spent almost two hours huddling: cuddling and licking his mate. He spent less than twenty minutes with the stranger and the rest of the time pottering around a third chamber – the vole equivalent of a garden shed. When the experiment was repeated but this time using the meadow vole, the male spent most of his time alone in the neutral chamber and although he visited his mate for slightly longer than the stranger, he was still only with her for about twenty minutes. Could the prairie voles spend so much time huddling because this released the oxytocin hormone and bonded the partners even closer?

Certainly in humans we know that oxytocin is around in increased quantities when we become aroused and at peak levels when men ejaculate and women orgasm. Perhaps this is why couples feel at their very closest when cuddling and recovering from making love. However, there is something else happening too. Scientists at University College, London, led by Andreas Bartels, took seventeen love-obsessed students and showed them pictures of their beloved and measured their brain activity using an MRI scanner. As expected, blood flowed to the pleasure centres of the brain. However, two other parts of the brain were suppressed: the amygdala and the right prefrontal cortex. The amygdala is responsible for fear and anger; the right prefrontal cortex is active in people suffering from depression. So it seems that being in love and lovemaking is not only highly pleasurable but also suppresses our negative emotions too.

Step Two: Repairing

At the beginning of a relationship, sex can be a wonderful way of making up after falling out. Unfortunately, as couples share more and more of their lives together and more issues naturally arise, it can become harder to forgive and forget with just a bout of passionate lovemaking. In fact, for many couples, sex can become another source of discontent rather than a solution. So how can established couples repair their relationship and return to a time when sex restored their love for each other? Once again the prairie vole holds the key: cuddling and the sheer amount of contact time.

When I ask couples who are dissatisfied with their lovemaking whether they cuddle, they are normally quick to dismiss the idea. Sure, of course they cuddle. Doesn't everybody? However, when I question them further, their cuddle is seldom more than a quick hug in the morning or accompanying a goodnight kiss. And how much time does the average couple spend together? According to the Office of National Statistics, it is very little. Once work, commuting time, sleep and watching TV have been deducted out of a normal week, three and a half hours a week is all that is left for shared social life, sport, hobbies and interests (or just twenty-four minutes a day).

So in Step Two in our journey to passionate, plentiful and monogamous sex, we will be concentrating on spending more time together and improving the quality and duration of your cuddles. But first there is some individual work that you and your partner need to undertake.

Preparing Yourself for a Richer Love Life

In my research into our attitudes to sex and what Britons do in bed, I was saddened that many people had low expectations of improving their love life: 35 per cent were not really confident and 14 per cent had no confidence at all. Unfortunately, we believe that we have to transform either ourselves (by becoming slimmer, sexier and more skilled) or our circumstances (by finding more time or getting the children off our hands more often). No wonder we feel trapped and dispirited. My message, however, is that great sex is not the preserve of the young, good-looking and knowledgeable. It is for everybody and the best news of all, the most vital ingredients of all, are within easy reach – locked inside each and every one of us. So what are these magic factors?

The answer will probably come as a shock because when I asked people what would most improve their love life, they gave all the predictable answers: 52 per cent said feeling closer to my partner; 53 per cent said better communication; and 38 per cent said more time. However, the two qualities guaranteed to revolutionise your love life – imagination and confidence – polled relatively low. So why are imagination and confidence so important?

Imagination

If we were in a fairy tale and you could have just one wish to improve your sex life, the best choice is to be blessed by a good imagination. I place imagination even before confidence – because unless you can first dream it, you can't do it. There are also secondary gifts with imagination – such as creativity (vital for keeping passion alive) and the ability to find a way around fears and inhibitions (and there will be plenty of those on the journey ahead).

If your heart sunk when I stressed the importance of imagination, you are not alone. When I go into businesses and charities – with my writer's hat on – to teach staff how to unlock their imagination, I can almost smell the worry and fear in the room: 'I was hopeless at stories at school', 'It's not for me', 'I can't spell' and 'People will laugh'. It is entirely different when I go into primary schools and encourage children to be creative and improve their writing skills. I take a large box filled with strange items and the pupils have to go up one by one and take something out. Afterwards, we go round the room and each child tells a story based on what they chose. In their imagination, a hollow bone that my dog has chewed becomes a telescope to see into the future, an orange squeezer is a spaceship and a key unlocks buried pirate treasure. However, once the pupils have reached secondary school, a bone is just a bone, an orange squeezer is for making orange juice and the key opens a front door. Although they tell great stories, these teenagers have lost the ability to escape into different worlds. Something about going through puberty makes us very grounded in the real world – which is strange when you consider how much we need that childish sense of wonder to keep our passion alive. So how can you turn back the clock and undo the damage of a school system focused on passing exams and work focused on getting results?

Think of your imagination like a muscle that has gone flabby but with a little training will soon become flexible, powerful and a real asset for improving your sex life. Here are three ways of giving your imagination a work-out:

1. Be more aware of your senses

Modern life is so hectic that we seldom stop and stare. And if we fail to notice anything during the daytime, what chance is there of being fully conscious during our dreams? Go somewhere that you won't be interrupted and either sit or lie down. Take ten minutes out of your day and, one by one, focus on the following senses:

- **Look.** Drink in all the sights around you. Become aware of the varied shapes and patterns – the angle of the park bench, the wrapper on a bar of chocolate, the colour of the flowering cherry or the pigeon perched on the eaves of the railway ticket office.

- **Listen.** Tune into the different sounds. Start with the loudest ones, perhaps the echo of footsteps in an atrium. What is the pitch? What is the pattern? How do the patterns change? What are the other sounds mixed in underneath? Perhaps traffic outside, birds or conversations? How do they echo round the space? What about the silence? Is that layered too? Can you hear wind through the trees or the hum of a cold drinks fridge in a café?

- **Touch.** Feel the texture of the grass beneath you and not just with your fingers but with the back of your hand or your forearm. Take off your shoes and enjoy the warmth of the earth under your toes. What about the texture of the chair you're sitting on? Is it smooth, rough, dry or possibly even sticky? Pick something up and feel the weight in your hand. Become aware of the different competing sensations, the warmth of the coffee cup and the coolness of the stainless-steel table it's on.

- **Smell.** We're generally only aware of the strongest smell but with a little time and practice, you'll begin to distinguish the layers here too. Close your eyes, so you can really immerse yourself. Can you smell the earth, freshly mown grass, concrete dust from a nearby building site, or maybe the almond croissant of the person at the next table?

- **Taste.** Run the tip of your tongue over your lips. How do they taste? Let your tongue roam over your teeth, get the saliva going. Can you find the after-taste of your last meal? Imagine eating it again.

- **Emotions.** What are you feeling? Joy, happiness, emptiness, regret? How many different emotions can you find? How do your feelings overlap?

- **Be aware of your awareness.** You don't have to live your life with your senses switched off. Find beauty where you least expect it – the shade of yellow on your neighbour's skip. Hear the music and rhythm beneath the clatter and hum of the nearby building site. Enjoy the texture of the spiky pot plant in your office foyer. Once fully conscious of these small wonders, you'll be more prepared for being sensual in the bedroom rather than expecting to go from nought to ninety when your partner make his or her first move.

2. Explore your dreams

Have you ever been in the middle of a dream and something bizarre happened, like you can fly or you've been introduced to the Queen in your dressing gown, and you've suddenly realised: 'Hang on, I must be dreaming'? You are doing something which Dutch psychiatrist Fredrik van Eeden (1860–1932) called lucid dreaming – being aware that you are in a dream rather than reality. So how can you harness this power to boost your imagination?

- **Get more rest.** The longer that you're asleep, the longer and closer together the dreams will be. While the first dream of the night is only ten minutes long, after eight hours asleep your dreams last between forty-five minutes and an hour.

- **Prime yourself to dream.** As you're lying in bed, about to drift off to sleep, tell yourself: 'I'm going to dream tonight and I'm going to remember it.' Repeat this instruction a couple of times.

- **Look out for the signs that you're dreaming.** The classic signals of a dream include: you're doing something strange (for example, breathing underwater), items in this world are strange (for example, dogs talk or pavements move), other people are acting strangely (for example, they have tentacles rather than arms) or you're in a strange context (for example, you're Madonna's lover or you're talking to someone who is dead).

- **Tell yourself: I'm dreaming.** Being aware that you are in the middle of a dream takes away any anxiety and allows you to explore this other world.

- **When you wake up, stay still.** Moving makes the dream harder to remember. In contrast, if you keep still, various fragments will return. Ask yourself: What was I doing in my dream when I woke up? What was I thinking? What did I feel? Recall the context and assemble all the clues about what happened. Then ask what happened before that and backwards. By reliving the dream in reverse, you'll remember more.

3. Write down your dreams
Keep a piece of paper and a pen by the bed and record what happened immediately after you wake up.

- **Scribbled notes are enough.** It does not have to be an essay, just a few words and prompts.

- **Describe the images and characters.** Just get a few vivid fragments down, rather than trying to explain the strange logic of the dream world or attempting to make sense of it.

- **Imagine you can move around in this world.** Taking the moments of recovered dream, what happens if you move the story forwards or backwards? What would happen if, for example, you went outside or pulled back a curtain? How do you feel? Write down all your discoveries.

- **The act of writing down fixes the dream.** Instead of the dream slipping away, it will stay with you. Later, you might like to write up the dream in a book – see below – or just keep a pile of notes. (In Step Five, we will look at how dreams can feed fantasies and you might like to refer back to previous lucid dreams.)

My own experience

Before exploring lucid dreaming, I could never remember my dreams. So when I was first introduced to the idea, I was sceptical. However, I decided to write down my dreams the moment I woke up and was amazed at how much detail I recalled. The following started as about fifty words scribbled down after the alarm went off.

'I'm the stage assistant for a beautiful mixed-raced model, she's rehearsing her strip-show and slowly peeling off a chic coffee-coloured jacket to a song called "You Can Have it All". She throws the jacket into the imaginary audience, pulls off a slip and reveals her body but all I can see from my viewpoint in the wings of the stage is her long, sculpted back. When the model comes backstage, she's clasping a blouse and the jacket to her breasts. They seem small, hard and beautifully formed.

'The performance itself is at a conference in a sports hall. Although the space is large, there's probably only twenty businessmen down the front. The music starts, but this time I stay on stage and dive down into the audience to retrieve her jacket. The model continues to dance around the stage but I've filled it with more and more empty boxes. She has a smaller and smaller space for her performance until she's dancing on the spot. The music ends with a triumphant: "You Can Have it ALL", but this time, instead of taking off her top, she bursts into tears and runs into the wings – which is also crowded with boxes and other ephemera. It's all my fault, what was I thinking about – all those stupid boxes? The model collapses into my arms and cries on my shoulder. She'd been fooling herself, she couldn't take her clothes off in front of all those businessmen.'

So what does the dream mean? It is important to remember that dreams are not simply letters from our unconscious – I don't have a secret desire to be a stripper's assistant – but the result of a complicated interaction between my conscious and unconscious mind. Freudian and Jungian analysts, who specialise in dream analysis, stress the importance of considering *all* the characters and items in a dream as each one respresents part of your personality or an internal struggle. Therefore, the stripper symbolises my worries, right at the start of writing this book, about how much I should reveal about myself and the boxes on the stage are my fears. Ultimately, however, the meaning of the dream is irrelevant because lucid dreaming has other benefits:

- **Lucid dreaming is a pleasure in its own right.** By valuing your dreams, you consider yourself worthy of a little indulgence – rather than someone who has a lot to get done.

- **Lucid dreaming makes you feel good.** My clients report being carried through the morning on a wave of bliss.

- **Lucid dreaming helps you look freshly at the world.** One client told me that as she dressed that morning, the sun shone through the blinds casting patterns across the duvet that looked like a giant bar-code. She must have seen this effect thousands of times but this was the first time she'd noticed the beauty of those shadows.

- **Lucid dreaming provides fresh material for your fantasies.** All too often, we use second-hand stimulation from movies or pornography. These might be effective – in the same way that fast food fills us up – but, ultimately, a home-cooked meal tastes better and properly sustains us. A lucid dream is fuel for your imagination.

- **Lucid dreaming helps make you a more sensual person.** In this way, you will have a richer palette to bring to your lovemaking.

The healing power of lucid dreams

Research at Stanford University has revealed that lucid dreaming occurs during the highly activated phase of REM (Rapid Eye Movement) sleep when there is also increased vaginal blood flow or erections. This explains why there is a sexual component to so many dreams.

Alice, thirty-eight, found it hard to achieve an orgasm when she was stressed. Unfortunately, the more she worried about climaxing, the more stressed she would become and the less likely to orgasm. After two weeks of lucid dreaming, she came to counselling with a smile and a story: 'I was in this horror movie full of zombies, vampires and werewolves. To keep out of harm's way, I was skulking down these ill-lit alleys but then I realised that I was in a dream – so nothing could really harm me. I ran across the road and round the corner where I found a bright, cheery pub. I remember thinking: "How clever of the monsters to lure people in and then make them submit to all their horrors." So I went in and wandered around the pub, it looked completely normal – except that they had blood as well as whisky on the optics behind the bar. I went into this small darkened room in the back of the pub and all these vampires were watching a TV. It was showing a porn movie and I found myself sucked into the movie. I was the centre of attention and the bright lights were on me. I felt incredibly aroused and sexual. The feeling intensified quite rapidly and I had an orgasm, the first in months. Then I woke up feeling wonderful.'

That evening, when Alice made love with her partner, she had no problem orgasming. Her experiences are not uncommon. Many of my clients have found lucid dreams can be a forum to rehearse solutions to problems and to overcome blocks – especially in their love lives.

Having covered the importance of imagination, it's time to move on to the second quality needed for a richer love life.

Confidence

In my survey, 100 per cent of women and 20 per cent of men thought their love lives would improve if they had a better body. Unfortunately, many people, like Jenny whom we met earlier, don't just stop at wanting to be slimmer or have better muscle tone, they actively hate their bodies. 'I didn't really like it before I had my daughter but now . . .' Her voice trailed off.

'I think you've got a lovely body,' said Mike sincerely.

'You don't have to look at it – well, you do, but not as often as I do,' replied Jenny. 'I'll be drying myself after a bath and catch myself in the mirror and shudder. Even when I'm dressed and my Caesarean scar is not on display, I still know it's there.' It was not surprising that she found it hard to relax and enjoy lovemaking (and preferred to keep the light off).

Over the past twenty-five years, I have seen an increasing number of people with poor body confidence. Perhaps it is not surprising that our sense of a 'normal' body has been distorted so dramatically – particularly for women. In colour supplements and magazines, we see impossibly slim airbrushed models and, in pornography, huge silicon-enhanced breasts and hairless vaginas. Meanwhile, the average man in the UK has a thirty-nine-inch waist but the latest shop dummies have only twenty-seven inches. At local swimming pools, the communal single-sex changing rooms have been removed – and replaced with individual shower cubicles – and many people arrive at the gym already dressed for their exercise class and wash at home. We simply don't see ordinary bodies any more.

That's why I've started showing pictures of naked men and women in my counselling sessions – which have been taken especially for sex therapy – so my clients realise that most people sag in certain places and that breasts and nipples can be different shapes and sizes. For most people, there is a huge sense of relief to compare themselves to normal people rather than models or movie stars. However, I would like to go a step further. Instead of just tolerating our imperfections, I think we should celebrate them and even consider them sexy. So how do we achieve this?

The last twenty-five years have not been completely harmful to our body confidence. There have also been some encouraging developments. Gay images were supposed to be fixed: Michelangelo's *David*, the blond beach boy, the body-builder and photographer Robert Mapplethorpe's *Leathermen*. However, in the late eighties, a new cult arrived: the bear. These were bearded, hairy and natural men. It started in 1987 with a magazine, appropriately enough called *Bear*, a pocket-format desk-top publication in San Francisco with a run of just a few hundred copies. The models were not young – mostly in their thirties, forties and fifties; most were hefty and quite a few cherished their bellies. Most revolutionary of all – bears liked other bears. So instead of dieting, waxing their backs and hiding away in dark corners, these men were letting it all hang out – quite literally – and founded a cult that has spread to every major city and town. Bears felt sexy and desirable and so became so.

Here is how you can pull off a similar trick yourself:

1. **Stop running yourself down.** One of the ways that women bond with other women, or make themselves seem less threatening, is listing their faults – 'stick insect legs' or 'my increasing expanse of upper arm' or 'this flabby belly hanging like a bean bag'. Worse still, it soon gets into an auction where everyone claims to hate themselves the most. Although this sort of behaviour will make you feel like a member of the gang, it does nothing for your self-confidence. Next time, simply refuse to enter the competition, walk away or change the subject.

2. **Stop running other people down.** Whole magazines are devoted to famous women's flaws with circles pointing out their 'skeletal backs', 'perspiration stains' and 'cellulite'. We imagine that by pulling celebrities down to our level, we'll somehow feel better about ourselves. However, it just feeds our own fears that we will never measure up.

3. **Stop imagining that a good body equals confidence.** I've twice been in the company of someone so overwhelmingly good-looking that heads turned. In the first instance,

my ballroom dancing club were giving money to the Samaritans. By coincidence a friend of mine was president of the local Samaritans and sat on my table with his committee – one of whom was so good-looking that I had five calls the next morning from other members asking about my 'gorgeous friend'. This 'gorgeous' man joined our club and one hot evening we chatted outside the hall while trying to cool down. He was wearing a T-shirt *and* a short-sleeved cotton shirt but he admitted he couldn't take it off because, he said, 'I've got ugly shoulders'. Many years ago, I was interviewing for a new member of staff and one of the candidates was a former male model. Once he'd left, most of my team – men and women – put their head round the door to enquire about the candidate. The women were particularly keen and thought he would be 'an asset' to have around the office. However, the former model believed he was good at nothing and had no self-confidence. Although these two people were undeniably good-looking, they suffered from the same frailties as the rest of us.

4. **Think laterally.** The great American novelist Norman Mailer married a woman half his age. His wife, Norris Mailer, discovered that he was being unfaithful to her with women who were either closer to his age – by that point he was almost seventy – or significantly overweight. When she asked him why he replied: 'Sometimes I want to be the attractive one.'

5. **Celebrate your achievements.** We've all done things which make us proud. It might be knocking three minutes off your personal best for running a half-marathon, closing a deal at work, or having the courage to phone

your mother and tell her you'd like to host Christmas yourself this year. Transfer that small moment of internal pride into a proper celebration by having a bottle of sparkling wine in the fridge ready to go or reward yourself with a special treat.

6. **Remember a time when you did feel confident.** Picture in detail the last time that you did feel good about yourself – it could even have been in a lucid dream. Really anchor that experience by remembering where you were and how good it felt. Think about where the confidence seemed to come from – your stomach, heart, head, hands, etc. Next, imagine moving it round your body so that every part is filled with confidence and raising and lowering the volume. Once you have a solid grip on the feeling, you can trigger it whenever you need it. Start by using this trick somewhere non-threatening (but potentially troubling), such as at a difficult meeting at work, and then progress up to feeling confident in the bedroom.

7. **Does it really matter what other people think?** Barry, thirty-eight, came into counselling because he had no confidence when meeting women. 'I'll be talking to someone and suddenly I'll be gripped by this thought: "She's thinking about my nose, how big it looks, that it's huge and dominates my whole face – the whole room."' Barry had been using the strategy of celebrating his achievements to cope: 'I tell myself: I've started a good business, it's doing really well and that I'm going to start to employ more people.' As Barry had been having these thoughts even when dealing with low-stakes situations – such as talking to someone in the office down the hall from his

company – I asked: 'Does it really matter what they think?' During the next week, he had been able to ask himself the same question whenever he'd starting worry about his nose. 'It really helped get everything into proportion. Why should I worry about someone whose good opinion I don't need?' By acting quickly, when the nasty internal voice started up, he'd headed off the problem and prevented himself plunging into obsession.

8. **Make peace with your body.** Instead of promising to accept your body when you've lost a stone or have better pectoral muscles, accept yourself as you are today. This doesn't mean abandoning your health and fitness goals. You still want to eat well and take moderate exercise, but stop putting off doing things until you've reached some magical target.

How Honest Should I Be With My Partner?

Often there is an official explanation for why a couple seldom make love – 'Our youngest has attention deficit disorder and is very demanding' or 'I'm stressed out with money worries' or 'We've a lot on our plate right now' – but normally these excuses are just a convenient cover. One partner would like to make love but something about their beloved is turning them off. So what's the best way forward? A white lie? Nobody gets hurt but sex remains infrequent and unsatisfactory? Or tell the truth and risk damaging the relationship for ever?

Gordon, thirty-two, and Maya, twenty-eight, are thoughtful and considerate. Gordon always thinks before he speaks – in case he says something hurtful. Maya looks up to Gordon and values his opinions about her art (she is a part-time potter, although she would like to go full-time) and his knowledge of marketing and networking (which has got her work into several group exhibitions). On the face of things, they are the perfect couple: able to put themselves into each other's shoes, involved in each other's dreams and ambitions, and mutually interdependent. Unfortunately, their sex life was a disaster.

'We make love about once a month,' explained Gordon.

'If that,' Maya chipped in, 'and I'm always the one to make the first move.'

'I'll give Maya her due, she's always very encouraging. She'll dance in an erotic way or put on sexy underwear, but I'm not often in the mood.' He smiled and shrugged his shoulders – as if it was just one of those things, like the weather, that we can't influence.

'How does that make you feel?' I asked Maya.

'He has very high standards – all his girlfriends have been outstanding.' She seemed to shrink into herself.

'I've never been unfaithful or ever given you reason to doubt me,' Gordon replied. I sensed there was something more and encouraged him to continue. 'But I don't want to hurt Maya.'

She had already reached for the tissues. 'I have some idea what he's going to say.'

'What good is it going to do?' he asked me.

It was obvious: Gordon was about to explain why he seldom felt desire for Maya. While it was admirable that he had kept back hurtful information, it had still leaked out – probably in hints, jokes or exasperated put-downs which were immediately taken back. Worse still, Maya had already been hurt. Her sexual confidence was low and being repeatedly knocked back had undermined her self-esteem. Indeed, the more we talked about sex – even in a general way – the more often she reached for the tissues. Not surprisingly, Gordon became more and more reticent. However, until his issues were directly voiced, Maya could not challenge him and the couple could not find a way of dealing with their problems.

So what did Gordon need to say?

'There are certain odours that I don't like,' he confessed.

When it comes to dealing with sex, it is important to call a spade a spade, so, slowly, I encouraged him to be more direct.

'Maya likes to be spontaneous about sex but if she hasn't had a shower for several hours, I don't like the smell of her vagina.'

'I know that unless we've just got out of the shower, sex is not going to happen,' said Maya.

The whole atmosphere in the room had completely changed. Maya had imagined something far worse, she had a chance to give her side and we could work on improving their love life.

Before you start confessing your issues to each other, it is important to ask yourself two fundamental questions:

1. **Can my partner do something about this complaint?**
   If your partner's behaviour is upsetting and interfering with your sex life, it is important to be honest and explain. Gordon's complaint – about smell – is fine because it is something that Maya could easily change. Other examples of acceptable complaints include 'making more of an effort and wearing stylish clothes when we go out as this puts me into the mood for lovemaking when we return' or 'Please cut your fingernails because the jagged edges hurt when you fondle my vagina'. However, I had to stop Gordon from making remarks about Maya's weight as that was not something she could easily remedy and, any way, it feeds directly into the second question.

2. **Are my criticisms fair?** All too often we are criticising something that our partner cannot change. For example, Gordon had put the blame for his waning desire on 'neither of us getting any younger or more attractive'. Although he tried to include himself, Maya was despondent: 'I can't stop time.' There is another way in which a criticism is unfair. Sometimes when we dislike something about ourselves, instead of accepting our frailties or trying to change them, we distance ourselves by rounding on our partner and complaining about the very same behaviour or fault in ourselves. (This is called projecting feelings on to someone else.) So, for example, Gordon admitted – later in counselling – that he had deep anxieties about ageing himself and had lots of negative feelings about his thickening waist and thinning hairline.

If you have answered yes to the two questions above, discuss your issues with your partner. However, remember to be *specific* (or your partner will imagine far worse) and to *own* the problems (or your partner will hear only criticism). For example: 'When you wear your winter nightie, I find it hard to get aroused' rather than 'You turn me off.' If you answered no to either question, please keep your issues to yourself – for the time being. It is unfair to dump on your partner or to dramatically undermine their self-esteem (and it is counterproductive to better lovemaking). But don't worry, I'm not going to ignore issues about attractiveness (and all the feelings associated with wrinkles and being too skinny or too fat).

First, these are only a problem if your lovemaking is based purely on lust (and my aim is to provide many ways into great sex) and second, I want to help you make love on a deeper level (so you're not just communicating on the surface but also with who your partner really is). In addition, there is more about making a fresh start with your partner in the exercise section.

Starting My Programme

Having understood how sex changes over time and what undermines it, and having removed some of the barriers to tackling your problems, we are ready to start the journey to passionate and plentiful sex:

Putting a ban on sex

The best way to improve your love life is to stop it. A lot of couples who come to me for counselling or who attend one of my workshops are puzzled. They sought my help because they were hardly ever making love and I'm going to stop them altogether? How can they ever improve, if they don't have a chance to practise?

There are three reasons for putting a ban on intercourse and other forms of sexual contact. First, it significantly reduces tension between a couple. Second, it helps couples get in touch with the full range of sensual pleasures – rather than rushing towards an orgasm. Third, it can change the way that you and your partner communicate. I know these are bold claims, so let's look at how banning sex revolutionised the relationship of Mike and Jenny from the previous chapter.

Mike had been so keen to make love that he had ended up applying emotional pressure. 'I couldn't stand Mike sulking, so after a while I'd back down and let him have what he wanted,' Jenny explained, 'and I'd just lie there like a sack of potatoes.' Mike did not find this sort of sex satisfying either.

He would much rather Jenny had been an active partner. He looked glum. I asked him what he was feeling but he couldn't put it into words.

'Is it better than nothing?' I asked.

'No, it is worse than nothing because I'm still frustrated,' he replied.

Between these unsatisfactory bouts of sex, there was virtually no physical contact between Mike and Jenny at all.

'I wouldn't mind a cuddle but I don't want to send out the wrong signals,' said Jenny.

They had fallen into a nasty trap – common in many couples with unhappy love lives – *all or nothing*. They either had full intercourse or stayed at opposite edges of the bed. There was no sensuality, no togetherness and no intimacy in their marriage. Worse still, had they continued down this path, Jenny probably would have closed down completely and started to refuse sex.

By agreeing to a ban on sex, for a while, Mike and Jenny could start afresh. Jenny could relax and enjoy a cuddle. 'I don't want to be cringing inside,' she told Mike, 'I want to want you.' Instead of hoping 'maybe this time', Mike could also enjoy the moment too. In effect, they would return to being teenagers again – enjoying heavy petting as a pleasure in its own right, rather than as a quick warm-up for intercourse.

When they returned the next week, they were both smiling. The tension and the arguments had significantly reduced and they had cuddled every night after their daughter had been put to bed.

'I felt so much closer to Jenny. It was nice to be held but it was even nicer to be able to show my love for her,' Mike explained. There had also been a significant breakthrough in their general communication.

'I don't like it when he surprises me from behind. If I'm in the kitchen, I'm in a world of my own, and although he is just being nice and giving me a hug, I go all cold inside,' said Jenny. 'I hadn't told him this before, because I didn't think it was important, but my last boyfriend tried to strangle me on several occasions. Although I'm not frightened of Mike, if I don't know he's there, it brings back memories.'

Mike had known that her boyfriend had been rough – but had no idea how bad their relationship had been. 'It also explained why she hates being kissed on the neck,' he said. These revelations not only brought the couple closer but also shone further light on to understanding their problem.

The intimacy of the cuddles had another positive knock-on effect: Mike and Jenny were more relaxed and spent more time together. At the weekend, they had taken their daughter to play in the park and Jenny had stepped back to give Mike time to play with her. They were behaving more like co-parents rather than Jenny taking the lion's share of their daughter's attention. As he talked about his daughter at the counselling session, I could see two competing sides of Mike. There was the brash builder, who I could imagine joking with his mates, and the more sensitive man who loved his wife so much that he was jealous of the way their child came between them. So I encouraged him to talk about his own father.

'He was a good man. Firm but fair,' he explained.

'Did he show his feelings? I asked.

'Real men don't show their feelings,' he joked, but I could tell he was deadly serious.

Unfortunately, Mike's upbringing and his hyper-masculine work environment had cut him off from most ways of expressing his tender side. His only 'socially acceptable' channel for communication was having sex (because 'real men' are also 'studs'). By closing down this option, with a ban on inter-course, he had begun to look for other ways of showing his feelings. At this point, it was just a glimmer but the beginning of something very important.

Hopefully, the experiences of Mike and Jenny will have either piqued your interest or helped put your doubts to one side for while.

A Month of Sensuality

This four-week plan sets out to repair and rebuild the loving bonds between you and your partner. (There is advice on getting your partner's cooperation and working as a team in the exercise section.) Take time to think about each week's activity and discuss with your partner whether there is anything that makes you uncomfortable and, if this is the case, make any necessary adjustments. It is also fine to stay with one activity for a second or third week but don't rush ahead.

Week One: The focus is on cuddling and sensual touching

- Flip a coin to decide who will go first.

- The one who wins the coin toss becomes the first person to say 'I would like to be touched'. This could be straight away or at a convenient moment over the next few hours or days. As long as the person asking to be touched does not pick an incredibly inconvenient moment – in the middle of cooking supper or bathing children – the other partner should put aside what he or she is doing.

- Go somewhere warm, quiet and private.

- The touchee lies down and the toucher explores his or her body. (If you would rather keep your underwear on that's fine.) The only forbidden areas are the genitals and the breasts – plus anywhere that is a problem area because of your partner's past.

- It is not a performance, don't worry about technique, but really enjoy looking at your partner's body. Let your feelings flow. (Don't be surprised if some strange ones, such as sadness, float to the surface.)

- Discover what kind of touching gets the best response. Does firmer pressure work better, or a really light touch – barely brushing the skin with the tips of your fingers? What about scratching his or her back? Mix up the sensations.

- The touchee should provide plenty of feedback but avoid talking (as this can sometimes be interpreted as criticism). If something feels good, don't keep it to yourself. Let out a sigh or a moan of pleasure. If your partner's touch is too firm, raise his or her hand slightly. If the touch is too light or tickles in an unpleasant manner, lightly push your partner's hand downwards.

- After fifteen minutes, swap over and the touchee becomes the toucher.

- Finish off with a cuddle – remember, sex has been banned for the time being – and discuss the experience and your reactions (especially the unexpected ones).

- Later in the week, the other partner is the person to initiate by announcing: 'I would like to be touched' and the whole exercise is repeated.

Week Two: The focus is on kissing

- My plan works by adding another layer of sensuality each week, so continue with the same activities as before, taking it in turns to announce: 'I would like to be touched.'

- Beyond a peck on the lips, many couples abandon sensual kissing in the rush to have an orgasm. With this distraction out of the way, temporarily, you can really focus on enjoying proper kisses.

- Start with the original formula: 'I would like to be touched.'

- After a few minutes of sensual touching, look for new places to kiss your partner. What about the neck or the elbow? (Remember, genitals and breasts are still forbidden.) Don't just go for obvious places to kiss, such as the lips, try others – the belly, fingers and armpits.

- Alternate the kissing with sensual touching, so that your partner is not certain what sensation will be next.

- Experiment with different kinds of kisses. Butterfly kisses land really gently and can come in quick succession. Slobbery kisses pull lots of flesh into your mouth. Nibbling kisses involve a light use of your teeth.

- The touchee remains in control; if it is unpleasant to be kissed somewhere, he or she can move their partner's head. Give plenty of moans and sighs, so that your partner knows what is particularly enjoyable (but please don't put on a performance, this has to come naturally).

- Towards the end of your fifteen minutes of sensual touching and kissing, try kissing on the mouth. Open your eyes, so it is a very personal experience.

- Once again, alternate between different kinds of kisses – on the lips and with tongues.

- After fifteen minutes swap over.

- As before, finish with a cuddle and a discussion.

Week Three: The focus is on advanced sensual touching

- Once again, combine this week's activity with the sensual touching and kissing.

- Extend the allotted time from fifteen minutes each to twenty minutes, but the task still starts with 'I would like to be touched'.

- With advanced sensual touching, look for different sensations by adding fabrics and implements. For example, a piece of velvet or fake fur. I've had clients who have used pastry brushes, feathers and even a couple who used sandpaper (lightly) on each other.

- The kitchen, toolbox and your local hardware store will be full of implements that could be used for purposes other than that which the manufacturer intended. Some couples get pleasure from surprising each other, while others enjoy the buzz of a shared shopping expedition.

- Mix up the different sensations and give each other plenty of feedback about what feels nice.

- There is another new element this week: the breasts.

- Towards the end of sensual time, the woman should guide her partner's hands to her breasts. By this point, you will be used to showing what feels nice and what is not stimulating. Don't be shy. Make certain your partner knows what works for you by getting his hands to shadow yours (still no verbal feedback during your love-making).

- When it is the man's turn to be touched, he should also guide his partner to his nipples towards the end of the twenty minutes. Just like in the female, there are lots of nerve endings here and a possible source of new pleasure. Try out different techniques . . . licking, nibbling, tweaking and even gentle pulling can be pleasurable. Start slowly and build up the intensity.

- Finish with a cuddle and a discussion.

Week Four: The focus is on having an orgasm together

- Start with the sensual touching, progress through kissing on to advanced touching. However, this week you can finish off with an orgasm.

- This is not achieved through intercourse – which is still banned – but by each partner simultaneously masturbating themselves.

- Many couples think this is the opposite of intimacy and many are shocked by the idea. However, sharing what, for many, is a secret activity can promote a profound connection.

- Maintain good eye contact. Watch how your partner pleasures him- or herself.

- Masturbation might feel very revealing or too private to share with your partner but, as you will discover, sex becomes boring because we keep too much of ourselves back.

- Pushing past the taboo about masturbation is what makes week four such a spectacular climax – in every sense of the word – to a Month of Sensuality.

Stops and starts

When working with clients on this programme, I always say that I expect there to be some weeks when they don't do their 'homework'. So please don't make achieving each week's goal a test of whether your partner is truly committed – that just ups the stakes and makes it harder to cope with setbacks. In fact, most people get stuck somewhere. It's partly that life gets in the way – family comes to stay or one partner is ill – but changing the habits of a lifetime and facing down our demons about our bodies and the negative messages about sex from our upbringing is tough. So be kind to each other, discuss what didn't work, try again or go back to where you felt comfortable. What matters is not how quickly you progress but how you deal with any obstacles. If you think of a setback as a learning opportunity, you can't go far wrong.

Summary

- Cuddling and touching are not only a good way of repairing damage caused by the stress of modern life but also of making your partner feel wanted, valued and important.

- Therefore the first weeks of my programme put a ban on sexual intercourse to channel all your communication into touch, stop you repeating the same old mistakes again, and help you strip down your lovemaking – before building up something better and more fulfilling.

- By temporarily taking direct stimulation to each other's genitals out of the equation, you will become aware of other centres of pleasure in your body.

- Bring all your senses: touch, smell, taste and sound – not just sight – into the bedroom.

Exercises

Setting Aside Time for Each Other

No relationship can thrive on snatched moments for very long. The following ideas will help you set aside time for each other and create the platform for improved lovemaking.

1. **Live mindfully.** Over the next week, observe how much time you spend together in the same room or space. So although you might both be home on Saturday morning, if one of you is in the garage and the other in the kitchen, that does not count. How much of this time is 'business' contact – by which I mean arranging what time to pick up the kids or what time you'll be back for supper? How much of this is 'leisure' time – by which I mean chatting about this and that (rather than giving each other instructions or passing on information), sharing pastimes, socialising with others or just hanging out together?

2. **Reassess your priorities.** It is easy to fall into the trap of putting our partner last. We imagine that he or she knows that we truly love him or her and therefore will not be hurt if we spend two hours on the phone to a friend in crisis. There are so many little things that need to done, he or she will understand if we just wipe down the kitchen surfaces or make that work phone call. We tell ourselves that our partner is an adult – and therefore can fend for him- or herself – while our sons and daughters need our attention. We forget that children are just passing through, but a partnership is for ever. Have you been taking your partner for granted?

3. **Realign your lives so they intersect.** Rather than making ambitious changes – like date night – which can easily be derailed, develop good habits that provide regular opportunities to be together. Intimacy or in-depth conversations cannot be scheduled; they arise naturally out of chunks of shared time. For example, when you get home, seek out your partner and chat over your day. If you're home first, put down what you're doing for five minutes and give your partner your undivided attention when he or she arrives. Make a commitment to share meals together (without the television on). Go to bed at similar times, so your body clocks are in sync.

How to Turn Your Bedroom Into a Sensual Space

I often ask my clients to describe their bedrooms and, in some cases, it is amazing that any lovemaking happens there at all. One couple had a dog which slept in a cage by the bed, apparently it yelped during the night and this way the husband could reach over and give the cage a knock with a slipper.

- **De-clutter your bedroom.** Look around your bedroom with fresh eyes. Has it become a dumping ground? Are the items on the bedside table – like flu remedies, folders from work and household bills – conducive to lovemaking? What about pictures? Do you really want snapshots of your children or parents on the wall?

- **Create the right atmosphere for lovemaking.** A lot of bedrooms can be very feminine (pink, flowery and lots of pleated fabric) or childlike (lots of stuffed toys). What sort of sexual energy does this create? Is there anything which might inhibit one or both of you? How could you make this a more neutral place on to which you can both project your fantasies?

- **Is your bedroom warm enough?** Nothing is less conducive to good lovemaking than being cold. Do you need to upgrade the radiator or get a heater for instant warmth?

- **Improve the lighting.** Scientists have discovered that making love exclusively in the dark or with harsh artificial lighting deprives us of a natural sexual stimulant to the brain – the pineal and pituitary gland – which are vital for arousal. Try to create natural and soft full-spectrum lighting in your bedroom.

- **Use music as soundproofing.** Installing a sound system in the bedroom is another good tip for reducing your fear of being overheard and for creating the right mood. Choose music with no strong theme, vocals and changes in beat. Making up your own sexy compilations can be fun and much better than the radio, which some couples use, complete with DJ chatter and commercials for double glazing.

- **Stimulate all your senses.** Don't overlook the importance of smell. This can range from opening a window for fresh air, through to scented candles and air ionizers. Think of everything possible to stop your bedroom from being the 'bored' room.

Making Amends for the Past

Until you can cooperate, it will be hard to work as a team on the Month of Sensuality and the rest of the programme. The following will help you achieve this goal and put the past behind you:

- **Acknowledge past problems.** The more something is not spoken about, the more power it accumulates. We talk about the 'elephant in the room' – something everybody is aware of but which everybody ignores. However, the Dutch have a better saying which really encapsulates the idea: 'a dead horse on the table'. It's right under our noses and the longer we ignore it, the greater the smell and the greater the problem. By contrast, speaking the truth is like opening a window. Not only does the smell fade but also, once everyone has accepted the origin of the unpleasant ordure, the horse can be given a decent burial. When acknowledging a problem, you don't need to summarise what happened or explain why something hurts – just a sentence or two. Make certain you own the feelings ('I am still hurting from your affair' or 'I find it hard to get on with your mother') rather than blaming someone else ('You hurt me when you cheated' or 'Your mother has never accepted me'). The first version simply reports your feelings and invites a discussion, while the second will make your partner defensive and encourages a row.

- **Apologise for your share.** However blameless you might feel about the origin of the problems, look at your contribution to the impasse. There is probably something that you regret – however minor. For example, staying with the previous example, 'I'm sorry that I took you for granted' or 'I shouldn't have lost my temper with your mother as it made things worse'. Don't add explanations, as these can seem like excuses and reduce the power of the apology. In addition, the power of saying sorry can be magnified by acknowledging how your behaviour affected your partner: 'and that made you feel unloved and alone' or 'and that made you feel pulled in two'. A fulsome apology – where you express sorrow, accept your part in the problem and demonstrate that you understand the impact of your behaviour – will encourage your partner to make a similar move.

- **Forgive your partner.** There are three attitudes which make forgiveness harder. First, forgiveness will let my partner off the hook (but only if you give instant forgiveness without understanding the underlying causes or seeking to solve them). Second, he or she might do it again (but does your constant disapproval and anger help to mend bridges or just keep the two of you apart?). Third, my partner does not deserve my forgiveness (if this how you truly feel, you are not ready to work on your love life yet. Read my book *Resolve your Differences: Seven steps to coping with conflict in your relationship* instead). After having looked at what forgiveness is *not* about, let's focus on what it really means. If forgiveness is truly given – and not coerced – it allows us to let go of resentment, blame and anger. Therefore, forgiveness is not just an act of generosity to our partner but a gift to ourselves. It frees us from the past, allows us to draw a line in the sand and to start afresh.

- **Ask for what you want.** Often we are frightened of being rejected, so we drop hints or hope our partner will *know* what we need. Alternatively, when we do ask we lessen the impact of a simple straightforward request ('I'm going to bed now, will you come up too?') with preambles or explanations ('We've been having a lot of late nights recently and I think it's important that we get a good rest . . .') that invite discussion, argument or our partner simply switching off. Sometimes we are so keen to build consensus that our partner is handed a ready-made get-out clause ('I know you're watching this programme . . .). If this sounds difficult, practise asking in low-risk situations (like at work) or for things on which your heart is not set and therefore any rejection will not be too painful.

- **Recruit your partner into my programme.** Use the lessons from this exercise to get your partner on side. Acknowledge past problems: 'I know our love life has been a bit predictable and although we enjoy it, we never seem to get round to it.' Apologise for your part: 'I've left you to make all the first moves' or 'I've often been too tired.' Forgive your partner: 'I used to be resentful because you would sulk if you didn't get sex, but I've decided to put that behind us and start again.' Ask for what you want: 'I've bought this book with a weekly programme to improve our sex life. Please read it, so you can understand the underlying philosophy.'

How to Deal With a Nightmare

The benefit of lucid dreaming – being aware that you are dreaming – is knowing that however scary something might appear it does not have the power to hurt you. Here are some strategies for dealing with your night-time fears and overcoming them:

1. **Relax and go with the experience.** Tell yourself, 'I'm dreaming and in a dream I can change the outcome.' If you're falling, for example, you could imagine landing somewhere soft and delicious – like a mound of rose petals. In this way, your fear can be turned into enjoyment.

2. **Adopt an attitude of intrepid curiosity.** Instead of running away, turn and face your pursuer. They will often turn out to be harmless or disappear altogether. Alternatively, you could make peace with your enemy and, for example, instead of swimming away from a shark, have a ride on its back.

3. **Look for a solution in your dream.** Speak to the characters or creatures in your dream. Who are you? Why are you here? Can I help you? This will help you learn something important about the anxieties that feed your nightmares.

4. **Be positive.** Combating your night fears will make you braver in the day and more courageous when tackling difficult sexual issues.

Central Task for Repairing:
French Kissing

Teenagers spend a lot of time worrying about the art of French kissing (or *baiser amoreux* in French) but adults forget how good it feels. Worse still, many couples only French kiss before intercourse. For example, Jenny, from earlier in the chapter, had crossed it out of her repertoire for fear of giving 'the wrong signals'.

So this task works in tandem with the Month of Sensuality. After week two, when you have started sensual kissing, bring kissing out of the bedroom and incorporate a good French kiss into the rest of your life together. (I find this works particularly well with couples like Jenny and Mike where housework, childcare and chores eat up the majority of shared time together. A French kiss is a good way of checking back into together and remembering that you are lovers as well as parents.)

So what's the secret of a good open-mouthed kiss?

- **Moisten your lips.** Dry lips do not move well together. No need for lip balm, just a light brush of your tongue over your lips. (It can also look quite sexually provocative.)

- **Mix it up.** Alternate deep kisses with shallower ones, concentrate on stimulating the lips, remember the tongue is very sensitive and light touching with the tip is particularly stimulating.

- **Hands.** Cup your partner's face, caress his or her shoulders, and wrap your arms round each other. Once again, find lots of different ways to touch but do not go for the breasts or genitals.

- **Keep going.** A good French kiss should last for at least two or three minutes. Allow enough time for the passion to rise, so it is not simply a social kiss hello or goodbye.

- **Stop and talk.** The idea is not to progress to making love; just finish off by giving your partner a compliment, positive feedback (I really liked it when you . . .) or tell your partner how much you love him or her.

- **Repeat.** It will take a while to break the habit that French kiss = sex. So experiment with different places and times to French kiss. If you are uncertain if an advance would be welcome, ask your partner.

Prairie Voles and Desire

How do prairie voles decide which mate to settle down with and dig a burrow with? In order to understand how these sociable creatures formed bonds, scientists at Maryland University set up a series of experiments. Young prairie voles are weaned at twenty-one days and ready to leave the nest. The scientists separated them into same-sex sibling groups for two weeks – rather like a prolonged vole stag and hen party – so that by the time the tests started the young prairie voles would be raring to go. The team, led by Dr Courtney DeVries, expected the females and males to behave in the same way – because the differences in behaviour between the sexes are reduced in monogamous species. However, the young female voles needed just six hours with a desirable male before they were ready to pair off but the young male voles needed fourteen hours before they could decide.

The scientists suspected that another hormone called vaso-pressin was linked to mate selection. They already knew that vasopressin was responsible for managing stress but what would happen if they placed their voles in a stressful situation? Might this encourage quicker bonding? So this time, the young voles were made to swim for three minutes in a small tank of water where they could neither touch the bottom or climb out.

Afterwards, they were fished out in a net and returned to their home cage for thirty minutes to recover before possible mates were introduced.

So was this the vole equivalent of swimming across a lake with a box of your beloved's favourite chocolates or a damp squid? Once again, there was a marked difference between the sexes. The males were quicker to choose and formed a stronger bond after the swim test. However, the females reacted completely differently to the water tank. They could no longer make their minds up within six hours and even when they did eventually pair off, they spent three times longer with stranger voles than the control group who had not been stressed by swimming.

In a second study into the influence of stress on mate selection, the team from Maryland monitored the levels of an adrenalin-like steroid called corticosterone (which is released into the body by vasopressin). Even under normal conditions, prairie voles have an exceptionally high level of this steroid – five to ten times more than another of their polygamous cousins, the montane vole. From studies of prairie voles in the wild, the team knew that the levels of corticosterone would quickly drop in young females as they got to know unfamiliar males. What would happen if the scientists intervened and stopped this process? So they took two sets of female voles who had just left the nest. With the first group, they injected extra corticosterone and with the second group, they blocked the natural production of this steroid. While the first group of females showed no interest in pairing off at all, the second chose a mate in record time: an hour or even less. So what happened when the test was repeated but this time using young male prairie voles? Just as with the swimming, the males voles responded well to the extra stress steroid but when it was blocked, they had still not bonded twenty-four hours after being introduced to an eligible female.

Vasopressin is also present in humans. However, scientists do not yet understand how it works in men but they speculate that it works in a similar way as it does in prairie voles. It is certainly secreted during sexual arousal. Vasopressin may also explain why men often make such jealous boyfriends or husbands and why, although men respond well to a challenge, stress is a complete turn-off to women.

Step Three:
Bridging

In my intake interview with new clients, I always ask about couples' love lives. By a long way the most common response is that one partner, normally the man, wants more sex so that he can feel close; meanwhile, the other partner, normally the woman, counters that she cannot have sex until she feels close. It is an argument that goes round and round in circles and many couples settle into an armed truce.

A typical example where one partner pressured the other for sex is Simon and Cassie. 'I'm really worried that we're drifting apart. We used to make love about once a week – although I would have liked more – but recently it is not even that,' explained Simon, 'It's like I have to beg to make love to my wife and if we have no togetherness, how can we move forward?'

Cassie saw the situation differently: 'But you don't pay me any attention – unless you want sex you don't talk to me; I feel that you don't listen to me or take my needs into consideration.' Because, like most men, Simon responded better to stress, he imagined that Cassie would also respond to his pressure to make love, but this strategy had, of course, turned her off. In contrast, Cassie, like most women, valued time together and talking to promote bonding. However, as we have seen from prairie voles, females take half the amount of contact time that men take to bond. Meanwhile, men need so much more 'togetherness' to feel intimate that all they can see is hours and hours of talking. No wonder they roll their eyes and long for the quick fix of sex. In effect, both sexes expect the other to need exactly what they do.

Myths About Desire

It should be easy to define desire. On a first date, we ask ourselves: 'Do I fancy him or her?' When we're in a committed, long-term relationship, we ask ourselves: 'Do I want sex?' We're constantly monitoring our levels of desire. Surely, it's something that we either feel or we don't – simple as that? Except, desire is more complicated than a simple on/off switch and our attitudes are influenced by a whole lot of cultural myths – most of which we're only half aware of.

Desire is natural

If we take a purely biological approach, desire is a tool to propagate the species. It is about relieving tension or scratching an itch. Alternatively, desire is a craving for sexual pleasure – something inherent in our personalities (Freud's idea of libido or sex drive) or part of being human (John Stuart Mill, the nineteenth-century British philosopher, who believed that we seek pleasure and avoid pain). There is nothing wrong with any of these ideas, except that they locate desire in the reptilian part of our brain – at the top of our spinal column – which controls basic functions such as breathing and digestion. It also hands over important decisions about our future to our hormones.

Alicia, thirty-two, came to see me because she couldn't find love. When we looked at her dating history, her relationships had either been intensely passionate (but with little or no common interests) or based on friendship (with little or no sex). She had just finished one of her passionate relationships or at least she was trying to: 'Jasper has been very good for me. He made me feel attractive and desirable again, and when you've got a small child that's no mean feat. However, I know he's not right for me. I'll end it, but he'll phone me up and persuade me to come out for a drink and I tell myself "Why not? Because I'm not really doing anything else." When I see him, there's this craving inside and I can't keep my hands off him. Obviously, we end up in bed, even though I know I'll feel terrible the next morning.' By contrast, the father of her child, Howard, had been one of her 'friendship' relationships: 'I really respect him and he's helped my career by being a mentor and opening doors. I liked him so much that I thought I should fancy him too and I talked myself into giving it a try – and that's how we accidentally had a child together – but the spark wasn't really there. What can I do?'

Like many single people, Alicia expected what I call 'big bang sex' to bind her and her partner together and launch them into a lifetime of loving togetherness. Unfortunately, it had bonded her to inappropriate men and made her overlook others with whom she could have had a lasting and fulfilling relationship.

It is not just singles but long-married couples who are prone to the 'desire is natural' myth. When Frank was forty-six, and had been married for twenty years to Gwen, he met Lucy at work. 'There was an immediate connection, something I hadn't had with my wife for years. We tried to fight it but the passion was stronger than both of us. We'd meet up and I'd be all ready to say "This must stop" or "This is wrong", but we'd start kissing or she'd slip her shoes off and rub her foot up my thigh and I'd be lost. We did split up once or twice but we couldn't keep away from each other.' Inevitably, someone saw Frank and Lucy in a wine bar and sent an anonymous text to Gwen. When the affair was discovered, Frank was forced to choose and left his wife. 'Gwen was devastated and I don't know if my daughters will ever forgive me – perhaps when they're older – but I couldn't keep on faking it and going through the motions.' However, when he came into counselling at fifty-two, he was beginning to think he'd made a big mistake: 'Lucy is very hard. She makes no attempt to get on with my daughters. Secretly, I think I made a big mistake but I can't go back because Gwen is happily remarried and my daughters tell me they're very well suited. Sometimes I wonder if Lucy sent that anonymous text to force my hand.'

Sex = intimacy

With this myth, the amount and the quality of sex is a reliable barometer of the health of a relationship and the level of intimacy between the partners. Certainly, sex is part of the way we communicate and reflects our longing to bond. In fact, nothing brings us physically closer than sexual intercourse where we penetrate or are penetrated by our partner. This version of sex does at least place desire in the mammalian part of our brain – in the midsection – which controls such emotions as anxiety and our fight or flight responses. However, we are in danger of becoming prisoners of our feelings.

'My partner, Malcolm, leaves all his stuff lying around our small flat – business papers, three-day-old mail, dirty coffee cups, the towel when he comes out of the shower – it's me who has to pick them up,' says Bryony. 'When he takes advantage of my good nature or when he just expects, for example, there to be enough bread in the fridge – without ever thinking of picking up a loaf himself, I don't feel close and I certainly don't feel like having sex – full stop.'

The other problem is that intimacy means different things to different people. When Rebecca, thirty, came into counselling, she was considering ending her relationship: 'I've really tried to get close to Thierry. I've told him things about my childhood that I've told nobody else. It was tough – because there were some painful times after Mum left and I didn't get on with my stepmother – but I thought it would bring us closer together. However, Thierry's never really opened up to me. He just says "There's nothing to tell", but it's like he's wearing a mask. He's kind and attentive but I don't know him.' Although their lovemaking had been very passionate – especially after Rebecca unburdened herself – she had become more and more withdrawn and the couple hardly ever made love (unless Rebecca had drunk too much).

Thierry was withdrawn and frustrated: 'How can we be close if we never make love?' While Rebecca used talking and trading personal stories to feel intimate, Thierry used touch: 'I'm telling her things all the time we're in bed: how much I love her, how much I desire her.'

'But you won't open up to me,' Rebecca moaned.

Although Rebecca and Thierry worried that their sexual difficulties were a sign that their relationship was fundamentally flawed, I saw them as a sign that they were struggling to grow. Rather than being satisfied with one of the ingredients of desire, they were seeking to expand how they expressed their sexuality.

The truth about desire

Desire does have a natural or biological component, but we can regulate our impulses in the brain and even if we find someone incredibly attractive, we won't start copulating in the street (like dogs). Being intimate is an important ingredient for desire but a straight link between what happens and our feelings overlooks the importance of our brains and how we interpret events.

For example, Margery, fifty-three, and Joseph, fifty-five, sought help after he had an affair while on a business trip. After a lot of talking, soul searching and two months of counselling, they were closer than they had been for years. 'We just have this little sex problem,' explained Margery. 'About twenty-five per cent of the time that we're making love, Joseph will lose his erection.'

'How do you react?' I asked.

'It doesn't happen when I'm giving him oral sex but sometimes when he's returning the favour. So naturally, I'm angry and hurt and want him to stop. I roll over to my side of the bed and try to go to sleep.'

This is how Margery viewed her desire:

event ⟶ feeling
losing erection ⟶ rejection

However, I wanted to know what was happening in her brain. So I asked, why she felt rejected.

'He didn't lose his erection when he made love to her,' she replied.

'How do you know that?' I asked.

'I don't know for certain, but he's told me that the sex was good, so he must have been aroused.'

'So you are interpreting his lack of erection as a personal rejection, that somehow you're not "good enough" for him.'

'She was almost twenty years younger and if I'd been "enough", he wouldn't have strayed,' replied Margery.

Although it was painful to spell out the links, we had a more accurate picture of why Margery felt rejected:

event ——————————→ interpretation ——————————→ feeling
losing erection ——————→ I'm not sexy enough ——→ rejection

Next, I started to challenge her interpretation of events:

'So your husband's affair was all down to you not being attractive enough?' I asked.

'No, of course not. He was away on business and would get lonely and my father's been ill and I'd been preoccupied with him.'

'And when you're giving him oral sex, where is your focus, on his body or your own?'

'On his body, of course.' Margery was puzzled.

'So you're not focused on your vagina and how lubricated it is? You're concentrating on your husband's pleasure.'

Margery nodded as she realised where my questions were leading: 'So he might be concentrating on me when he's pleasuring me.'

I went on to explain that even for men in their twenties, erections and desire come and go during lovemaking. Men in their fifties will often need more stimulation to become physically aroused; it is not a reflection of how much they love or desire their partners. Finally, men of any age who become anxious about their erection will find it more difficult to perform – regardless of how they feel about their partner.

'That feels like you've lifted a weight off my shoulders,' said Margery.

event ————————→ interpretation ——→ feeling
losing erection ————→ natural part
                        of lovemaking ——→ unconcerned

By acknowledging the role our thought processes play in desire, we are acknowledging the part of our brains which makes us human – the neo-cortex in our forehead. We are alone in the animal kingdom in placing meanings on sex beyond the biological or moving towards what we like and avoiding what we dislike. This is what makes intimacy and sexual desire so incredibly complicated, and the reason why humans have the longest post-puberty sexual development.

In other words, desire has three important ingredients:

Touch
Thoughts
Feelings

Sex is possible with just one or two of these qualities. For example, touch alone can provide a stimulating but probably empty one-night stand or someone might talk themselves into giving in to a long-term partner and having 'just get it over with' sex. However, all three ingredients need to be working together for passionate and fulfilling lovemaking.

What inhibits desire

There is nothing sadder in counselling than when a couple realise that while one partner was lying frustrated and unfulfilled on one side of the bed, the other was having almost identical thoughts on his or her side. Sometimes they have been trapped in routine, six times a year and bury the problem-style sex for over twenty years; when all along both wanted something better. However, there is hope. Once you move away from the simplistic idea that you either feel desire or you don't, it's possible to understand all the everyday things which keep you and your partner apart.

Performance anxiety

A small amount of anxiety and uncertainty can be a spur to good lovemaking. Hence the relative ease of sex with some-one new or kiss-and-make-up sex after a row. However, high levels of anxiety – 'Am I doing this right?' or 'Will she know that I'm inexperienced?' or 'I hate my body' – can kill even the most accomplished touch and prevent desire building. Worse still, anxiety is catching. If one partner is anxious, the other partner will become anxious too and the couple will get into a vicious circle. Lesley, twenty-eight, had always been worried about making love: 'Sex was never talked about in our family but there was an unspoken message that I should be a virgin on my wedding day. I suppose this was some-where at the back of my head because whenever things between me and my boyfriend, Gavin, headed towards inter-course I would tense up.' Although nothing was said, Lesley's body language was communicating loud and clear. 'I was really worried about hurting her,' said Gavin. 'I thought I was doing something wrong and put it down to being young and clumsy and ignorant.' So he would either lose his erec-tion or make a half-hearted attempt at penetration. Instead of talking about their individual worries – and how they fed off each other – they 'managed' their anxiety by avoiding inter-course altogether.

Time and again, I counsel couples where each is anxious about whether they are 'good enough' in bed. Men's anxiety tends to focus on whether they can 'satisfy' their partner and women's tends to focus on their bodies. Unfortunately, rather than talking about these fears and releasing the tension, each partner will find coping strategies – for example, turning off the lights or focusing on technique rather than on the person – which means that neither partner is really 'present' while they are making love. And if you're only half there, the sex will only be half as good – and there is little opportunity for desire to flourish.

Unresolved emotional issues

If you are not talking about something important outside the bedroom, it is unlikely you will be connecting inside the bedroom. Although many couples blame 'communication' problems for their lack of desire, all too often they are communicating very effectively – after all, there is nothing clearer than a turned back or functional, but absent, sex (physically there, but emotionally somewhere else). Both say 'I don't want to get close'. What people mean by 'communication' problems is that they have not been able to *resolve* their differences. When Sarah, twenty-eight, fell in love with Jeremy, thirty-seven, she accepted that he had been married before and had a seven-year-old daughter. Although she got on well with the daughter, she objected to the way her mother kept interfering with their lives.

'She will phone up at the last minute and change the time or even the date for the access visit – which completely disrupts our plans.'

Jeremy didn't think the problem was so serious. 'I've tried to lay down the law more with my ex and she has been a lot more considerate recently.'

Sarah nodded her head and although I wondered if the subject was really closed, we focused on other issues (mainly helping Sarah and Jeremy argue constructively) and their low levels of desire. Although both were committed to the Month of Sensuality (see Step Two), there were lots of excuses – most of which sounded perfectly plausible – but no progress. When they had only managed one half of week one's exercise, where Jeremy had initiated the touching, I suspected 'unresolved emotional issues'. In fact, in the next counselling session, everything came back up to surface again.

'I'd gone to pick up something I'd left at work, so I wasn't there when Jeremy's ex came to pick up their daughter. The arrangement was that she wouldn't come into the house – as I don't like the idea of her snooping around my home because she's in our life enough already,' explained Sarah. 'You can imagine my surprise when I returned and found her in my kitchen.'

Jeremy was trying to be calm but it was obvious that they'd been over this a million times already. 'We were talking about the summer holidays and I needed to check something on the calendar, it seemed easier to sort it out there and then. It was only a moment. It's not like she was free to open any of the cupboards.'

I suddenly had a picture in my mind of Sarah and Jeremy making love and his ex walking into their bedroom and sitting at the end of the bed. So I asked: 'Is Jeremy's ex inhibiting your desire?'

'I don't feel safe enough to let go,' said Sarah in a quiet voice.

So we stopped working on their love life and concentrated on resolving this issue. Several weeks later, when Sarah had not only attended her stepdaughter's birthday party at

Jeremy's old house but had also enjoyed the occasion, and all the underlying issues had been properly explored, the desire returned and the couple were able to graduate from my programme with a passionate and fulfilling love life.

It is not just unresolved issues between the couple but each partner's individual problems that can inhibit desire. Angela, twenty-eight, had been living with her partner for five years and although their sex life was 'okay' and 'all right', she wanted to be able to relax and truly enjoy their lovemaking. Even a couple of weeks into working together, when most people have got over their natural reserve and embarrassment about talking about sex, I sensed that Angela was still holding back. So I talked about the protective barriers that everybody puts up to stop others taking advantage, and asked how high hers were at that very moment. Angela pointed to her forehead, while her partner, Adrian, pointed to just above his waistline.

'I know I should be able to trust you,' Angela said to me, 'and Adrian too, but I find it hard to let myself go and be truly vulnerable.'

'It seems like you're having trouble letting go of your desire too and becoming sexually needy – because it would not only reveal your vulnerability but also risk rejection too.'

Slowly Angela talked about the legacy of having a father with Asperger's syndrome (a mild form of autism) and how, when he was stressed, he'd explode with irrational anger. It had left Angela wary, even if someone just raised their voice, and highly defensive.

Once I'd helped her become more aware of her barriers, when it was appropriate to raise them and when not, she found herself able to relax more in bed and their lovemaking improved.

Fused sex lives

The next scenario, which inhibits desire, comes as a shock to many couples who think being close is an asset. However, it is possible to be so close that it can spoil your lovemaking – either by turning you into brother and sister (the opposite of feeling sexy together) or being so responsible for each other's sexual happiness that you're overwhelmed (after all, it's hard enough to negotiate your own sexual hang-ups without being responsible for your partner's too). So what exactly do I mean by 'fused'?

In every relationship, there needs to be both 'we' and 'I' – too much 'we' and the couple lose track of their individual identity, while too much 'I' means there is no relationship (just two people sharing a home). Meanwhile, we might love our partner and want the best for him or her but we can't run his or her life and we're certainly not his or her therapist.

Caroline and David were in their late thirties and had been together for over fifteen years when they entered counselling for their low-to-no-sex relationship. They lived in a small flat, both worked from home and David was helping Caroline launch a business. However, it was not just their business lives that were fused. Whenever, Caroline got stressed and upset, she would unburden herself to David: 'I had a difficult childhood – my parents split up when I was a teenager and my mother married a man whom I hated – so I can easily get overwhelmed and let it all out.'

There's nothing wrong with sharing a problem but, for Caroline, it normally came out as a torrent with one problem sparking another. 'The other day I got worried about a problem with the business and how hard it was to work together and if we can't work together could we cooperate and have children? What if our whole relationship is doomed?' After an hour of pouring out all her fears and escalating worries to David, Caroline felt much better. Unfortunately, David, who up to that moment had been doing all right, became overwhelmed and sank into depression. Like many fused couples, Caroline and David let their own and each other's anxiety undermine their relationship. So what's the alternative?

Self-soothing is one of the most important ideas in this book – and key to establishing a good sex life. The idea is that on a day-to-day basis we are responsible for dealing with our normal day-to-day problems. This does not mean keeping your feelings to yourself – it is fine to report your feelings: for example, I'm feeling low and stressed – but avoid dumping on to your partner: 'Nothing ever goes my way, I can't cope, I'm never going to finish, etc.' While reporting keeps your partner informed, dumping risks 'infecting' your partner with your anxieties and stress.

When Caroline was unable to soothe her own anxieties and centre herself, David felt obliged not just to listen but also to take on all her problems and solve them.

'When Caroline is upset, I get upset, and it starts a vicious circle because I get more and more stressed,' says David. 'Perhaps she's right: if we can't sort out an accounting system for her business, perhaps we are doomed. I'm trying to solve the accounts problem and our whole relationship at the same time. So I'll get snappy or, more likely, switch off and walk away – as it is the only way to process everything.' In fact, David found it just as hard to self-soothe as Caroline. Instead of being able to tell himself: 'I love Caroline but I'm not responsible for sorting out every detail of her life', he started to panic, become infected by her anxiety and resort to another unhelpful alternative to self-soothing: blanking out.

So how does a fused relationship create problems in the bedroom? In David and Caroline's case, they would worry so much whether the other was having a good time that neither could relax and enjoy themselves. Worse still, their relationship was so important, and they were so frightened of each other's disapproval, that it became almost impossible to experiment. The resulting sexual boredom further exacerbated their low levels of desire. However, once Caroline and David learned to self-soothe and stabilise their own fears, they stopped being overwhelmed or infected by each other and their desire quickly returned. (See the section for healthy and unhealthy ways of self-soothing in the exercises below.)

Another example of a fused couple with sex problems is Craig and Nicola who are both in their mid-twenties. When they did make love, it was pleasurable and rewarding. Unfortunately, it happened only once every six weeks or so. The more they talked, the more fused they sounded until I had a picture of two people sharing genitals rather than his penis belonging to him and her breasts and vagina belonging to her. When I asked Craig if he ever masturbated alone – especially as they had sex so seldom – he was quite shocked. 'I think that would be very selfish and, anyway, if I satisfied myself, I'd probably have even less desire.' Nicola, who was generally responsible for initiating their lovemaking, would often playfully grab his penis if he came out of the shower – especially if he had an erection. 'I'm never certain if she's just mucking about and I'll get all worked up for nothing or really interested, so I tend to freeze up.' Meanwhile, Nicola would complain that when they cuddled, Craig would go straight for her breasts: 'He hasn't said as much, but it's like he thinks he's entitled and that's a big turn off.'

What Promotes Desire

When taking a history of every couple who comes to me for counselling, I find the couples who report a good and fulfilling sex life have five things in common:

1. **Investing time.** If sex is the last thought of an exhausted mind and the last act of an exhausted body, it is unlikely to be inspiring. My sexually successful couples prioritise enough time together to tune in to each other. Time and again, clients, particularly female clients, attribute a session of good lovemaking to: 'I felt really relaxed.'

2. **Self-validation.** If you rely on other people as the prime source of feeling attractive, sex can become not an expression of love but proof that you are desirable. Worse still, over time, your partner's praise becomes less and less effective – because 'He would say that, wouldn't he?' or 'She's just saying that to fob me off' – while the interest of strangers becomes more and more powerful (making you vulnerable to an affair). While people who need others to validate them are a black hole and suck in sexual energy, people who are secure in their own skin, and like themselves, have sexual energy to give out.

3. **Good eye contact.** No wonder all cultures use make-up to draw attention to the eyes. Good eye contact is important for initiating sex and shows that someone is truly present in the moment. Sexually successful couples keep their eyes open during foreplay and communicate how they're feeling ('Go faster, yes, more please') and monitor how the other is feeling (the raised eyebrow, the

questioning frown or the look of pure bliss). Peek-a-boo games where you hide your face and suddenly reappear (such as the ones we play with babies) can also create laughter and build desire.

4. **Being in the moment.** Sexually successful couples clear their mind of other concerns and worries, and are therefore aware of the feelings building in their body. (If you have an overactive mind, see the exercise section for advice.)

5. **Good communication.** It is important to share thoughts and relevant feelings, so if there are problems or if there is something that needs to be changed, both partners know they will be listened to and their concerns will be taken on board.

Bridges to Desire

Sex is easy at the beginning of a relationship. Pure lust helps us over any general inhibitions and hang-ups – like messages from the Church or our parents that 'sex is shameful'. Unfortunately, the ease of early lovemaking and the Hollywood/romantic novel myth of being swept away by our feelings stop us from understanding how we move from the mundane reality of being a couple – nappies, laundry, bills – into the bliss of sex. That's why it is so important to be aware of how passion builds and of the four phases through which it travels:

- **Desire** (positive anticipation and feeling that you deserve sexual pleasure)

- **Arousal** (being receptive and responsive to touching and intimate stimulation)

- **Orgasm** (letting go and allowing arousal to naturally culminate in pleasure)

- **Satisfaction** (feeling emotionally and physically bonded after a sexual experience).

At the beginning of a relationship lust almost hardwires us into the arousal stage, so we don't need to be aware of desire and how to feed it. We just magically fall into each other's arms. By the time the honeymoon period finishes, most couples have found other bridges from day-to-day life (of earning a living, running a house and bringing up children together) into the desire stage (and the sensual world of lovemaking). Unfortunately, the couples who depend on just lust are left stranded, frustrated and blaming each other. So what are these bridges and how do they work?

The most important bridge to desire is **casual touching** – for example, holding hands in the street, a neck message while watching TV or nibbling each other's ears. This is the bedrock for a healthy love life. The good news is that if you have completed the previous stage – and enjoyed a Month of Sensuality – you have already added this bridge to your repertoire. For Mike and Jenny, from the first two chapters, this had been a revelation: 'I really enjoyed having the pressure taken off,' said Jenny. Previously, she would have had to decide if she was aroused the moment Mike first touched her – which seldom happened unless she had had a few drinks – now they had a proper bridge to desire. They could either enjoy the non-demanding touching, which is pleasurable in its own right, or decide to have sex.

While every couple enjoys the first bridge from everyday life into lovemaking, the next one is always more controversial. When I tried to convince Adam and Hannah, in their late twenties, that sex needs to be **planned** – like any activity – Hannah sighed: 'It's better when it's spontaneous and natural.'

I agree, but those qualities alone cannot sustain desire.

Adam was more pragmatic: 'Remember when I got those tickets for U2 in concert? We looked forward to that for ages and somehow it made the evening even better.' Indeed, anticipation is important for building desire. After I probed further into Hannah's worries about a 'sex date', she asked: 'But what if I'm not in the mood?'

This is important because feeling obliged is a barrier, rather than a bridge to desire. Fortunately, they had completed their Month of Sensuality and Adam agreed that cuddling and fondling would be enough intimacy if Hannah did not want to go further. Ultimately, planning ahead was a success.

'We stayed in and I cooked us a nice meal. Adam had downloaded some new music and we danced in the living room and one thing led to another. Actually, it felt quite natural,' explained Hannah.

For couples who feel self-conscious about planning ahead, I often include another 'bridge': **play**. When we were children, play was at the centre of our lives and a gateway to learning and team building, and was an opportunity to let off steam: all of these qualities are just as important for good lovemaking. Unfortunately, as adults we forget how creative – and how much fun – playing can be. So I've had couples building dams across streams, having food fights and playing on children's swings together. These games break down barriers and help partners see each other in a new light and this is ultimately very sexy. There is another bridge that is very similar to play: **flirting**. It involves teasing each other, pet names, jokes, double-entendre and compliments.

The next bridge from the practical into the passionate is a surprise to most couples: good lovemaking needs **distance** as much as closeness. Charlotte and Edward, in their fifties, had not made love for over six months and described themselves as best friends. 'I always know what Edward is thinking,' claimed Charlotte. 'She's right; she does,' Edward agreed. They did lots of things as a couple – fine dining, a busy social life – but very little apart.

'We hold hands when we go shopping and he's very considerate – opening doors – but I wish . . .' Charlotte drifted into a sad silence.

'There are more important things in a marriage,' Edward chipped in.

I doubt that's what Charlotte meant but she smiled in agreement. Instead of being two individuals, albeit in a relationship, they had become one amorphous couple – frightened of allowing each other to be different. The first step was to encourage them to argue more – the quickest and most effective way to release submerged passion. Next, I asked them to witness each other's separate lives.

Edward went to a conference where Charlotte was speaking. Charlotte watched Edward play tennis – an interest he'd given up when their children were young.

'I really admired how he really went for each shot and he looked quite sexy in his shorts too,' Charlotte laughed.

'And I saw the respect of Charlotte's colleagues,' explained Edward, 'it was like looking at her through fresh eyes.' Soon after these visits, Charlotte and Edward reported passionate lovemaking again. It is when we see the distance between us and our partner, and recognise them as a separate person who is independent of us, that there is enough space for desire to return.

Ultimately, there are as many bridges to desire as there are couples. However, some common themes that emerge:

- We use different bridges at different stages in our relationship.

- If you use the same bridge over and over again, it will wear out and become less reliable for transporting you into the sensual world.

- The happiest couples have a range of possible bridges and choose the most appropriate one for the occasion.

Can We Remove the Ban on Sex Yet?

Each of the six steps for turning okay sex into passionate sex has a particular lesson. The aim of a Month of Sensuality was to make you aware that your whole body is a source of pleasure – not just the breasts and genitals. There is another important lesson embedded into this next step – which I call a Fortnight of Wickedness – that might be missed if you rush headlong into having intercourse again. Holding back also will help you focus on each moment along the way, rather than miss out on the passing delights because you are too fixated on the final destination. Having said that, I think it is important to be flexible with my clients.

Each couple at my counselling centre gets a slightly different variation that suits their particular needs. Everyone does the Month of Sensuality but after that, everything is up for negotiation and some couples start to have intercourse again. Think about all the issues, read the rest of the book, and discuss the options together. If you decide to follow my programme to the letter but slip up, don't worry. Humans are contrary creatures and banning something makes it that bit more desirable! Just return to where you fell off the wagon and repeat that step.

A Fortnight of Wickedness

Up to this point, you have ignored your genitals, but now they are about to take centre stage. Some people find this rather uncomfortable – particularly if they prefer their lovemaking under the bedclothes. Stephanie, forty-two, had pursed her lips when I outlined this next task: 'It all sounds rather dirty.' At which point, I quoted Woody Allen: 'Is sex dirty? Only if it's done right.' By this I mean we have to make peace with and enjoy every part of our bodies before we can abandon ourselves to being passionate.

Week One: Show and Tell – Part One.

- Before you start touching each other's genitals, you need to look at your own – really look at them.

- Stand *alone* naked in front of a full-length mirror and look at your reflection. If you don't have a mirror that shows at least head to knees, it's probably time to buy one.

- Take a full inventory of what you *like* about your body – say it out loud or write it down.

  This is a hard task – partly because we have been trained from earliest childhood not to be big-headed and partly because we only see images of 'perfect' bodies in the media (which have normally been airbrushed or altered). Women find this task difficult, especially if they bond with friends by running down parts of their own or other women's bodies.

- Look again at your reflection and aim for five good things. For example, Stephanie reported: 'I have a cute belly button and my bottom has a nice curve but . . .' I could tell she was about to add something negative, so I stopped her. This is not about what could be changed or improved. It is five things that you *like*. Finally Stephanie added her nipples, her fingers and her long neck. She started crying: 'That's probably the first time I've ever looked at myself without adding "but" . . . Why am I so hard on myself?'

- Next focus on your genitals. For men, look at your perineum (the sensitive ridge between your anus and scrotum). Cup your testicles and feel their weight. Roll back your foreskin, if you have one. Look at the tip of your penis, squeeze it and watch how it opens and closes. For women, spread your labia majora (the outer lips of your vagina) and peer inside. Pull back the hood from your clitoris and examine it as closely as possible. A large number of women, like Stephanie, go through life without examining this sensitive spot. (A hand mirror might help.) Stephanie found this a revelation: 'It wasn't dirty after all. In fact, it was really rather pink and pretty.'

Week One: Show and Tell – Part Two

- Later in the week, the two of you should stand *together* naked in front of the mirror.

- Flip a coin to decide who talks first, the winner goes through all the things about her or his body that he or she likes. Talk about your genitals, too, and show some of the discoveries. Maybe you will need the hand mirror to show the more intimate or overlooked parts of your bodies. Give your partner a tour – preferably with a running commentary.

- Don't worry if this is not remotely sexy. The aim is to introduce your partner to every inch of your body and your genitals are no different than, for example, your knee.

- Look carefully at how your partner handles his or her genitals. This will provide clues for the future for what he or she enjoys.

- Swap over and the second partner talks about his or her body and what he or she likes.

- The final stage is to give compliments to each other. Looking in the mirror, tell your partner: 'I've always liked . . .' or 'I never knew how beautiful your . . .' Fill in the blanks.

- When given a compliment, don't knock it back or run yourself down. Just thank your partner and return the positive feedback.

- When you have finished, give each other a hug and get dressed.

- Discuss what the experience was like and share any surprises.

Week Two: Focus on Arousal

- Decide who will be toucher and who will be touchee. Start with the same touching and kissing as last month.

- After ten to fifteen minutes, you can start to explore your partner's genitals.

- Be gentle and remember how your partner touched her or his genitals.

- This is a sensual pleasure; not a means to an end but an end in itself, so take your time. Alternate different kinds of touching: firm, light. Tips of fingers. Quick. Slow. In circles or up and down or in and out. (The touchee is still in control. If something is too intense, he or she can word-lessly move the toucher's hand or press down/pull up to vary the pressure.)

- Allow enough time to experiment – up to fifteen minutes – alternating touching genitals with other parts of your partner's body.

- Don't worry if your partner does not have an erection all the time or her vagina is not constantly lubricated. The penis is still sensitive when flaccid and so is the vagina even when not engorged.

- Swap over, so the toucher becomes the touchee.

- Focus on your arousal and how it flows and ebbs. Enjoy the moment. Intimacy does not have to end just because the penis is not constantly erect.

- Finish with a cuddle rather than an orgasm.

The main lesson from a 'Fortnight of Wickedness' is how desire comes and goes. Men, in particular, are focused on whether they have an erection or not. The fear of losing potency makes men rush through sex and focus on reaching orgasm rather than on their feelings. Women, too, worry that when they lose desire, it is gone for the evening, or they give up when they are unable to climax within some self-imposed time limit. This task will offer proof that erections and desire fluctuates but will come back – especially when there is no fixed goal.

Summary

- One of the biggest barriers to a fulfilling love life is the belief that sex should be 'spur of the moment' and 'natural'. This idea of an 'instant fit' and 'skin-to-skin' compatibility makes it harder for single people to forge deeper and lasting connections and can bond them with unsuitable partners. It also encourages long-term couples to wait until desire sweeps them away.

- Desire needs three ingredients: touch (an animal connection), feelings (a heart connection) and thoughts (a brain connection). Couples need to find a balance between being too independent (and having no relationship) and becoming fused (where each partner's sense of themselves is reflected through the other's eyes). The goal is to become inter-dependent.

- Knowing and making peace with your genitals, and feeling comfortable sharing them with your partner, is an important ingredient for good lovemaking.

Exercises

Challenging the Myth of Spontaneous Sex

We are so preoccupied with spontaneity that we tend to close our eyes to just how much planning goes into being spontaneous.

1. Looking back at your most recent 'natural' lovemaking:

- What facilitated the right mood? (For example, arranging for the children to be out; booking a table at a favourite restaurant; jetting away to a romantic destination.)

- How much preparation? (For example, wearing the right clothes, washing or personal grooming – like leg or bikini waxing.)

- What other ingredients went into creating the spontaneity? (For example, the bottle of champagne in the fridge or putting on favourite music.)

2. Total up the number of phone calls, emails, purchases and decisions that went into being spontaneous:

- How do you feel about the result?

- Who is shouldering most of the burden?

- Is it you or your partner? How does that make you feel?

3. By relying on chemistry or some unspoken magic to carry you into the sensual world, you are not taking responsibility for your own lovemaking. So ask yourself:

- What is stopping me from owning up to how much I need and enjoy sex?

- What lessons have I been given about sex – from my parents, friends and our wider culture?

- Without really thinking about your answers, from the top of your head, complete these sentences: When it comes to sex, nice girls . . . When it comes to sex, good boys . . .

- How could responsibility for lovemaking be more evenly shared?

The Art of Self-Soothing

When children fall over, whether it really hurts or not, they burst into tears and one or both of their parents run over and 'kiss it better'. One of the most important parts of growing up is learning how to self-soothe rather than expecting someone else to sweep us up in his or her arms. Unfortunately, self-soothing is one of the hardest things to achieve and the myth that 'love will solve everything' encourages us to expect our partner to step into the role that our parents once held (although if our partner does get somewhere close to meeting this expectation we often accuse him or her of being 'suffocating' or 'controlling'). The whole concept of soothing is further complicated because there are constructive and destructive strategies:

Destructive ways of soothing

Blanking: This strategy includes denying there is a problem, shutting down or rationalising everything away.

Self-medicating: Using alcohol, recreational drugs, work, etc. to distract attention from your underlying problems or to manage stress.

Dumping: Instead of taking responsibility for your own problems, you expect someone else to come to your rescue (and then get angry when they don't rise to the challenge).

Acting out: When children have problems at home – for example parents divorcing – they often 'act out' their problems by being disruptive in class or take their anger out by bullying smaller or weaker pupils. Adults act out by losing their temper with the wrong person or the right person but over something trivial, driving too fast or plotting revenge.

Constructive ways of soothing

Acknowledging: Sit quietly and become aware of the feeling and what it is trying to tell you.

Processing: When the feeling is strong – or induces panic – concentrate on your breathing as air is inhaled in through your nose and exhaled out again. When you are calmer, start to assess the problem and what can be done about it. Going for a run or walking the dog can similarly help to process and understand the feelings. Once you have processed the feelings and isolated the relevant issue, your partner is more likely to listen rather than be overwhelmed by a pile of problems and switch off.

Engaging: If you cannot find an immediate solution, where could you get information or advice? Think about your specific needs. For example, if the car has been broken into you might need to contact the police, your insurers and a glass repair company – rather than dumping the problem on your partner.

Reporting: Keep your partner and loved ones informed of your feelings – 'I'm tired' or 'My boss is a nightmare and I'm at my wits' end' – so they don't feel excluded or imagine they've done something wrong. It also invites your partner to offer help, advice or support.

Choosing: Ultimately reaching out to your partner becomes a choice, not a necessity. When it is a large problem – such as bereavement, redundancy or serious illness – it may well be sensible to ask for your partner's help to soothe.

Switching Off a Spinning Wheel Mind

Many people find it hard to disengage their brain and listen to their body. Some cannot relax until all the chores have been done, and others are too busy churning over the events of the day or particular problems. They are like a hamster on a wheel, constantly running but getting nowhere. So what's the alternative?

- **Accept that over-thinking is counterproductive.** There comes a point when further ruminating just confuses or promotes bad decision making.

- **Unload your thoughts.** When left to go round and round in your brain, thoughts and jobs-to-do get bigger and bigger. So put everything down on paper, as if you are taking dictation from your brain – don't censor or edit, just get it down.

- **Review your thoughts.** First of all, you'll be surprised that there is less on the page than you might have expected. Look for words like 'should' and 'must' and question the beliefs. For example: 'Why must you clean the kitchen before you make love?' Who says? Where does this belief come from? Is this belief right? Look for statements that are simply not true and cross those off. For others, be like a barrister and look for the evidence for the 'facts' on your piece of paper.

- **Put off coming with up a solution or doing that 'must-do' job.** Having accepted most pressing tasks are no such thing, put off, for example, checking emails or tidying up until later. In the same way, put off thinking about a pressing problem. In many cases, you will have forgotten the problem the next day.

- **If the problem returns, simply push it away.** If you've begun to make love and a thought pops into your head (for example 'We're out of coffee'), imagine pushing it out of your brain (rather than thinking 'I could pop into the supermarket on my way back from work tomorrow'). You will be surprised how easily these thoughts disappear if you don't allow them to take hold. If, however, you find this technique difficult, consider meditation classes and train your mind to be still.

Central Task for Bridging:
Planning Intimate Time Together

There are many bridges to desire but the most over-looked must be planning. Maybe it is a legacy of our Victorian past but many people are only happy when they are swept away by their emotions – and therefore do not have to take responsibility for their desires. Of course, spontaneous lovemaking is wonderful and exciting, but if you wait until both of you just happen to be in the right mood, at the same time and in the right place . . . you can end up waiting a long, long time. Alternatively, a little planning can solve all these problems.

When I set up this task, my clients are sceptical: 'What if I'm not in the mood?', 'I don't want to be obliged' or 'Isn't it all a bit clinical?' First, there is no obligation to make love – only to be physically inti-mate. You could have a bubble bath together, slow dance to some favourite music or get out a bottle of body oil and give each other a massage. Second, setting aside time for each other is proof that you value each other and, once alone together, your mood will probably change. (It's a bit like going for a meal and not being particularly hungry until you arrive at the restaurant and look at the specials.) Third, I am not suggesting that all your lovemaking is pre-planned but this becomes one of your bridges to desire.

Here are a few guidelines for a sex date:

- Put a date in the diary.

- Set aside at least an hour – preferably more.

- Agree that the date does not have to end with an orgasm but that it would be nice. (If you are sticking to my programme – which I would advise – this would be tandem solo masturbation.)

- Make arrangements, so that you will not be disturbed. (If you have teenage children, you might like to book a hotel room or arrange for them to sleep over at a friend's house.)

- Think of ways to make your time special. What about favourite foods? How could you create a loving atmosphere?

- The more energy you put into your date, the more enjoyment you'll get out of it.

Prairie Voles and Habit

One of the most promising areas of research into the brain chemistry of prairie voles is that of addiction. Scientists at Florida State University were interested in how the reward circuitry for pair bonding – the nucleus accumbens and ventral pallidum located in the front of the brain – are also the primary target of all drugs which people abuse. They knew that drug addiction is linked to genetic factors and availability of drugs but could there also be a link between drug seeking and social interaction? So they set up an experiment to see if our gregarious prairie voles would choose to hang out in the place where they received a drug reward, rather as previously when they opted to be in the section of the cage with their mate.

So sexually inexperienced prairie voles were put into a two-chambered cage. The first chamber was made out of black plastic and had a solid metal lid. The second chamber was identical but made out of white plastic with a wire mesh lid that let in light. The two habitats were linked by a plastic tube. Would the voles prefer the darker or the brighter habitat? First the young males were placed in the cage, one half in one chamber and the other half in the other chamber, and allowed to roam freely. Left to their own devices, they chose the bright habitat. (When the experiment was repeated with young females, they had no preference.) In the second half of the equation, some of the young males were injected with amphetamines in the dark cage. Instead of choosing the bright habitat, these drugged-up voles spent most of their time in the black plastic cage – possibly even smoking Gaulois cigarettes and discussing French existential philosophy. The female voles needed far fewer drugs to choose the dark cage where they received the amphetamines. (This is because females are generally more sensitive to psycho-stimulants.) In future studies, the scientists will test whether voles which have bonded are less likely to become addicted and hopefully use this to improve treatment of and prevention of drug abuse in humans.

There are also some lessons for maintaining a passionate and plentiful love life from this experiment. First, it shows the links between love and craving (especially noticeable in the heady early days of falling in love). This also explains why we are so devastated if our partner constantly refuses sex – it is like going through a drug withdrawal. Second, I am fascinated that the female voles needed less stimulation to light up the reward part of their brain. Could this explain why many women, in my office, report that they prefer cuddling and could quite happily do without the bigger endorphin hit of an orgasm? Finally, this study shows that pleasure is habit-forming. While the voles always hung around the dark cage, we tend to have sex in the same place, at the same time, in the same way. If love truly is a drug, then we need to change the dose (or change things around) or sex will follow the same law of diminishing returns.

Step Four: Sustaining

Over the past three chapters, you have understood more about your own and your partner's attitude to sex, repaired any damage caused by miscommunication and the stresses of modern life, and begun to deepen your bond. This step is aimed at maintaining your progress and stopping you from slipping back into bad habits.

'On the face of it, our sex life is fine. We make love, normally once a week, and it's okay,' explained Claire, forty-five, who came alone for her first session, 'except it makes me feel further apart from Derek than ever before. Sex seems to be another box to tick: great, that's over, what next? We don't seem to connect and I'm feeling lonelier and lonelier. It didn't use to be like this.'

The more she talked, the more I had a picture of two bored people going through the motions. 'Derek is very considerate – attentive to my needs, gentle and skilled and when I listen to some of my girlfriends talk, I know I should be happy but . . .' She tailed off.

Lovemaking doesn't have to become boring. Food doesn't get more boring – or snorkelling, or other hobbies – the more you experience it. We get bored in the bedroom because we get scared. Our partners learn so much about us from living together and raising children with us that to share too much more feels like being swallowed up. Alternatively, we worry that if our partners knew the real us that they won't like us any more. So we show less and less of ourselves until we become, in our partner's eyes, a one-dimensional caricature rather than a fully rounded individual.

Once again neuroscience can explain not only why we are so convinced that our partner will never surprise us again but also a way forward to solve this dilemma. The brain's job is to make sense of the world and generally it likes to simplify and find one solution. However, when there are multiple potential interpretations, the brain has the ability to meet the challenge and hold all these ideas at the same time. For example, Vermeer's masterpiece, *Girl with a Pearl Earring*, is one stable image. However many times you look at this painting, it will not move or change. Yet because there are lots of different, but equally valid, interpretations of the expression on her face, this picture continues to fascinate us three hundred and fifty years later. The girl's look is both inviting but also distant. Her eyes seem both sexually charged but chaste. She appears resentful but pleased by our attention. Vermeer's genius is that he managed to convey all these expressions at the same time. No wonder other creative people, like Tracy Chevalier, whose novel imagines how and why the painting was created, have been inspired by Vermeer. Academics are still debating whether the pearl is real, the significance of the turban and the identity of the girl. In contrast, pictures with a single interpretation might hold our attention for a moment but, however beautiful, they are seldom worth a second look and we soon lose interest. The secret of sustaining our love lives, therefore, is to present ourselves to our partners in all our complexity.

Not just our love and our understanding but also our fears and our jealousy, and to trust them even with our darker side.

A Fortnight of Variety

The aim of this part of my programme is to make lovemaking more varied and to allow you to see your partner in a new light. For many couples, there is just one destination: full genital intercourse. This creates two problems. First, knowing where something ends is not only predictable but also promotes boredom. Second, the stakes are raised and initiating lovemaking becomes riskier. In the split second after one partner starts fondling the other's thigh – or whatever signal for sex is used – the second partner has to make an instant calculation. Does he or she fancy intercourse? Can he get an erection? Can she be bothered? More times than not, the answer is no.

However, if a hand sneaking across the bed is an invitation to a range of sexual possibilities from cuddling at one end through to intercourse at the other, the chance of a positive result is significantly increased. Across the next two weeks, you have the opportunity to extend your range of sexual options:

Week One: Different Strokes

- Start with the usual combination of sensual pleasuring and kissing with one partner being the toucher and the other the touchee.

- However, this time, the touchee should start to play with his or her own genitals – as he or she begins to be turned on – demonstrating what he or she likes.

- The toucher puts his or her hand over their partner's, so that he or she can understand the rhythm and style that is most enjoyed.

- After a couple of minutes of shadowing with the toucher's hand over the touchee's, the toucher takes control and masturbates their partner.

- Experiment with different ways to give your partner pleasure, slow down and drive him or her wild, then speed up and increase the intensity.

- Finish off by giving your partner an orgasm, if he or she wishes – but please treat an orgasm as an optional extra rather than the goal of this exercise.

- Switch places and the toucher becomes the touchee.

Week Two: Oral Sex

- Some people find oral sex a problem because they are worried about cleanliness. So this week's activities starts in the shower together. Spend time soaping each other down, cleaning each other's hair and finally washing each other's genitals.

- This last part allows you to ensure that your partner is clean – but showering together can also be fun in its own right.

- If you are the toucher, start with pleasuring your partner's whole body before fondling his or her genitals.

- Making love should not always be such a serious business! Some couples build up to oral sex by garnishing each other's genitals with fruit or ice cream.

- When receiving oral sex, the touchee can guide their partner's head but please do not give verbal feedback.

- If the touchee wishes, you can finish by giving him or her an orgasm either orally or, if you prefer, manually.

- Swap over and repeat.

In the early stages of my programme, you escaped from 'all or nothing' by enjoying cuddling for its own sake – which helps with the stress of twenty-four-hour life as you're seldom too tired for kissing and cuddling. Once into this sensual world, you could be ready for much more and with the Fortnight of Variety, you have added extra sexual destinations and the foundations for delving deeper into what you both enjoy. After you have completed these exercises, you are ready – if you have not done so already – to remove the ban on intercourse.

The Three Kinds of Lovemaking

In the fifties, William H. Masters and Virginia E. Johnson started their ground-breaking research recruiting couples to have sex in their laboratory and monitor what happens to their bodies during orgasm. However, it was not until the late seventies that psychologists began to look at the meanings we place on lovemaking and what makes the difference between functional sex (where someone orgasms) and rewarding sex (which is emotionally as well as physically satisfying). Professor Donald L. Mosher, from the University of Connecticut, was the first person to scientifically study what went on inside people's heads (*Journal of Sex Research*, 1980). He based his theories on what was already known about how the brain responds to hypnosis and asked recruits to fill out detailed questionnaires about their attitudes to sex. I have taken Mosher's research and adapted it in light of my experience working with couples.

My clients find the three kinds of lovemaking a particularly helpful tool because it not only provides a framework for them to explain to each other what they enjoy but also is inspiration for exploring other sexual possibilities. Before I lay out the concept, it is important to say that one kind of lovemaking is not inherently superior to another – it's down to what suits our particular personality, our sexuality (what we find sexually pleasing), our experiences to date and which of the messages about sex from the media, Church and our family we have adopted. So what are these three kinds of lovemaking and how can they help keep marital sex passionate?

1. Trance
In this kind of lovemaking the focus is inward looking and centred either on giving or receiving pleasure. Someone using trance drifts into their own private world. If there is talking, it is normally to give instructions or feedback. If there are any fantasies, they are normally without a script but full of sensual images, colours and shapes. For people who enjoy trance lovemaking, sex is an altered state of consciousness, or being transported to a different planet. 'I love to sink into lovemaking and relax into a world where the colours are brighter and more focused,' explains Janine, thirty. 'Sometimes I'm lying

on a warm beach with the waves lapping at my feet or running through the woods, faster and faster until all the leaves float off the trees.'

Likes: Slow-pacing and repetitive movements (round and round, up and down) helps people who enjoy trance love-making to relax and let go. The ambience is incredibly important. Sensitive lighting, warmth and music all help to create a calm and peaceful mood. However, the most important ingredient is privacy and having no outside distractions (such as the children coming home unexpectedly). This style of lovemaking is affectionate and is about mutual pleasuring. The perfect orgasm involves intense sensations and losing track of both place and time.

Dislikes: Pillow talk or being asked 'Do you love me?' stops trance love-makers from surrendering to their feelings. Sometimes, they can find kissing on the lips too invasive because it pulls them back down to reality. They don't enjoy sex games and find it hard to share their fantasies as they are often visual, wordless and almost hallucinatory.

Levels of trance: One of the most inspired parts of Mosher's theory is that not only are there three types of lovemaking but also each type has several layers (which I have distilled down to five). When I discuss levels with my clients, there is a natural desire to head for the highest one (as if sex was an Olympic sport) but I always stress there are advantages to each and every level. So what are the five levels of trance?

- **Casual:** You are relaxed enough to shut out everyday concerns (eg., the ironing and composing that work email) and have begun to interpret your partner's gestures as sexual (so that a touch or a look becomes erotic or romantic rather than consoling or friendly).

- **Routine:** Reality begins to fade away (rather than you making a conscious effort to shut off). Both partners are focused on sex – rather than kissing and cuddling. The awareness of the world around – critical for everyday survival – is relaxed as you become more receptive to pleasure. However, it is still easy to be distracted by a noise downstairs or suddenly remembering something important.

- **Engrossed:** You have completely abandoned everyday reality and have begun to sink down into the trance. Nothing short of a knock on the door or your car alarm going off outside will stop you now.

- **Entranced:** At this level of trance, you and your partner might be in your own separate worlds but the connection is so strong that there is no division between giving and receiving pleasure or touching and being touched. You are locked in a loop where your partner's pleasure increases yours and vice versa. Only someone shouting 'FIRE!' will stop you from reaching orgasm – and maybe not even that!

- **Ecstatic:** There is total absorption in the trance. All the boundaries disappear. The connection is not just with your partner but also with every lover in the world (and maybe throughout all time). Sex has reached an almost spiritual level and the need for an orgasm fades into insignificance.

How to go deeper: When I explain the five levels of trance, my clients immediately want to challenge the idea that all levels of trance are equally valid. (They suspect it is the sex therapy equivalent of 'everybody should have prizes'.) After all, who wants to settle for Casual or Routine? My first defence is that it is impossible to reach the deeper layers without going through the first two. Second, the lower levels of trance can be a platform for launching into another type of lovemaking.

If you have been following the programme laid out in this book, the Month of Sensuality already will have introduced you to some of the pleasures of trance. In this chapter's exercise section, 'Progressive Relaxation' will also help you progress to a deeper level.

Otherwise, my advice is to take it slowly and allow plenty of time. The key is getting the ambience right and using lots of repetitive strokes (occasionally changing direction, pressure and area of skin covered). If any images float into your mind, focus on them and try and brighten the colours, imagine what is round the corner and heighten the overall experience.

Concentrate on all the sensations of lovemaking, so touch becomes a caress not a tickle. Heavy breathing becomes sensuous (and a sign of just how turned on your partner has become). Smells and tastes become appetising and animal rather than disgusting. Finally, the naked body is not embarrassing but vulnerable and erotic.

2. Creative

In this kind of lovemaking, sex is an adventure. The mood is playful, fun and dramatic. Mosher called this Role Play but I find this term too narrow as these lovers use a whole range of practices to keep their sex life vital and adventurous. While for many couples fantasy is something only whispered (or more probably kept private), creative couples share and act out their desires together. While, in trance, the emphasis is on repetitive patterns and soothing movements, in creative love-making, it is on variety (especially of techniques, positions, props and toys). Common role plays include teacher and naughty schoolboy or schoolgirl, doctors and nurses, prison guard and prisoner, whore and customer, jockey and pony, and sultan in the harem. The possibilities are endless but many have a power element – although it is not always obvious who is control. Jack, forty-two, is gay and likes to spice up his love life by occasionally playing a game. 'My partner and I are the groom and best man sharing the same bed on the night before the wedding. Whether it is having had too much to drink, last-minute nerves, or just overwhelming desire, one of us will "seduce" the other. He will pretend not to be "like that" and ask "Why are you touching me there?" but it doesn't take long before the groom relents and we make passionate love. Sometimes I like to pretend I'm straight and sometimes to be the "gay" best friend coming out about his secret desires but, whichever way round, the drama is always very satisfying.'

Likes: These people feel good enough about themselves to step out of their everyday identity and adopt a different sexual persona. Some couples only talk about their fantasies – for example, being discovered making love somewhere public – others will act them out (and take a blanket into a secluded park or drive to a lovers' lane). Many couples dress up to truly get into the role and have props to set the mood (for example, a lump of sugar for the pony) or use toys to provide variety in their lovemaking (for example, handcuffs for the prison scene). A peak sexual experience is when, instead of playing a role, each partner becomes the role. This is eyes open, lights-on lovemaking. Talking is important for pulling each other deeper into the fantasy or as part of assuming another character. These couples are the ones least likely to restrict their lovemaking to the bedroom – after all, the world is full of intriguing possibilities.

Dislikes: The worst outcome for lovers of creative play is when a partner just goes through the motions or reminds them of who they really are. Other dislikes include mediocre, lacklustre and repetitive sex, or when one partner drifts off into a private world before the fantasy has had time to breathe and establish itself. Creative lovers accept that their partner is not an actor but hate holding back, rating skills, or allowing an internal critical voice to take hold. Laughter is fine – because this kind of sex is joyful – but not laughing at someone's desires or how they choose to express them.

Levels of creative play: Once again there are five levels, and each person has to find the level at which they feel comfortable. To progress deeper into role play does not necessarily mean complicated props, a kinky imagination or a lack of inhibitions, but the desire to throw yourself into and enjoy the game.

- **Casual:** At the most basic level, when you cannot, or feel unable to, explain the fantasy to your partner, this is a private experience. Unfortunately, this means no props, sexy talk or opportunity to deepen and develop the scenario. Common casual role plays, where the partner is excluded, include imagining making love to a celebrity or an acquaintance. With some cooperation, for example, putting on sexy lingerie, there is still a complete cut-off between the character (sensual woman) and the real self (bored and doing it to keep the peace).

- **Routine:** Both partners are clearly aware of the game but one or both are going through the motions or imagining the character in a non-sexual role (for example, a whore doing housework). Another example of routine role play is where the fantasies have been played so often that they have become stale and predictable or not been allowed to develop. Alternatively, the roles are unfocused and traditional – as if the couple are 'playing' dutiful husband and wife, rather than accepting each in all their contradictory complexity.

- **Engrossed:** Instead of playing a role, you become the role and stop worrying about what each other thinks or whether you're doing it 'right' and just enjoy yourselves. All the cares of the day are thrown off and there is a childish sense of play and wonder.

- **Entranced:** The action flows without either of you thinking about or directing the scenario. It is like you can communicate without words – facial expressions, sounds and movement are enough – as you push each other to the heights of passion. When an orgasm comes, it is dramatic, lusty and often takes you by surprise.

- **Ecstatic:** There is such a fit between the role and you that it reveals something deep about yourself or you learn something new about your partner. For example, Jack grew up in the Caribbean – where there was a lot of homophobia – and his bridegroom fantasy allowed him to challenge the idea that everybody was heterosexual. Fully formed role play can also be healing too, as 'coming out' to the bridegroom allowed Jack to put the pain of rejection (by some of his real friends) into a sexual game where he is always accepted and rewarded.

How to go deeper: Although pretending to make love to someone other than your partner can provide an orgasm, and be a pleasant 'holiday' from everyday life, it is not a long-term answer to a disappointing sex life. There also can be comfort from routine lovemaking in long-established roles but it is easy for one partner to get bored and, in the worst case scenario, be tempted by an affair. However, there can be a lot of resistance to going deeper. Jack's partner, Sean, had been cautious about playing Jack's games. 'Where is it going to end, that's what I want to know. Are you going to want me to tie you up and beat you?' This is a common misconception and Jack was able to reassure him that he had no interest in sadomasochism.

The best creative play either has a strong match with who you are or offers a holiday from your everyday life and the beliefs handed down by your parents or the Church. For example, if you believe that 'nice women do not enjoy sex', it can be liberating to play a bad girl. If you believe that 'a man should give women orgasms' it is a relief to play a helpless schoolboy. In my experience, you have to reach a certain level of maturity to fully embrace the joys of role play. It takes time to grow into ourselves and even more time to find enough self-belief to be able to play with this hard-won identity – without losing touch with the real you.

Set aside plenty of time to talk with your partner about your desires and fears about creative play. The exercises from earlier in the book should have improved your overall communication. So hear each other out, ask questions and be sure you've heard each other correctly before dismissing any ideas. Maybe, with a few changes, you could enter into your partner's imaginary world.

Another vital ingredient for going deeper is being able to read your partner and thereby pace the levels of sexual tension. There is advice about this in the exercise section. (See 'Developing Sexual Intuition'.)

So what holds us back? It is normally a fear of failure or not being good enough; after all, we are not actors or skilled in improvisation. Having worked with actors (on the plays I've written) and been trained to 'role play' clients with relationship problems (as part of my therapist training), I have two pieces of advice: *Don't block* and *Don't wimp out*. Blocking is where someone says 'We're on the Moon' and you say 'No, we're not, I can see the supermarket car park.' Instead you could reply, 'That's why we're floating' or 'Isn't it beautiful?' Wimping out is where you say 'I can't do this' or 'I'm not creative'. Instead of blocking or wimping out, try silencing your inner critic and going with the flow for a while. Remember, what counts for creative lovers is not the skill but how much you enter into the spirit of the game.

3. Partner-focused

For these couples, making love is not the isolation tank of trance or the theatrical props and setting of creative play, the focus is on their relationship and how they feel about each other. There is a lot of affectionate sweet-talk and intimate conversations before, during and after sex. These couples enjoy valentines, love songs, romance and closeness. The style is eyes open, lots of kissing, cuddling and full body contact. No wonder they consider sex to be a loving merger. Rick is forty and has been married to Elaine for ten years: 'I really like the deep connection of lovemaking, watching the pleasure across her face as I enter her and the sharp intake of breath. I love teasing her by slowing down when she wants to go faster, so she has to beg for release. Afterwards, we cuddle and I feel rejuvenated and ready for anything.'

Likes: Anything that deepens a loving bond and helps one to 'really know someone' is always popular with partner-focused lovers. They read romantic novels and enjoy 'soppy' films. It goes without saying that foreplay is incredibly important to help them get in the mood. Although lovemaking is normally in the bedroom, they also like 'romantic' settings like on a four-poster bed or in front of a log fire. These are sensual people who enjoy satin sheets, lingering touch and mouth-open kissing. Traditionally, this style has been considered the woman's choice but I have plenty of male clients who prefer this kind of lovemaking.

Dislikes: There is nothing more upsetting for partner-focused lovers than their lover going through the motions or not being 'present' – especially if, like Rick, they get pleasure from giving their partner pleasure. Partner-focused lovers are often reticent to try role play or take it as a form of criticism ('Why aren't I good enough?') or feel 'their special connection' will be challenged by dressing up, props or toys.

Levels of being partner-focused: The depth of partner-focused lovemaking depends on the quality of the bond between the lovers – at the lower levels it could be a one-night stand or casual on-going sex, but the deeper levels need a long-term commitment. However, it is not just the nature of the relationship that affects this kind of lovemaking but also the emotional maturity of each partner.

- **Casual:** At this level, the other person is a sex toy to produce an orgasm and sometimes to satisfy needs that are not necessarily sexual – such as revenge on an old partner ('This will make him jealous' or 'This will show her there're plenty more fish in the sea') or for money, power or social-standing. In effect, there is no real engagement with the partner beyond them being a means to an end. The focus is firmly on your pleasure and your orgasm.

- **Routine:** At this level, the other person is a comfort blanket and the closeness and physical pleasure help you feel better after a hard day in a cruel world. This is generally more tender than casual partner-focused sex but often the partner is a prop for private fantasy (either standing in for someone famous or the new colleague at work, or imagining something exhibitionist/forbidden together) rather than being invited to share the fantasy. Ultimately, if your partner enjoys the sex, that is a bonus rather than a necessity.

- **Engrossed:** The partner is a mirror, the compliments and sweet-talk bolster your ego and make you feel good about yourself. Through his or her eyes, you are beautiful or desirable – even though you don't always believe it yourself. There is a lot of focus on surface qualities and you admire your partner's physical attributes and his or her skills as a lover. Although you do not necessarily want your own and your partner's fantasies to match, or more likely feel unable to let them share yours/are frightened to ask about his or hers, you are a considerate lover, keen to match and pace mounting levels of excitement. This is the first level where each partner's pleasure is equally important. Mosher, however, describes this kind of lovemaking in a poetic but telling way: 'Sex is a duo sonata, and not a concerto, in which the genitals are the lead instruments.'

- **Entranced:** Your partner is a real person at this level. Finally, you can take off your mask and be who you truly are and your partner can do the same. There is an acceptance about each other's weaknesses as well as strengths, until even blemishes and imperfections are beautiful because they are a part of him or her. This is truly lovemaking with eyes open and the lights on. The fantasies are shared, romantic, poetic and an expression of your love for each other.

- **Ecstatic:** At this level, the other person has a spiritual dimension. Lovemaking is a mystic union between yourself and your partner. The boundaries between the two of you have dissolved into a loving merger where 'now and then' and 'here and there' are transcended. This is the world of Tantric sex where orgasms are often irrelevant.

How to go deeper: Although casual and routine partner-focused lovemaking does not sound particularly appetising (especially if a lot of your sex fits this category), there is still a place for it in a fully rounded relationship. However much you love each other, there will be times when you fall out and have 'I'll show him/her' angry sex together. Sometimes, greedy, don't-care-about-the-other-person lovemaking can be a turn-on for both parties. Equally, there are occasions when comfort-blanket sex is just what the doctor ordered.

I sometimes meet couples who want their lovemaking to *always* be entranced and although there is nothing wrong with this goal, it can ruin your sex life. These couples are deeply in love and care too much for each other's pleasures – to the point that they are sexually constipated. To achieve this level of union, they need plenty of free time and to be purged from the stresses of everyday life. The result is that they seldom make love unless on holiday. Finally, I should point out that ecstatic partner-focused lovemaking is not for everybody (and is probably beyond the scope of this book).

Having made those provisos, how do you go deeper? The answer will probably be a shock: argue more. We live in a society that is uncomfortable with anger and rows. However, they bring buried issues up to the surface and create a sense that something must be done. It might be 'nicer' to turn the other cheek and pretend something does not matter but it is not honest. Remember, the deeper levels of partner-focused sex involve taking the mask off and trusting that your partner will accept all of you – not just the 'nice' bits. Ultimately, having an argument with your partner is one of the most intimate things you can do, because it shows you care enough to engage rather than pretend everything's okay.

What if Our Styles of Lovemaking Don't Match?

When I explain the three kinds of lovemaking to clients, some couples worry that unless they agree on their preferred style their relationship is doomed. However, I am quick to reassure them that ultimately it does not matter.

First, there is plenty of overlap between the different kinds (particularly at the deeper levels). For example, deep trance can become very partner-focused and creative play sometimes reveals more about yourself than partner-focused sex (because it can bring the painful, difficult or rough edges of our personality to the fore). Second, a range of enjoyed kinds of lovemaking – rather than just sticking to one – can help sustain passion and interest in your sex life.

Trance and creative play

When I explored the three kinds of lovemaking with Janine, whom we met earlier in this chapter, and her partner Greg, it became clear that while she enjoyed trance, he liked the idea of creative play. So I sent them away to experiment. They returned the next week all smiles, which was a good sign, but it turned out that things hadn't gone quite to plan. Greg takes up the story: 'When Janine goes off into her trance, she often finds herself by water or the sea – carried away by the power of huge waves. As she was reading a book about Vikings, I suggested that we pretend . . .' At this point, he looked a little embarrassed.

'What's the matter,' I asked.

'It's very personal.'

'That's the beauty of fantasy, it reveals so much about yourself.'

Greg took a deep breath: 'So we pretended that I was a marauding Viking who'd ransacked the village and had taken Janine back to my boat for a bit of rape and pillage.'

'We had a wonderful time and a real connection, honestly,' said Janine.

'But when we were kissing and cuddling afterwards, Janine explained that they didn't have masts on Viking longboats. In my sexy talk, I'd somehow crossed over into *Pirates of the Caribbean* and she was tied to the rigging and forced to walk the plank unless she submitted to my evil plans. For a second, I was upset – because I'd put a lot of effort into the story – but then we laughed and had another cuddle.'

So how can a trance and creative play couple complement each other? The creative partner needs to keep the 'script' as simple as possible so that it does not intrude too much on the unstructured fantasies of trance partner. Meanwhile, the trance partner needs to be aware that creative lovers enjoy a variety of settings for sex and often enjoy dressing up. As Greg had tried to enter her world, Janine decided to return the favour. The next week, she arranged for the children to stay over at their grandparents' and placed the duvet in front of the open fire in the living room and circled it with candles. (This fulfilled her need for privacy, security and sensuality.) She also put on a lacy garter and suspenders and some of her best jewellery.

'I'm not certain what made me add the necklace but it just seemed right,' said Janine.

'I was completely thrilled,' said Greg, 'partly because she'd been to all this trouble but mainly because she looks so beautiful by candlelight.'

It also inspired a fantasy for Greg where he was a highwayman who had been seduced by a lady so that he would let her keep her jewels. Remembering how intrusive Janine had found the details last time, he kept the lusty talk to a minimum – just calling her 'My lady' and telling her how beautiful she looked as the necklace sparkled in the candlelight. The evening had been a complete success and helped them find a compromise for the future where Greg had variety and Janine had the rhythmic foreplay which allowed her to slip deeper into the sensual pleasures of lovemaking.

Other suggestions: Light bondage – hands tied with a silk scarf – can provide the stimulation for creative play and the slight restriction can heighten the pleasures of the trance. Similarly, light spanking – hardly more than a pat or a tap – can feed the patterned play for trance *and* the power fantasies often attached to creative play.

Trance and partner-focused

In the case of Rick and Elaine, whom we met earlier, the main source of conflict was that Rick felt Elaine would slip off into her own private world of trance and that he was marooned on the outside looking in.

'Sometimes, it can feel very lonely making love to Elaine because I feel she's not really there,' explained Rick.

'But I'm really enjoying myself – until you keep asking me to open my eyes or "look at me",' countered Elaine.

Once they understood that theirs was quite a common dilemma, and that there was no right or wrong way to make love, the heat was taken out of their fights. It was time to find a middle way.

So how can a trance and a partner-focused couple complement each other? With these couples, I try and lengthen the amount of foreplay. In this way, the first ten or fifteen minutes of lovemaking can be dedicated to kissing, eye-contact and loving endearments that are so important to partner-focused lovers but which can be intrusive when someone is deep into their trance. This allowed Rick to feel a strong enough connection with Elaine so that he did not feel quite so abandoned as their lovemaking progressed.

My next task was to help Elaine give some feedback to Rick.

'Do you feel turned on?' I asked.

'Of course. But I keep quiet because I don't want to wake the children.'

So I encouraged Rick and Elaine to use background music to mask any sounds while they made love and allow Elaine to 'give voice' to her inner-feelings – not in a *When Harry met Sally* fake-orgasm way, but naturally, to vocalise what was inside. This strategy was a great success.

'Being able to let go and moan and sigh, allowed me to fall deeper into all the lovely sensations,' explained Elaine.

'Not only did I enjoy her reactions, which were really lovely, but I also became more aware of other signs of her enjoyment – like the heavy breathing,' said Rick.

Other suggestions: Put extra emphasis on after-play – the kissing and cuddling after orgasm – as pillow talk, and a few good reviews, are important for partner-focused lovers. This was particularly effective when Elaine shared the images that Rick had helped create in her trance and gave him feedback about what she particularly enjoyed.

Partner-focused and creative play

This combination has the most potential for conflict. With partner-focused lovemaking, the relationship is centre stage and anything else is seen as either a distraction or, worse still, not just undermining the sex act but threatening the whole relationship. During counselling, Sean, the partner of Jack who enjoyed the wedding-night role play, found the courage to say something that had been troubling him:

'It's like I'm not enough for him. I worry that he'll stop playing and actually start seducing straight men.'

'What would that be like?'

'Devastating. I don't know if I could cope with the rejection.'

Jack wanted to interrupt and tell him it was only a fantasy, but I stopped him. It is important to allow your partner to give full voice to his or her fears.

'What does devastating mean?' I asked Sean. 'A quivering piece of jelly that could barely function?'

'No. Of course, I'd be able to function – go to work, that sort of thing.'

Once Sean had confronted the reality of his fears – something horrible but which would not destroy him – he was able to listen to Jack's reassurance.

'I'm not interested in straight men. What would we have in common? I love you.'

Although, the peace had been restored, I was aware that Jack had fears too. People who enjoy role play want variety (lots of different positions, techniques and places to make love) and tend to become easily bored by the same eyes-open, face-to-face routine that is a central part of partner-focused lovemaking. So how would Jack feel if there was no opportunity for fantasy and role play?

'Everything would be very vanilla.'

I asked him to explain more.

'There're hundreds of different flavours of ice cream, for example, and I might not like them all, but I don't think I want to return to the world of my childhood where there was only vanilla or possibly strawberry – if you were lucky.'

Sean wanted to reassure him but once again I stopped him.

'What would only vanilla sex be like?'

'Dull, boring, routine, going through the motions,' he replied.

'What would that be like?' I asked. 'You'd get fed up and stop having sex?'

'I'd never get that bored.'

Once both partners' fears were out in the open, and not as overwhelming as they first thought, they were ready to find a way forward.

So how can a partner-focused and a creative play couple complement each other? If you're partner-focused, concentrate on how much role play reveals about your partner. In this way, you can reframe the experience into something intimate that deepens your understanding of each other. If you enjoy creative play, be aware that your partner will feel most comfortable in a role when it is closest to his or her own identity (or does not challenge his or her sense of who he or she is). So think carefully, before you ask.

Other suggestions: There are lots of ways of fulfilling creative lovers' need for variety but where partner-focused partners can still feel valued and the relationship is centre stage. These include making love in places other than the bedroom, experimenting with different techniques, and food play. Smearing each other with yoghurt and licking it off, running a piece of ice over each other's skin on a hot night or eating fruit off each other's body and passing it backwards and forwards with passionate kisses are enjoyable in both types of lovemaking. Finally, be grateful that although you and your partner have different ideas about sex at least the issues are out in the open and can be discussed.

Forced Matches and Other Destructive Scenarios

To help my clients get in touch with their preferred type of lovemaking, I take them through a questionnaire (see the exercise section). When I ask certain questions, I can almost feel the pressure in the room for each partner to come up with the same answer. I've even made couples do the test back-to-back, so there are no 'meaningful' looks passed between them. I accept it can be distressing or even disturbing to discover your partner is not your identical twin, but it is better than a forced match. Time and again, I discover couples doing not what they want but what has *not* been ruled out. If this sounds familiar, how do you get round the problem?

When it comes to experimenting with sex, we have a deep-rooted fear of stepping off the primrose path. Popular stories from Adam and Eve to Little Red Riding Hood tell us that one mistake and we'll be thrown out of the Garden of Eden or gobbled up by a hungry wolf. Yet wouldn't it be thrilling to dance with the wolves and maybe, just maybe, you'd like to be a wolf yourself? Except you'll never know how far into the woods you'd like to stray until you have the courage to set off on your own journey of discovery. Remember, you are only *experimenting*, not signing a binding contract to pursue this style of lovemaking for ever.

Game Theory, the study of cooperation and the underlying strategies that shape human behaviour, offers insight into the other two patterns that undermine passionate and plentiful lovemaking. The first of these is called 'Chicken' after the scene in *Rebel Without a Cause* where James Dean and his rival race stolen cars towards an abyss. The loser is the first person to jump out. It explains how the world got to the edge of a nuclear war over the Cuban Missile Crisis with the

Russians refusing to remove their missiles and the Americans refusing to remove their blockade. However, this 'game' is best illustrated, for our purposes, by the classic dilemma of two strangers walking towards each other down a narrow street. For each person, the positive outcome is when the other steps into the gutter to let them pass (and gets their shoes muddy). The worst outcome is if neither backs down and they are stuck in the narrow street. There is, of course, a neutral outcome where both parties step aside.

When I look into the sex life of many couples, I find they are playing a version of Chicken where each partner wants a different kind of lovemaking (normally one prefers straight-forward partner-focused sex and the other would like more variety or role play). All too often they are trapped by brink-manship – which leaves each partner at opposite sides of the bed – until one partner backs down and they have the sort of sex that the other wants. Normally, this puts the partner least interested in sex in the driving seat as he or she can always 'win' a war of brinkmanship. There is a different version where the most interested partner effectively blackmails the other, for example, after an affair, to step-up their lovemaking for fear of losing him or her again. Although this might create a positive outcome for one party, it undermines the long-term health of the relationship and everybody loses.

The other game is called Battle of the Sexes. The classic scenario, this time, has a couple where one wants to go the movies but the other wants to go to a sporting event. In some ways, this game is like Chicken. However, there is a twist; as they are a couple both would prefer the other to come with them – rather than attend their first choice activity alone. In what game theorists call the 'perfect' version of the game, the couple discuss the alternatives. In the 'imperfect' version, there is no discussion and each partner hopes the other will suggest their preferred choice.

In his book about game theory, *Rock, Paper, Scissors* (Hay House 2008), Len Fisher gives a personal example of this dilemma. Len is Australian and his wife is British, so they divide their time equally between the two countries and enjoy two summers. However, Len prefers to be in Australia and his wife, Wendy, prefers the UK, so each would ask the other for a little longer on home territory. Many couples face this Battle of the Sexes dilemma with their lovemaking. Both partners are happy to go along with the other's preferred type of sex – so the choice is between two reasonable outcomes – but they would still rather have their own way. If this sounds familiar, how do you break any potential deadlock? (Hopefully, in your relationship, you can discuss sex – so it is 'perfect' rather an 'imperfect' version of the game.)

The Fishers tried to do a cost-benefit analysis of their dilemma and decided that Len would go to Australia a little earlier and stay on for a while after Wendy returned to the UK. He got a lot of work done but he didn't enjoy the time apart. Meanwhile, Wendy had to shut up their UK home on her own. So Len decided to resolve their problem by adopting the strategy of Israeli-American game theorist Robert Aumann who won the 2005 Nobel Prize in Economics for his understanding of cooperation and conflict. His solution for Battle of the Sexes is simple: both parties agree to a random way of determining the outcome. For example, cutting cards, flipping a coin or playing Rock, Paper, Scissors. So the Fishers' annual dilemma is resolved by tossing a coin. If it's heads, Len stays in England and comes to Australia at the same time as his wife. If it's tails, Wendy comes to Australia earlier with Len.

However, there is another way forward and one which draws on the neutral outcome of Chicken (where both parties step aside). I call this 'Giving and Receiving'.

Giving and Receiving

Many couples get stuck in very strict roles. Traditionally the man will 'do' the woman – by this I mean give pleasure and drive his lover to the heights of an orgasm. Similarly, with gay and lesbian couples, one partner will have the active role and take charge of their lovemaking. However, the partner doing the giving can find it hard to let go and receive pleasure back. By contrast, someone who is 'done' will enjoy the surrender of lovemaking and is only too happy to receive. Unfortunately, this partner does not experience the pleasure of giving or have the opportunity to harness the full power of her, or occasionally his, sexuality.

One of the best ways of sustaining good lovemaking is learning the power of swapping 'doing' and 'being done'. It also helps circumnavigate the problems of forced matches, Chicken or Battle of the Sexes as lovemaking becomes a partnership with an outcome where both partners win.

Giving
This involves the following:

- Generosity

- Initiating or proposing sex

- Taking the lead on what happens during sex

- Setting the pace

- Seducing

- Tasting

- Moving into your partner (or, if it is a woman in this role, impaling herself on to her partner's penis, tongue or fingers).

- Sending your partner over the edge

- Zoning in on his or her responses

- Enjoying his or her moans and sighs and getting a buzz off his or her pleasure (as much as your own)

- Power

Receiving
This involves the following:

- Allowing yourself to be seduced

- Surrender

- Total absorption in the ecstasy of the moment

- Devotion

- Opening yourself up. (For a woman, letting your partner enter you with his penis, tongue or fingers. For a man, this can involve the woman being on top and setting the pace for intercourse by raising herself up and down or tensing and relaxing her vaginal muscles. With oral sex, it means letting her lick and tease your penis rather than thrusting into her mouth. For gay men, receiving includes anal intercourse. Incidentally, many heterosexual men enjoy their partner inserting her finger into his anus and massaging his prostate gland.)

- Letting go: 'Take me I'm yours.'

- Freedom

Problems giving and receiving

It takes a certain amount of confidence to enjoy both roles. Unfortunately, some men find it hard to let go and 'be done'. As one sex therapist remarked on a training day I attended: 'Some men use sex to screw their penis on tighter.' Everybody laughed, partly because it was such a graphic way of explaining men's fears that giving up control of sex will somehow unman them but mainly because we recognised the fear in our clients or maybe in ourselves.

Similarly, some woman find it hard to let themselves go completely – fearing it will be unladylike. Others are embarrassed to show their full potency and womanly potential (often for fear of hurting their partner's ego). Ultimately, both men and women are frightened of their sexual power and of truly controlling or truly surrendering to the pleasures of lovemaking.

Summary

- Sex becomes boring when we are frightened and don't let our partner see our full complexity.

- There are three types of lovemaking. In trance, sex is like meditation and focused on inner pleasures. In creative play, sex is dramatic and as varied as the mood and the fantasy creates. In partner-focused lovemaking, sex is about union and an orgasm will be the most intense when the couple feel closest.

- With each type, there are five levels of intensity. At the basic levels, sex can happen with almost anyone – as long as they have the necessary skills. However, it takes a loving and committed relationship to achieve the full intensity of each type of sex.

- Enjoying both receiving and giving allows couples to go deeper into the three kinds of lovemaking, to the place where being partner-focused, trance and creative play overlap and intertwine, and lovemaking is no longer about game playing or winning or losing but about cooperating.

Exercises

Progressive Relaxation
Anxiety inhibits good sex, but feeling relaxed promotes it. The following exercise will help you achieve the right frame of mind:

1. **Set aside time to relax.** Ideally, you should lie down on a flat surface. However, progressive relaxation can be slotted into idle moments at work or commuting. In these situations, do the exercise sitting down – with your feet firmly on the ground.

2. **Attend to your breathing.** Put your hands over your ribcage and feel your lungs expanding and contracting. Allow your breathing to deepen and imagine that every time you exhale all the stress flows out of your body.

3. **Progressively tense and relax each of your muscle groups.** Start with your toes, tense for ten seconds and release and repeat. Next move on to your knees, then buttocks, then stomach, shoulders, arms, neck, jaw, eyes and forehead. Pause between each muscle group, take a deep breath and let it out with a sigh.

4. **Allow your body to go limp.** Make certain every muscle in your body is as relaxed as possible and then return to part two of the exercise and go through parts three and four a couple of times.

Developing Sexual Intuition
We live in a rational world that likes everything proved, tied down and explained. So intuition – knowing something

without knowing how – is always going to be a slippery concept. It is doubly difficult when it comes to sex. On the one hand, there is a great emphasis on knowledge and skills. Magazines are full of 'sex tips' for driving your man wild or satisfying any woman. They perpetuate the myth that if only you know how to squeeze, pull and manipulate the genitals in the right way you'll lead a happy, fulfilled and orgasmic life. The result is that I meet many people who are worried that they are not 'experienced' enough or that their partner has more 'experience' and they will somehow be found wanting. For them, 'trust your instincts' and 'do what feels right' sounds like a cop-out. If you fit into this category, please put your cynicism aside for a moment. On the other hand, couples rarely talk about sex and just hope that their partner will know what they enjoy or what's lacking in their relationship. In a sense, they have pinned everything on their partner's sexual intuition and, to be honest, it has let them down. If you fit into this category, please put your worries aside for a moment too. The previous part of my programme will have helped you communicate better and provided some clues for what turns you both on – and thereby laid a proper foundation for intuition.

1. **Think back to previous examples when you've trusted your instincts and it's worked.** For example, the moment when you've just known your partner wanted his toes licking and you've had him thrashing around the bed in a mixture of agony and ecstasy or when some sixth sense made you hold back and only partially penetrate her vagina, over and over again, until she begged for more. If you can't think of a sexual example, cast your net wider – because we all have intuition. For example, I was waiting for a train and a

colourful couple arrived on the platform and struck up conversations with random strangers. Normally I head for the most peaceful carriage but something told me to choose theirs. By the end of the journey, I had an idea for a play which led directly to a production of my work at one of the UK's leading theatres. It would never have happened if some voice inside my head had not told me to sit within hearing distance of that couple.

2. **Stop screening out.** We live in a noisy, intrusive world, so we screen out fellow commuters who insist on having long, boring conversations at the tops of their voices, or distract ourselves with a game on our mobile phone. With so much screening out, it's hard to open up and listen to ourselves. So make a conscious choice to leave your personal music system at home, put down your newspaper and provide the space and opportunity to develop your intuition. What does your intuition say? If you experiment and follow your instincts, what is the result?

3. **Open yourself up.** Moving from general intuition, pay attention to the details next time you make love. So if you're a rationalist and think intuition is really reading the small changes in body language – your partner's pupil size, breathing, body odour – make certain that you notice the signs. If you believe in a psychic link, imagine dropping your barriers and flowing into your partner. Are you drawn to touching a particular part of his or her body? Do your fingers itch to do something?

4. **Learn the difference between intuition and your desires.** If, while making love, your sexual intuition

suddenly tells you, for example, to call your partner Daddy, Mummy or Baby (and engage in some age play) or to blindfold your partner to heighten all his or her physical sensations, how do you know if this is your partner's secret desire or your selfish libido speaking? The answer is to go slowly – try calling him Daddy or make her close her eyes – and watch the reaction. If your partner flinches and his or her muscles tighten up or the breathing is fast and high in the chest, you've got your answer and should stop. If, however, the breathing is heavier, and he or she is groaning, babbling, grinding his or her body against the bed or up to meet yours, you've got a green light.

Test Your Sexual Style

For many people there is a difference between their preferred style of lovemaking and what they and their partner normally do. To help you discover your true sexual style and whether it matches your partner's, I have adapted the following questionnaire from Mosher's original 'Sexual Path Preferences Inventory'. Look through the following statements and which of the options best matches your opinion about making love. Don't take too long on this exercise, take the first idea that pops into your head and remember there are no right or wrong answers. Think what you would *truly* enjoy the most, not what you *should* answer.

1. When it comes to the right ambience for lovemaking, I would prefer:

    a) sex in a romantic context where my partner and I are feeling loving towards each other;

    b) sex in a setting close to nature – for example, a field

of long grass or on a beach – assuming we were totally alone and could be sure of not being disturbed;

c) sex in a dramatic setting – for example, a New Orleans brothel, a harem or a medieval dungeon.

2. When it comes to technique, I prefer:

a) my favourite position for intercourse: face-to-face with the one I love;

b) a wide variety of positions for intercourse;

c) slow and rhythmic movements which allow me to enjoy the shades of pleasure during intercourse.

3. My ideal sex is:

a) a drama that begins with attraction, develops a plot filled with intrigue, mystery and sex play and ends with a tumultuous orgasm;

b) a trip into a world of sensory images and tingling nerve endings;

c) an expression of love for my partner.

4. I'm most likely to be in the mood for passionate sex when:

a) I'm physically relaxed and mentally receptive;

b) I'm feeling really loving towards my partner;

c) I'm feeling playful and adventurous.

5. When it comes to the perfect place for making love, I would choose:

a) a semi-public place to make secret love;

b) somewhere that ensures total privacy;

c) somewhere that has special meaning for me and my partner.

6. When it comes to foreplay, my first choice would be:

    a) kissing the face and the lips and the neck;
    b) plenty of accomplished oral sex;
    c) anything where the pacing and repetition permits us to become absorbed in the moment.

7. In an ideal world, my sex partner would have:

    a) a flair for experimenting and good technique;
    b) the ability to flow with my mood rather than trying to dictate how sex is done;
    c) lots of love to give.

8. The pillow talk that I prefer is:

    a) moans and sighs or something like: 'That feels good';
    b) compliments and best of all: 'I love you';
    c) urging, begging or directing me: 'Harder, take me, more, more, yes.'

9. When it comes to fantasies, I'm most likely to enjoy:

    a) the idea that my partner pledging his or her love and devotion through sex;
    b) the novelty of imagining different activities, settings and people;
    c) using my imagination to sink further into the sensual experience.

10. If I was forced to choose my favourite recipe for good sex, it would be:

a) a wide variety of sex practices and positions for intercourse;

b) the love we feel for each other;

c) intense involvement in the sexual and sensual sensation of the moment.

11. If I was going to play music during sex, I would choose something:

a) soft and low that facilitates the mood without setting a pace to be followed;

b) lyrical, romantic and poetic to match my partner's loving mood;

c) dramatic and exciting rhythms which frame and feed my fantasies.

12. With which of the following statements do you most strongly agree?

a) An ideal sex partner knows exactly what I like and want now.

b) I enjoy a partner who is open to playing different roles so we can keep our lovemaking varied and exciting.

c) If my partner cannot look me in the eye before, during and after sex, I suspect the attraction is to my body and not to me.

13. Which of the following emotions do you most associate with sex?

a) love;
b) excitement;
c) enjoyment.

14. For me sex is:

   a) the merger of two into one;
   b) setting aside the pressures of daily life and being transported into a world of pleasure;
   c) a cathartic drama that helps me process and cope with the demands made on me in the real world.

15. For me the best orgasm is:

   a) a moment of total surrender to intense pleasures;
   b) an overwhelming dramatic shock which releases my sexual tension;
   c) a unique moment of fusion when my soul cries out its love and my longing for my partner is fulfilled.

Results

1. a) Partner-focused	b) Trance	c) Creative Play
2. a) Partner-focused	b) Creative Play	c) Trance
3. a) Creative Play	b) Trance	c) Partner-focused
4. a) Trance	b) Partner-focused	c) Creative Play
5. a) Creative Play	b) Trance	c) Partner-focused
6. a) Partner-focused	b) Creative Play	c) Trance
7. a) Creative Play	b) Trance	c) Partner-focused
8. a) Trance	b) Partner-focused	c) Creative Play
9. a) Partner-focused	b) Creative Play	c) Trance
10. a) Creative Play	b) Partner-focused	c) Trance
11. a) Trance	b) Partner-focused	c) Creative Play

12. a) Trance   b) Creative Play   c) Partner-focused
13. a) Partner-focused   b) Creative Play   c) Trance
14. a) Partner-focused   b) Trance   c) Creative Play
15. a) Trance   b) Creative Play   c) Partner-focused

How to interpret your results

- Total up the number of responses for each type of love-making. Most people will have one preferred type and a secondary one. Although, from time to time, I've come across people who are versatile and have a spread across all three.

- Discuss with your partner what you have discovered about your preferred style and what surprised you.

- Concentrate on the similarities between you and your partner. Where do you match? Is there an overlap between first and second preferences?

- Compare your current couple lovemaking style with your preferences. What ingredients could you include, from time to time, to enhance and deepen your sexual repertoire?

- What's stopping you from enjoying your preferred type? Don't just blame your partner but look at your upbringings and the messages you were given about sex. What would help you shed these restrictions and embrace your true sexuality?

Central Task for Sustaining: Take Charge/Surrender

Once you have completed the Fortnight of Variety, and begun to expand your range of sexual destinations, it is time not only to reintroduce intercourse (if you haven't already) but also to discuss who initiates sex in your relationship.

- Who is most likely to take charge and either suggest sex or start the seduction process?

- Talk to each other about what it is like to be in charge. What are the advantages? What are the disadvantages? (For example, risk of rejection.) Is it always clear when the person initiating is asking for sex and when he or she is asking for another form of being intimate?

- If you are the person in charge of initiating (most of the time), what would it be like to give up control and wait to be asked? How would your partner make his or her desires clear? What are the fears about waiting for your partner to initiate? How long do you think you might have to wait?

- If you are the person who normally waits to be seduced, what would it be like to initiate, to express your desire or to ask for sex? What are your fears? What is exciting about the prospect?

- Make a contract and swap roles, so the person who normally takes charge surrenders and the person who normally surrenders is in control. If it is you who is waiting to be asked, there should be no hints, comments or anything else that suggests impatience or pressure (even jokes count). Remember, this is total surrender.

- Are there other ways that the person in charge of initiating could retain control during lovemaking too? What changes would allow each of you to fully experience the pleasures of giving and receiving?

- Afterwards, look back and evaluate. What have you learned? Did the person who normally initiates have to wait as long as he or she expected, or just a few days longer than usual? Did he or she feel truly desired, for once? Did the person who normally waits to be asked feel empowered and in charge of his or her sexuality?

Prairie Voles
and Evolution

The prairie vole and the montane vole are almost identical. While our prairie vole is five to seven inches from nose to tail, the montane vole is half an inch to one and a half inches longer. The prairie vole has grey to dark brown fur mixed in with yellow-and-hazel-tipped hairs, giving it a peppery appearance. The montane vole has brown fur, washed with grey and yellow. To be honest, you'd need to hold them up against a colour chart to tell the difference. However, evolution has taken these two close cousins in completely different directions.

Tall grass prairies are harsh environments. There is not much food or water and therefore there is a low density of prairie voles, typically around forty per two and a half acres. Montane voles live in alpine meadows, mountain valleys and similar grassy areas by streams and lakes. With plenty of food and water, two and half acres can support 375 to 560 voles. Such a mild habitat favours promiscuous males who abandon their mates to seek out additional sexual partners and therefore maximise the chances of passing on their genes.

By contrast, the male prairie voles enhance their likelihood of success by nesting with one female and raising multiple litters together rather than risking not finding another fertile mate. In addition, food scarcity, and the fact that a vole makes a very attractive meal for a snake, means that it is better to have two adults raising the young. So while one parent forages for food, the other can defend the nest.

At the Centre for Behavioral Neuroscience in Atlanta University, Dr Tom Insel discovered that it was not just the amount of vaso-pressin – the bonding hormone produced in the brain of most mammals including humans – but the distribution and number of receptors in the brain (which read the signals encoded in the hormones) that affects behaviour. Insel has succeeded in taking the relevant gene from a monogamous prairie vole and placing it into the less social mouse, and although the males did not become monogamous, they showed a dramatic increase in the amount of time spent with their females rather than alone.

Although a multitude of genes are likely to be involved in the evolution of monogamy, this is an important step in identifying the links between DNA and brain chemistry and our behaviour. 'Perhaps it will turn out that mutations in the same gene have occurred many times in evolution,' says Insel, 'leading to altera-tions in patterns of social interaction and facilitating monogamy under special socio-ecological conditions.'

Step Five:
Unlocking Your Fantasies

Nature is incredibly economical. Ultimately, nothing happens without a purpose and slowly but surely science is opening up a greater understanding of what it means to be human. Brett Kahr is a senior clinical research fellow at the Winnicott Clinic and has gathered the sexual fantasies of eighteen thousand adults who either filled in an Internet questionnaire or had a face-to-face interview – this research is published as *Sex and the Psyche* (Penguin 2007). He believes that virtually all men and women have private sexual fantasies. On his Internet research, 96 per cent of the men and 84 per cent of the women were happy to report that they fantasised, but the number increased significantly when he conducted private interviews. In fact, Kahr met only a handful of women who insisted that they did not fantasise and after a five-hour interview, even they started disclosing their sexual fantasies. If fantasies are universal and part of what makes us human, what purpose do they serve and how can we harness them to improve our lovemaking?

There are two levels of fantasy. The first, we are happy to reveal to our friends or our partners. These will often feature famous faces, are generally quite 'respectable' and reveal very little about us. The second level we will only share with great reluctance (possibly only to a researcher or anonymously in an Internet chat room). In sharp contrast to our public fantasies, these are detailed, dirty, and sometimes disturbing.

Top five fantasies that we're unlikely to reveal down the pub:

33 per cent: Playing a dominant or aggressive role during sex
29 per cent: Playing a submissive or passive role during sex
25 per cent: Being tied up by someone
23 per cent: Tying someone up
17 per cent: Blindfolding someone else

What do we fantasise about?

Although our sex lives, in reality, can be disappointing and dull, in our imaginations we are always desired, uninhibited and unconstrained. So it is no surprise that the respondents to Kahr's survey came up with thousands of different fantasies. Some of the scenarios were simple (just a few images and one partner), while others were complex (with long involved plots and a huge cast) – and quite a few involved Her Majesty the Queen. At first sight, this was the strangest discovery that I made while researching this book. However, as the main driving forces behind our secret fantasies are authority figures, religion and our childhood, it is perhaps understandable. The Queen is Head of State, Head of the Church of England and symbolically mother to her people.

To give a clearer picture of our fantasies, I have grouped them together into ten main categories – although some fantasies overlap.

Our partner

According to Kahr, a significant proportion of the British public fantasise about their regular partner during sex: 10 per cent every single time (Men 11 per cent and Women 8 per cent), 16 per cent very often (Men 18 per cent and Women 14 per cent). However, there is quite a difference between how younger people, who have not been with their partner so long, and those aged 50+ responded. With those aged 18–29, 14 per cent fantasise about their partner every single time but with people aged 50+, it was only 6 per cent. These fantasies include having 'stamina to make love in every room in the house (fifteen) in a continuous session' and 'sex with my husband just like it was before we married'. In my research, I found many people fantasise about their first time with their partner: 'I remember that look on her face as I was poised to enter her, full of lust and abandonment – such a sexy combination,' said Scott, forty-seven. 'I pushed her legs further back, so her pussy was completely exposed. I teased the entrance with the tip of my cock and she moaned. I gave her this look "do you want it", she tried to buck up and capture me but I shook my head. This would be on my terms and at that moment, she smiled and we melted into one another. That was over fifteen years ago and I still get off thinking about it.'

Another popular partner fantasy is making love in romantic places. 'We're on this beach at midnight. It's warm and tropical and we can hear the cicadas in the bushes as we walk down the cliff path to the sea,' said Sophie, twenty-eight. 'My husband takes my hands and swings me round, faster and faster, until we fall together laughing in a heap on the sand. We start kissing and it gets more and more passionate and urgent. The tide is coming in. I can taste the saltwater on his lips and I'm feeling hot inside but the cooling waves are lapping over my naked feet. He pulls me up the beach and pulls my clothes off at the same time. In the moonlight, I have this perfect body and he kisses me all over. I come without him touching me down there.'

People other than our partner

Although our partners would like to believe that we are thinking of them while making love, this not necessarily the case. In fact, 9 per cent of *Sex and Psyche* respondents never thought of their regular partner during sex (Men 8 per cent and Women 10 per cent) and 19 per cent thought of them not very often (Men 19 per cent and Women 20 per cent). Our fantasy partners can range from nameless men or women (who are won over by our prowess or just overcome by lust) through famous people and, perhaps more disturbingly, neighbours, work colleagues or friends.

'I have these fantasies about Ben Affleck,' says Tracey, thirty-one. 'Not the real actor, but this character he played in a movie where he's a bank robber. There's this scene where he can't sleep and does pull-ups on a bar by his bed dressed only in his loose-fitting pyjama bottoms. In the film, the scene can't last more than a few seconds but in my fantasy it lasts much, much longer – as I lick the sweat off each of his lean muscles. Yummy. There's another scene where he screws this assistant bank manager whose bank he's just robbed, but he's gentle and considerate – even though he's got all these dragon tattoos across his shoulders and biceps. Sometimes, I look over my partner Rob's shoulders when we're having sex and pretend to trace those tattoos on his back with my fingers – even though I'd hate it if Rob really did get some done. I always climax really hard when I have this particular fantasy.'

All of us, if we're honest, wonder how life would have turned out if we'd made different choices, stayed with an ex, taken a different career path or married somebody else. Our sexual fantasies provide a reasonably safe environment to live these out. Here is an example from my research into fantasies. 'My little brother recently got married again to a much younger woman with these really pert breasts,' says Roy, fifty-eight. 'Sometimes, in the summer, she doesn't wear a bra and you can make out her nipples through her lacy top. I doubt she does it to turn me on, but that's the up-shot. A couple of months ago, my brother and his new wife shared a holiday cottage with us in Devon and on more than one occasion, my wife and I could hear them making love down the corridor. Ever since then, I have these fantasies were she puts on this almost see-through top and lures me into her bedroom where we rut like animals. In real life, I would never overstep the mark, and I doubt she'd have anything to do with an old thing like me, but I've only just got to think about this story and it gets me instantly hard.'

Group sex

If sex with one person is enjoyable, for many people in Kahr's survey, adding extra players into the fantasy makes it even better. In fact, 30 per cent of his respondents fantasised about a threesome, 20 per cent about attending an orgy and 11 per cent about swinging or partner-swapping. 'They have these clubs in Paris called *échangiste* where couples explore their fantasies. I've never been, of course, just read a lot about them,' Toby, thirty-five, told me. 'Being French, they do this really well. It's not a tacky knocking shop and my girlfriend is dressed up as if we were going to a five-star hotel. All the men in the club really fancy her, because she's the most beautiful and classiest woman in the place. So they keep on coming up to us at the bar, kissing her hand and asking my permission to ravish her. We turn them away and enjoy our champagne cocktails and canapés. When the sexual tension, from all these men with their tongues hanging out, gets too much, I lead my girlfriend to a large bed and invite these men one by one to lick her out. When she's really hot, I allow a man with a huge dick to impale her and after that it's open season and she takes on all comers. Finally, I mount my myself and pound her well-used pussy until we both have this enormous climax. When my girlfriend finally straightens up her clothes and make-up, and we leave, all the men in the club are jealous because she's going home with me.'

According to Kahr, who is a Freudian psychotherapist and believes our personality is shaped by childhood experiences, people who enjoy group sex fantasies are more likely than the general population to have had a committee of adults bringing them up. He also suggests that these fantasies help us explore repressed homosexual and lesbian desires.

Lesbianism/homosexuality

In Kahr's research 91 per cent considered themselves heterosexual, 3 per cent homosexual or lesbian, 4 per cent bisexual and 1 per cent undecided. However, when he changed the categories for a pilot study (conducted by YouGov) of 3,617, the nation's sexuality became a little more fluid. Only 85 per cent of the population considered themselves heterosexual, because 7 per cent identified as heterosexual but bi-curious and 1 per cent as homosexual but bi-curious. It seems that, for many people, their sexuality is a grey area and when it comes to fantasies we are even harder to categorise. For example, Patrick, twenty-four, imagines his best mate is sharing his girlfriend with him: 'In the fantasy, it's not his real girlfriend, but she's got giant breasts and I'm kneading my cock between them while he's plugging away at her cunt. After a while we change over and it's really nice being naked together, showing off our dicks – and although we don't touch each other or anything, when I go down on her I can still taste his dick in her cunt juices.'

At first sight, men who fantasise about two women making love would seem to be gold-standard heterosexual. 'I'm watching two gorgeous women make love, they don't know I am there and as they get more turned on, I get more turned on – until I can't help but moan. They spot me in the door-way and insist that I join in,' says Timothy, thirty-six. Ethel Spector Person, Professor of Clinical Psychiatry at Columbia University, believes that men imagine themselves as one of the women so there is no masculine competition; no brother, no father and no boss. Kahr, however, believes that lesbian fantasies suggests that the man did not receive enough mothering when he was a child.

Voyeurism

Unless our parents split up when we were very young, we grow up witnessing our parents' love affair (or lack of it). The health of their relationship is so important to our well-being that we are tuned into every up and down and notice every kiss and every cuddle. No wonder we grow up to have fanta-sies about peeping through keyholes and watching other people make love: 23 per cent of the population have fanta-sised about watching two or more women having sex, 21 per cent about watching a man and a woman having sex, 13 per cent about spying on someone undressing and 7 per cent about watching two or more men having sex.

Ray, thirty-six, has a favourite voyeuristic fantasy: 'I'm living in one of those New York skyscrapers – at least in my dreams. A beautiful woman – with long flowing auburn hair – moves into the apartment across the road and on the first night forgets to draw her curtains so I can see her undressing. Just as she's about to take off her bra and panties, she notices me watching. I don't turn away but pretend I'm enjoying the view of downtown. She doesn't get angry or draw the curtains, just turns her back, slips off her bra and disappears under the cover. The next night, I'm watching and the same thing happens, except this time she's not wearing the bra and panties but a red corset and matching suspenders. The night after, she strips completely and pushes her full breasts against the window – leaving steamy smudges. On the fourth, she shows off her fanny and masturbates – licking her fingers, covering them with fanny juices and smearing them across the window. On the fifth night, the apartment is dark and empty. She's moved out but I still cum loads.'

Many voyeuristic fantasies overlap with the next category.

Exhibitionism

Exhibitionism is a healthy part of growing up. Boys show off their newly acquired biceps and most girls flaunt their breasts in tight tops or sweaters. So it is not surprising, perhaps, just how much further we are prepared to go in our fantasies. The *Sex and the Psyche* survey showed that 8 per cent of British women have a fantasy of displaying their breasts and 4 per cent of uncovering their genitals in public. Nineteen per cent of the public have fantasised about being watched during sex. Eleven per cent want an even larger audience and to star in a pornographic movie. Interestingly, the younger half of the survey were twice as likely to have exhibitionist fantasies.

There is something about transport that brings out this sort of fantasy. In my research, I've had reports of making love on top of cars (in the drive of the parents of the man's girlfriend), on the Welshpool and Llanfair Light Railway and, of course, the mile-high club.

'In my fantasy, it is late at night. Most passengers are asleep and I'm standing at the galley chatting to one of the stewardesses,' says Ross, thirty-four. 'One thing leads to another and we start kissing passionately. She whispers to me to come to the toilet in five minutes, knock twice and she'll let me in. When I follow her instructions, she's totally naked except for black stockings. I flash my giant knob and we set to. Pretty soon, the whole plane is rocking. Suddenly, there's a knock on the door. Another passenger wants to use the toilet. "Don't let that bother you. Come on! Come On!", she screams. Afterwards, she straightens her uniform and pushes past the man waiting to get into the toilet. He smiles because it must have been obvious what had been happening. As I walk back to my seat, all the passengers applaud and that's when I shoot my load.'

Fetishism

Fetishism is defined as an erotic thrill provided by the presence of a physical item. The classic examples include rubber, leather and high heels. Dressing up in the clothes of the opposite sex is popular in fantasies too – with 6 per cent enjoying this fetish. The Internet has probably played a part in widening the number and types of fetishes. 'Furries' like dressing up as animals or cartoon characters and some have special access points in the costume to facilitate sex. There is also a small subset who are aroused by stuffed toys. Other fetishes include balloons (blowing them up, sitting on them and popping them with sharp objects), infantilism (wearing nappies and being treated as a baby or a toddler – sometimes of the opposite sex) and sploshing (being aroused by foods or slimy substances which are generously applied to naked skin).

Anouschka, twenty-eight, went to a summer music festival and, on the spur of the moment, agreed to mud wrestle with one of her friends. 'There was nothing sexual at all, we laughed loads. But it must have sparked something because I started getting these fantasies. The lights are low and a huge inflatable bath has been filled with olive oil or something slippery and tasteless. I take off all my clothes and I launch myself into this pit of wriggling bodies. Soon I'm covered in gunk and slipping and sliding over all these other limbs and shapes. I close my eyes and sink into this warm embrace of ever-moving, ever-changing flesh. Occasionally, I might brush up against a hard penis or a forgiving breast but it's not about intimate body parts, rather something more primeval, as if we're a bucket of eels.'

Humiliation

The next few categories of fantasies we are highly unlikely to tell our friends down the pub about. However, just because we are unwilling to admit to them in public, does not mean that they are not popular or widespread. Although there is no specific category for humiliation in the *Sex and the Psyche* research, several humiliating fantasies are measured. Thirteen per cent of the population fantasise about being forced to masturbate. Nine per cent enjoy the idea of forcing someone else to masturbate. Thirteen per cent fantasise about being forced to strip and eleven per cent about forcing someone else to strip. Six per cent fantasise about urinating on someone and six per cent about being urinated on.

Maggie, thirty-eight, is one of the people whose fantasies include an appearance by HM Queen. 'It's late at night and I'm looking around The Queen's Gallery, Buckingham Palace, or perhaps the Queen's Picture Gallery, and there's this good-looking guy – perhaps he's an art critic because he's got glasses and is peering at all the paintings. We get talking and the conversation turns from the semi-naked Madonnas and nymphs to my figure. He's very complimentary and has soon persuaded me to compare and contrast. One thing leads to another and we're naked on the bench in the middle of the gallery having passionate sex. Just as he's about to enter me, the Queen walks in. She is either enjoying a private late-night viewing of her paintings or taking a short cut. She lets out a sharp intake of breath and you can tell she's not pleased that we've despoiled her home. We stand up, exposing our naked bodies, clutching our clothes. She claps her gloved hands and guards appear from nowhere and drag us protesting and apologising away. I know it sounds strange,' she added, 'but it always works for me.'

Violence

On top of the violence implicit in a dominant or submissive fantasy, there are other people who enjoy the idea of pain – both giving and receiving it. Eighteen per cent of British men and seven per cent of British women fantasise about spanking someone, conversely eleven per cent of men and thirteen per cent of women fantasise about being spanked. Seven per cent are interested in using a whip, paddle, cane, slipper or strap. Mandeep, thirty-three, is Sikh and his family does not know that he is gay. 'I have this fantasy where I'm stripped to the waist, I've uncoiled my turban and my hair falls down over my shoulder – even though I'm supposed to have my head covered in public. This skinhead, who also has his shirt off, appears and starts whipping my back. Lash after lash, but I have no choice. I have to take it. He's really getting off on my cries for mercy, but he doesn't care. He just hits me harder and faster. Sometimes, I'm on the ground and he's kicking me with his Doc Marten boots. The pain is incredible but, in my fantasy, so is the pleasure and I can't tell where one ends and the next begins.'

The forbidden

Transgression is an important part of all fantasies and as what is socially acceptable changes, so does the nature of our private psychodramas. Take, for example, the work of the French author Raymond Radiguet (1903–1923), whose semi-autobiographical novel, *Le Diable au corps* (*The Devil in the Flesh*) is about a married woman who takes a fifteen-year-old boy as her lover. It caused a scandal when it was published in 1923, not because of the underage sex, as we would imagine, but because the woman was married to a soldier who was risking his life on the front line.

When many states in the USA had anti-miscegenation laws – barring blacks and whites from marrying or having sex – interracial pornography was extremely popular. With interracial marriage becoming commonplace and political correctness taking hold, the new transgressive edge is 'racial play' where race insults are added into sex. For example, in Mandeep's fantasies, the skinhead would shout the very taunts which young white men used when he was growing up. Other racist sexual scenarios include slave auctions and Nazi interrogations of Jews. Since the arrival of AIDS, where semen can be potentially life-threatening, gay pornography and sex blogs have focused on actors and diarists seeing how many 'loads' they can take anally or orally. It seems nothing is so forbidden that it cannot be fuel for our fantasies.

Indeed, every category of fantasy flirts with taboos – even Sophie's tender lovemaking on the beach involves sex in a public place and Scott's fantasy about the first time with his wife has undertones of dominance and submission. Although fewer people have transgressive fantasies – about humiliation, violence and bondage – they are by no means uncommon. In fact, only 38 per cent of the population have *never* had one of these fantasies.

Why Do We Fantasise?

Our sexual fantasies reveal a lot about us. However, our reactions to other people's fantasies probably tell us even more. We are either horrified and think 'what sick and twisted people' or become aroused and possibly even jealous because our own fantasies are not as sexually liberated. So it is no surprise that the experts are divided too. In the first camp, there are the therapists who believe fantasies allow dark thoughts to be expressed harmlessly. The second camp believes a violent fantasy is a sign that someone is struggling to deal with aggression in the non-sexual part of their lives – and therefore needs help. Perhaps the best way to settle the argument is to look at the various roles fantasies can play in our lives. Once again, there is a degree of overlap.

Self-comfort
Everybody fantasises for different reasons but at the core is one simple concept: sexual fantasies make us feel better about ourselves. Sophie, in her fantasy about making love to her

partner on the beach, has a 'perfect body'; Roy, while imagining sex with his sister-in-law, is no longer an 'old thing' and Toby gets an ego boost from possessing the woman that everybody else desires at the sex club. Fantasies also relieve the boredom of daily life, provide a respite from our troubles, calm us down and help us sleep. Olivia, in her late thirties, has one particular favourite: 'It's the World Snooker Championship and the champion is having a disastrous game. At the interval, he goes back stage and finds me in his dressing room – semi-clothed. We make wild passionate love and he goes back onstage and wins.' I was not surprised to discover that Olivia had a very dominant mother and low self-esteem. However, in her fantasies, she is not only extremely desirable but can also turn around a sportsman's game.

Play

Children are encouraged to play and be creative. Unfortunately, when we grow up and have to earn a living, play is seen either as a waste of time or codified into sports and competition. The sense of doing something – just for the fun of it – is lost for the majority of adults. So it is no surprise, really, that many fantasies echo childhood play: throwing food about, getting messy together or becoming animals. In this light, Anouschka's bucket of eels sounds almost pre-sexual – just rolling on the floor and play-wrestling with friends or kicking off shoes and socks and climbing into the sand-pit. In the creative industries – acting, advertising, writing, etc. – people are encouraged to play games as a way of generating ideas. In our sexual fantasies, play can bridge the gap between the adult worlds of paying bills, saving for holidays and getting a good night's sleep to be fresh for work, and the childish ability to be in the moment and have fun together right now.

Transition

One of the main tasks of growing up is to slowly separate from our parents. As we know from watching babies and small children, being apart from your mother can arouse plenty of anxiety. Donald Winnicott, an English paediatrician and psychoanalyst (1898–1971), studied interactions between mothers and children, in particular, picking up and handling a baby and how a mother could be metaphorically 'holding' a child even when she was not there – for example, by singing or talking to the baby from the next room or providing what he called a 'transitional object' – such as a teddy bear – to offer symbolic mothering. In this way, a transitional object, or what is more commonly called a 'security blanket', means a child does not feel entirely abandoned.

Our need to be 'held' and kept safe explains the popularity of bondage – tying someone up or being tied up – and some of the fetishes. In his study, Kahr tells the story of a man with an intrusive mother who, when he was a child, would burst into his bedroom without knocking and allowed him no private space. So he would masturbate in the cupboard under the stairs – surrounded by plastic raincoats and rubber wellington boots. As an adult, his fantasies always had beautiful women in boots and rubber as they were the 'transitional objects' from his teenage solo pleasure into the complex adult world of relationships. Many sexual tastes are set even younger – almost pre-sexual – which explains the popularity of shoe and foot fetishes as these objects are directly in the eye-line of small children who spend a lot of their time on the floor.

Wish-fulfilment

Although we think there is a straightforward relationship between our fantasies and our desires, in reality, it is far more complex – otherwise the number of guards at Buckingham Palace would need to be doubled!

Many of our fantasies are simply better in our head, as Sophie found out when she went on holiday to Maui: 'The moon was glistening on the waves and our bodies – very romantic until we discovered it was also glistening off the backs of two or three hundred sea crabs. What's more, they seemed very curious about what we were doing and started crawling towards us.' Other fantasies, like Ross having sex on the airplane, would probably lose the stewardess her job, lead to a lot of embarrassing questions, and possibly even a jail sentence.

With a great swathe of fantasies, the people and the events are symbolic or about something else altogether. For example, I doubt Patrick really wants to share his friend's girlfriend – even his pleasure imagining showing off his penis is unlikely to be an unconscious homosexual desire. Such fantasies are normally about the need for recognition from a distant father.

With Roy and sex with his sister-in-law, this is more likely to be tied up with childhood sibling rivalry than wanting to start a sexual relationship. Equally, fantasies about someone much younger or from our past might not be an instruction from our subconscious to go out and find them but a nostalgia for when we ourselves were young and firm.

Therefore, if you are thinking of turning a fantasy into reality – for example, starting an affair with a friend or work colleague – please think twice. Although we place a lot of emphasis on 'going with our instincts' or 'trusting our feelings', these are not necessarily a reliable guide to what's best for us. Studies by the psychologist Arthur Aron of the Stony Brook University in New York suggest that stress hormones distort our romantic perceptions so people misinterpret physical cues – notably the fear and thrill of flouting conventions – for the sensations of falling in love.

Avoidance of a painful reality

Imagining we're James Bond or Wonder Woman and can perform heroic or extraordinary feats in the bedroom is perfectly harmless. However, it can also stop us having to face up to painful realities such as receding hairlines or sagging breasts. And the anxieties are not just about our looks. Every man worries about satisfying his partner, whether consciously or unconsciously, and every woman has anxieties about being good enough, too. Instead of facing these fears – and doing something practical about them – many people self-medicate through their sexual fantasies.

For example, Timothy, through his lesbian scenario, proves he is 'all man' – and has no problem maintaining an erection – by satisfying not one woman, but two. What's more, his lesbian lovers are so turned on they abandon each other and turn all their attention on Timothy. A common male anxiety is that it takes two penises to satisfy one woman. In the sex club fantasy, Toby compensates by going to the opposite extreme and offering his girlfriend to everybody in the club. Even the men with 'huge' penises cannot satisfy her, she has to wait for intercourse with Toby to orgasm.

In the same way, fantasies about people other than our partner – especially if this is the only way that we can become aroused or achieve orgasm – might keep our sex life nominally alive, but they avoid us having to look at the painful reality of our relationship and making changes.

Early warning system

There is a flip side to using fantasies to avoid painful reality: they can just as easily be an early warning system.

Often, we are so busy earning a living, bringing up children and running a home, that we don't realise that our life is somehow off-kilter. Over time, the stress mounts, but we tell ourselves that a long lie-in at the weekend, a holiday, or completing a project at work will sort us out. Although on the surface everything is okay, underneath our body is crying out for us to stop or our soul is facing an existential crisis – because the gap between the life we need to lead and the one we're actually living has become too great. For other people, an event today will reawaken an unresolved crisis from the past but instead of attending to it, they plough on regardless. Whatever the cause of the distress, our unconscious mind can start sending distress signals that surface through our sexual fantasies.

Russell, thirty five, had always clicked with Ruth, a woman whom he knew through work. He had occasionally fantasised about her – nothing remarkable about that – but the urge got stronger and stronger. 'When my wife was giving birth to our third child, I kept seeing myself in the corner doing all sorts of wonderful things with Ruth. It was most unsettling.' Instead of wondering why the fantasies had become so powerful, Russell took them as straightforward instruction and six weeks later started an affair with Ruth. In counselling, Russell finally admitted that he did not want to be a father again and how much he longed to be free of his responsibilities. He had tried to tell his wife but the taboo about not wanting or not loving your children was too strong. However, Russell's problems went deeper. When I looked at his birth order, I was not surprised to discover that he was the third child and that his parents had split up when he was five years old. Russell immediately reached for the tissues and for the first time in our counselling sessions started to cry.

'What caused that?' I asked, when his tears subsided.

'I suppose I always wondered if I caused my parents' split. You know, the extra stress of three kids. The straw that broke the camel's back.'

Russell had been carrying this burden for thirty years and although his sexual fantasies had raised the alarm, he had chosen to ignore it. Fortunately, he confessed his infidelity to his wife and worked hard to resolve both his marriage and his personal issues. As often happens, voicing his fears was half the battle and Russell went on to repair his relationship with both his wife and his newborn son.

Mastery of trauma

I never cease to be amazed at the creativity of the human mind and how many people use sexual fantasies, either consciously or unconsciously, to master an old trauma by turning a painful memory into a pleasurable one. Maggie's fantasy about being discovered by the Queen made complete sense when she told me about an event from her childhood. 'My mother was a feminist and believed that I should know about my body and how it functioned. So when I was about twelve, she gave me this "right on" book about sexuality. It was really interesting and inspiring and I made myself this small dildo. I hid it in my drawers but she found it and called me to my bedroom to enquire: "What's this?" It was obvious what it was but I made up some excuse about a school project. I was so embarrassed. She knew I was lying and I knew she knew, but nothing more was ever said,' explained Maggie. Through her fantasies, Maggie had turned a humiliating experience into a pleasurable one – after all, what is more comforting, reassuring and enjoyable than an orgasm?

Mandeep's fantasies of being thrashed by a skinhead and sometimes goading him to give more punishment takes his teenage fears of being attacked and subverts them. Instead of being a helpless victim, he is inviting the pain and, in a roundabout way, he is finally in control. Other people lessen past shame and humiliation through their sexual fantasies by becoming the person meting out the punishment.

A milder example of using fantasy to replay and heal old wounds comes from Hannah, forty-eight, whose first sexual experience was hurried, rough and disappointing: 'In my fantasies, I lose my virginity to the pop star David Cassidy. He is kind and gentle; when I cry, he pats my eyes dry with a lace handkerchief. He also helps me tidy up afterwards, rather than going off to watch football with his mates – like what happened in reality.'

Discharge of aggression

Many fantasies are riddled with aggression about being 'ridden hard like a horse and put away wet'. Even romantic novels are full of violent images like 'ripping her clothes off' and being 'thrown on to the bed'. As previously discussed, sex is all about control and submission – after all, a penis, tongue or finger enters the vagina, mouth or anus – so violation is always going to be part of the equation. However, on a deeper level, humans are aggressive creatures and these socially unacceptable feelings have to be discharged somehow.

Sigmund Freud (1856–1939) believed that our sexual fantasies serve as the fulfilment of primitive, unbearable wishes and protect our minds from all sorts of uncomfortable thoughts. Carl Jung (1875–1961), the other father of psycho-therapy, talked about our shadow side: 'The thing a person has no wish to be.' Into this disowned part of ourselves, we deposit all the uncontrollable instincts, the destructive impulses and the characteristics we consider unwanted or inferior.

Although everybody has a shadow side, most people deny or repress it. One of the ways our anger towards our partner can leak out, in a relatively manageable form, is through our fantasies. For example, Toby making his girlfriend satisfy every man in the sex club is very close to punishing her. It also begs a question about how well he deals with unresolved anger in his day-to-day life.

Michel Foucault (1926–1984) a French philosopher inter-ested in sexuality and erotic transgression, goes one step further and links pain and pleasure together. The idea is taken up by Geoff Mains in his book *Urban Aboriginals* (Gay Sunshine Press, 1984). In this sociological and anthro-pological study of the leather subculture in North America, Mains described how a mood of trust between partners (rather than brutal attack) and a gradual build-up of care-fully and precisely placed pain can be transformed into sexual ecstasy. In the mid-seventies, scientists had discov-ered natural chemicals in our bodies named endorphins and enkephalins. These are used by nerves to communicate with each other, activate the body's internal pain-control system and create a morphine-type substance in the brain – respon-sible for a feeling of euphoria or trance. Mains explained that sadomasochism (or SM) provided not only a safe way to discharge aggression but also that the associated endor-phin rush triggered by flogging, spanking, etc. increased practitioners' desire for more pain. Interestingly, he linked these relatively new sexual practices in eighties' America with ancient religious rites which promote ecstasy such as the Dervish (Sufi whirling dancers) Hopi Sun Dance (Native Americans who pierced participants' chest with pegs) and fire-walking (which can be traced back to the twelfth century BC and to cultures as far apart as Greece and China).

Balancing ourselves

Well-balanced people have less hidden in their shadow side and access to the whole range of human emotions and characteristics – from tenderness to aggression, from being controlling to being vulnerable, from nurturing to being nurtured, from generous to selfish and from fixed to flexible. Unfortunately, society and our culture gives us all sorts of messages: big boys don't cry; nice girls don't enjoy sex too much; don't be too needy; don't show weakness. The list is endless but the result is the same: narrowing the range of acceptable feelings. Furthermore, it is easy to get trapped in a particular role and, for example, to dedicate your life to looking after others (and forget that you have needs too).

One of the ways we cope with the contradictions of human nature – beyond shoving the parts we find unacceptable in our shadow side and forgetting them – is expressing the other parts of ourselves through fantasy and our sexuality. Naomi is a respectable wife and mother but her imaginary lovers are often rogues – the sort of boys that lived at the other end of the village when she was growing up, and that her mother had placed strictly off-bounds.

One of her favourite sexual fantasies involves making love to the bad-boy character from her favourite soap opera on the luggage carousel at Heathrow airport: 'These are men who don't play by the rules, great for a fling but not the sort who marry and have children.' In effect, Naomi is wondering what would have happened if she had not settled down straight after university. Although basically happy with her choices, she can compensate for lost opportunities with a rich parallel fantasy life.

Ross, who dreamed of joining the mile-high club, is generally unassuming and does not like to push himself forward at work: 'It's safer being one of the back-room guys rather than one of the "stars" in sales and having your neck on the line all the time.' However, in his fantasies, he can satisfy his need for praise and attention by receiving a round of applause for seducing a beautiful stewardess.

Experimentation

When we were teenagers, touch alone was enough for us to feel desire. The older we become, the more important it is that our feelings and, in particular, our thoughts and fantasies, are all in alignment. So as we learn more about ourselves, we need to be certain our sex life matches who we have become or would like to be. Unfortunately, this can involve making changes and just thinking about that is disturbing and challenging. Jeanette, thirty-eight, had always considered sex something more for men than women: 'When I stop and think, I got some pretty screwed-up ideas from my mother. First, it was my job to please my partner. Second, it wasn't ladylike to let yourself go too much,' she explained during her counselling session.

'The first half sounds like a performance. The second half, that you shouldn't throw yourself into the role but hold back.' I remarked.

'My husband and I masturbated together, like you suggested, and I showed just how I enjoyed sex. It was really wild but, afterwards, I felt dirty and ashamed.'

'How would you like to be?'

'I don't know – vocal, uninhibited.'

'Writhing around – not just lying there?' I asked.

Jeanette nodded and looked glum. The gap between how she behaved in bed and how she'd like to behave seemed unbridgeable. So I suggested allowing herself to fantasise – as this is a safe arena to experiment with ideas that we hope for or fear.

The next week Jeanette looked happier: 'In my fantasy, I was moaning, gasping and shouting all these obscenities to spur my husband on. It was such a turn-on that I couldn't help myself and moved up to meet his thrusts. My husband noticed the difference and I think he was pleased.'

Over time, Jeanette was able to bring more and more from her fantasy into her real lovemaking – but it is unlikely that she would have had the confidence without first trying the ideas out in her head.

Self-punishment

There is sometimes an element of punishment for crimes real or imagined in our fantasies. For example, Mandeep did not feel completely comfortable with his homosexuality – as it is not acceptable in Sikhism – so his skinhead flogging fantasy allowed him to express his sexuality and be punished for it at the same time. Sometimes the reasons for self-punishment are more obscure. For example, some people experience humiliating or degrading fantasies after being promoted at work. Why should this be? Freud suggested that nobody wants to be more successful than their parents, so unwittingly self-sabotage their careers or, more healthily, compensate for their promotion by being put down in their fantasies.

Defences against intimacy

We all long to get close to someone. It is a basic human need. However, letting someone into our life lays us open for possible rejection or being taken over by them. Many people are profoundly uncomfortable with intimacy – normally due to a difficult childhood or their parents' acrimonious divorce – and either have a series of short-term relationships with unavailable men or woman or spend long chunks of time alone. I have counselled men who have one-night stands and short flings but find that solo masturbation with their fantasies provide the most satisfying orgasms. Alternatively, some widows feel a relationship with another man would be being unfaithful and retreat into their fantasies – often based around memories of their deceased partner.

I have also met divorced men and women who have been so profoundly affected by their break-up that they retired from relationships altogether and get their closeness from their children and friends. Once again, fantasy plays a consolation role in their sex lives. (If this is your situation and you'd like to change it, there is more help in my book *Heal and Move On: Seven steps to recovering from a break-up*).

How Fantasies Can Improve Your Relationship

For a lot of people, the reasons why they choose one fantasy over another is simply unimportant: 'Yes, it turns me on – but so what?' They are simply not interested in understanding their sexuality better. However, fantasies are more than just academically interesting or a window into our psyche. They are an important tool for creating a passionate and plentiful sex life – in the following three ways:

Repair

When couples are having a disappointing love life, it is hard to communicate problems in a way that is both sensitive enough not to bruise delicate egos but robust enough to be properly understood.

Dionne and Jacob, in their late thirties, were both teachers – although Dionne had been promoted to Deputy Head at her school. They prided themselves on being a modern couple and split childcare down the middle. The result was that Jacob was a very engaged father and had a close relationship with his children. In the counselling room, Dionne was very forceful: 'I don't want a relationship like my parents, where my father was a bully and my mother did everything to appease him.' Meanwhile, Jacob was sensitive, understanding and would often glance at Dionne before saying something he feared might be controversial: 'Our sex life is adequate and fine when you consider the impact of having two children, but I don't think either of us really enjoy it. I ask Dionne what she'd like me to do but she says she doesn't want sex by numbers.'

I had a picture of Jacob desperate to please and Dionne being angry and resentful. To check my hunch, I asked about Dionne's promotion and whether she was under increased pressure. She nodded. I already knew that she did the majority of the disciplining of their two children and had a veto of where the family went on holiday. My suspicion was that although Dionne kept an iron control over the rest of her life – and very little happened without her stamp of approval – she actually wanted to surrender the control in the bedroom (and thereby balance herself up). Unfortunately, she could not articulate this need, felt it was politically incorrect or that somehow Jacob should know what she needed. Rather than opening up a complex and potentially painful conversation, I decided to ask about her fantasies.

I was not surprised that Dionne climaxed to images of crusader knights – nasty, brutal and selfish – who tied virgins to altars and took what they wanted. In effect, her fantasies were the complete opposite of her 'polite' sex life.

'How could you incorporate those ideas into your love-making?' I asked at the end of their counselling session. When they returned the next week, I could tell from their body language that things had gone well.

'I told Dionne to get up those stairs and I'd give her a sorting out,' said Jacob. 'I meant it half in jest but actually it was a complete turn-on. And who would have thought that thinking about my own needs was much sexier than ignoring them?'

Subvert

Despite the feminist revolution and men becoming more aware of their feelings, many myths about sex are still alive and well. For example, men are in charge of sex and should have all the knowledge (and any lack is somehow 'unmanly'); women are responsible for pleasing a man (and taking charge is somehow not feminine). Playground messages about sex are still incredibly unhealthy. A teenage boy who has lots of partners is a 'stud' (and looked up to by his mates) and a teenage girl is 'easy' (and ostracised by her mates or subjected to bullying and verbal put-downs). No wonder sex – even in a loving relationship – is incredibly complicated. Fortunately, fantasies provide a way to 'play' with these messages and ultimately to subvert them.

Daniel, thirty, and Katie, thirty-two, had been together for three years when the shine came off their relationship and, fearing that they'd fallen out of love, they came into counselling with me. Their sex life was routine and uninteresting. In a nutshell, Daniel was in control and Katie surrendered. What would happen if Daniel just laid back and let Katie take control?

'It seems rather ungentlemanly not to give her pleasure.' said Daniel.

'So what?' I replied. 'It's not for ever, just a little experiment.'

'It might be fun,' added Katie – with a gleam in her eyes and she went on to talk about some of the sex toys that she still had from her single days.

'Why haven't you used them with Daniel?' I asked.

'I didn't want him to think I was that sort of girl or, I suppose, to feel in competition,' she explained.

'So now he knows and do you think less of her?' I asked Daniel.

He shook his head and his eyes were sparkling.

They returned the next week and explained how Katie had turned on her vibrator and used it to explore around Daniel's scrotum and the perineum (the small ridge between the anus and the beginning of the penis which Alfred Kinsey identified as one of the key male erogenous zones). She also held the vibrator against the underside of his penis.

'The pleasure was so intense, I tried to stop her,' said Daniel.

'But I knelt on one hand and held him down with the other,' said Katie.

She had been fully in control and he had surrendered, and they had both subverted their respective sexual stereotypes. It was like watching them throw off a layer of protective armour and becoming truly intimate – and therefore more loving again. (There is more about sexual stereotypes in the exercise section.)

Enlarge

If you ate the same diet every day for years on end, you would get bored and long for something spicy and unexpected. Yet couples will have the same sort of sex as when they were first married – even if that was twenty-plus years ago. Fortunately, we seem to be enlarging our range – according to the National Survey of Sexual Health and Behaviour based at Indiana University (*Journal of Sexual Medicine*, October 2010). They identify over forty combinations of sex acts but focus on five basics: penile–vaginal intercourse, solo masturbation, mutual masturbation, oral sex and anal sex. Amazingly, 6 per cent of men aged 25 to 29 claimed to have indulged in every single one the last time they slept with someone. It could be boasting but then 16 per cent of 18- to 24-year-olds and 8 per cent of 50- to 59-year-old women reported using four of the five techniques the last time they had sex.

'The findings demonstrate the enormous variability that occurs in the sexual repertoire,' says Debby Herbenick, one of the report's authors. 'Vaginal intercourse was still the most common sexual behaviour but we have an evolving and varying definition of what it means to have "had sex".' Indeed, when the National Health and Social Life Survey was carried out by researchers at Chicago University in 1988, 12 per cent of American women aged 25 to 29 has experienced anal sex in the last year, whereas in this most recent study that figure has almost doubled to 21 per cent (and that figure also applies to the 30 to 39 age group too). Although most of the Indiana survey is concentrated on the five 'basics', I am equally interested in the forty combinations of sex acts – because with so many choices how can anyone ever be bored?

Fantasy is a particularly useful gateway to enlarging your repertoire. After Ray discussed his voyeuristic fantasy in the skyscraper to his partner, she agreed to strip while he watched and then tease him by pleasuring herself. Meanwhile, Anouschka – who had a fantasy about being in a bucket of eels after trying mud wrestling – had a naked food fight with her partner and afterwards they licked each other clean. (For more on enlarging your love life, see 'What is sex?' in the exercise section.)

What to Do if Fantasies Are Troubling You

For most people, fantasy is a source of harmless pleasure; however, for a significant proportion of the population their fantasies are deeply disturbing.

It could be that they involve other people and this feels, in the words of former US President Jimmy Carter in his famous 1976 *Playboy* interview, like committing 'adultery in my heart many times'. Personally, I think even the happiest marriages need a private space. Otherwise, we are overwhelmed by the day-to-day intimacy of living together and raising a family.

If you find your fantasies suddenly changing, getting out of control or you start fancying other people – this does not necessarily mean that your relationship is in crisis. However, it does suggest that something is out of kilter. Possibilities include: mid-life crisis, a bereavement, career doldrums, depression, drinking too much, a new baby or unresolved issues with your partner.

With aggressive and transgressive fantasies, the picture is more complicated. Imagining watching other people make love is fine but peeping through our neighbour's bedroom curtains is a gross invasion of their privacy. Getting turned on by the thought of putting someone over your knee and spanking them is harmless but forcing someone to submit is assault. The key question is what purpose are your fantasies are serving. On the one hand, they could be a way of balancing oneself up, mastering trauma or a way of safely discharging negative emotions. Therefore, they could actually reduce the risk of going out and committing an illegal or harmful act. On the other hand, repeatedly masturbating or having sex while imagining aggressive or transgressive acts could reinforce the fantasies to such a point that someone starts seeking out specialist pornography which, in turn, can normalise something 'forbidden' and encourage crossing the line between fantasy and reality.

If you are concerned that you might be falling into the second category, ask yourself three questions about the activity that you are considering:

1. **Is it safe?** (Are you likely to spread life-threatening conditions like HIV or Hepatitis C? Could someone be damaged or hurt? Or is the humiliation and pain merely symbolic or pleasurable?)

2. **Is it sane?** (Are you breaking the law?)

3. **Is it consensual?** (Does your partner freely agree to explore your fantasies or are you putting undue pressure on him or her? Alternatively, are you going behind your partner's back – in which case, there would be no consent? Think through all the issues surrounding consent as it is more complicated than at first sight. For example, if you decide to have exhibitionist sex, there is a difference between going to a specialist club where membership

implies consent and having sex in a public place where anyone could stumble across you – and therefore it is impossible to gain consent.)

Ultimately, if your fantasies are troubling you, it is better to speak to your doctor and get specialist advice or help than to ignore your concerns and end up harming yourself or others.

Should I Share My Fantasies With My Partner?

Sex is such a personal matter that just talking about it seems terribly exposing. Therefore, most people's automatic response is to keep their fantasies to themselves, partly because they are private (and even in our 'share everything' society some things remain sacrosanct) and partly because they are worried about stirring up a hornet's nest of questions: Will my partner still love me if he or she knows about my dark side? Will he or she be insanely jealous? What if my partner isn't jealous? Can I cope with my partner's dark side?

Yet playing safe and holding back feelings is how most couples fall into the polite sex trap where lovemaking is more about obligation than passion. So how do you decide what is best for your relationship?

When not to share your fantasies

Naomi, married for almost twenty years and with two teenage children, believes that fantasies should remain private: 'Just because you've entered into a legal contract with someone does not mean that they own your fantasies too. I've never cheated on my husband but I think it would be a failure of the imagination if you went to a party and did not imagine how someone would look like without their clothes or you were not ambushed by wild, exciting thoughts.' Even if her fantasies did not include real people that her husband had just met, she would still not share them: 'It's my private space; a room of my own.'

Ultimately, it is easy to list reasons for not sharing fantasies. However, I find it far more interesting to explore circumstances where it could happen.

When it might be possible to share fantasies

Even if your partner is naturally jealous or wedded to partner-focused sex, it is still possible to reframe your fantasies so that he or she is centre stage or does not feel compromised. For example, Elaine, whom we met in the last chapter – who liked trance lovemaking but whose partner, Rick, was partner-focused – had fantasies about being ravished by anonymous hands and tongues. She knew that if she told Rick he would think that he was, in some way, not enough. So instead of her looking for a way to share the fantasy – as a precursor to acting it out – I asked Elaine only to think how she could incorporate the fantasy into their lovemaking.

'What if he blindfolded me, so I couldn't see?' she suggested. 'I would be more at the mercy of my other senses – like touch and hearing. He could walk around the room and I wouldn't know where he was, when he'd be about to touch me or where – that would be a real turn on.'

So instead of sharing her fantasy, Elaine shared an idea inspired by it and returned the next week with news about it.

'It was better than I imagined,' she said. 'We undressed each other downstairs in front of the fire, slowly and lovingly. Rick then blindfolded me and I was completely at his mercy.

He had to guide me up the stairs and help me find the bed. The level of trust between us was incredible and I was right – my other senses were really heightened. Afterwards, we agreed that we must do it again.' In the end, it did not matter where the idea came from or how they came to enjoy blind-fold sex – just the end result.

Other couples sanitise their fantasies or do not spell out the full extent of their darkness. For example, Dionne's fantasy about crusader knights and helpless virgins is actually a rape fantasy – although neither she nor Jacob used this word. (These kinds of fantasies are quite common. Researchers Lisa Pelletier and Edward Herold from the University of Guelph in Ontario found 51 per cent of women have fantasies of being forced to submit sexually. This research was duplicated by Donald Strassberg and Lisa Lockerd who studied 137 college women and found that the women with fantasies about being forced experienced less guilt about sex and were open to a wider variety of experiences than those who did not.) I also wondered if Dionne's images – conveniently set a long time ago – had been borrowed from a movie or a book rather than her private collection of fantasies. In other words, a more socially acceptable stand-in for something far darker. Who knows? Ultimately, it does not matter because she communicated what was necessary to Jacob and their sex life was dramatically improved.

There are some circumstances when it is easier to share fantasies. These include in the recovery period from an affair – when everything in a couple's love life is up for negotiation. Similarly, after a couple have been to the brink of splitting up, I find both partners keen to find new ways of relating. Other opportunities, surprisingly enough, include being preg-nant. Many couples worry that sexual intercourse will damage the foetus – even though this is not a problem unless the woman has a history of cervical weakness or a low-lying placenta – but still want to be sexually intimate. If you do decide to rule out intercourse, this can be a good time to explore fantasies and expand your repertoire.

Finally, reading a book like this one can be the catalyst for developing what I call Erotic Intelligence and discovering something new about your own or your partner's sexuality.

How to share your fantasies

If you decide that opening up would benefit your sex life, here are some pointers to help keep the discussion positive and productive:

- Have a clear sense of what your fantasies are about and what you are trying to achieve before talking to your partner.

- Tell your partner what you enjoy about your current sex life. This strategy is called 'Appreciative Inquiry' and instead of identifying problems and solving them, starts by celebrating what does work. Then ask: how can we make things *even* better?

- Share your fantasy or the desired new ingredient for your sexual repertoire. Ask about your partner's ideas and personal fantasies.

- When discussing difficult subjects – especially when we fear rejection – it is easy to hear an outright NO when our partner means MAYBE or YES but with reservations. (To get round this problem, look at the First Impressions Cards in the Exercise Section.)

- Accept that your partner will have different fantasies and just because yours and his or hers are not identical, is not a catastrophe. Give each other the benefit of the doubt when something is unclear or uncertain and keep talking.

- Be flexible. Your fantasy does not have be realised 100 per cent. Maybe your partner's reservations will prompt a rethink and promote ideas which could be even more satisfying.

A Fortnight of Expansion

Over the previous steps, the exercises and tasks have allowed you to strip down your lovemaking to the basics of touching and kissing, improve communication and slowly rebuild up to intercourse again. This part of the programme goes to the root causes of marital sexual boredom and shows how to keep challenging yourself and your partner to be more open, more intimate and to bring more of yourself into the bedroom. This chapter might have already fired your imagination about new elements to introduce into your lovemaking but you might like to visit a specialist sex aids shop or website together. Other places that could provide inspiration are a hardware or DIY store (often much cheaper than specialist stores) or even a supermarket.

Partner A chooses: In the first week, Partner A is in charge and will make suggestions for something which you have either never done before or haven't done for a long time – this could be an activity or a spicy extra ingredient, for example: food, talking dirty, dressing up or particular props, toys or equipment. Partner B will do his or her best to go along with the idea and even if he or she has reservations, talk through any fears – rather than dismiss the idea out of hand. If there is a stumbling block, how could it be overcome or how could the idea be modified?

Partner B chooses: In the second week, Partner B is in charge and makes suggestions. Partner A does his or her best to go along with the experiment or finds a way to embrace the underlying idea.

Be kind to each other; it takes a lot of courage to open up. If you have trouble deciding who goes first, flip a coin. Finally, if you come up with some simple but effective ideas that might appeal to other readers of this book, please visit my website www.andrewgmarshall.com and share your experiences.

Summary

- Fantasy can be a useful resource for keeping desire alive. Ultimately, your imagination is your most powerful sexual organ.

- Fantasy helps us embrace the inherent paradox of sex: it can be both pure and down and dirty; tender and carnivorous; primitive and spiritual; about losing yourself and finding yourself; something that can both fill you up and leave you drained and empty.

- Sometimes what frightens us the most is the very thing we need to do.

- Stability and staying in your comfort zone = boredom.

- Challenging yourself, growth and novelty = passion and commitment.

Exercises

What is Sex?

When American President Bill Clinton swore under oath that he did not have sexual relations with Monica Lewinsky, he was telling the truth – even though she had performed oral sex on him and he had pleasured her with his cigar. In the strict legal sense, he did not have sexual relations – because that was defined as penile–vaginal intercourse – but most of us would certainly consider their activities as sex.

This brings me to the nub of this exercise: what is sex for you and your partner? On many occasions during the induction session at the beginning of counselling, I have couples report that they have not made love for three months or more but later discover they have masturbated each other or had oral sex during this supposedly barren time. 'Doesn't that count as sex?' I ask and they blush and nod. Time and again, couples under-report or dismiss part of their lovemaking because they have not specifically labelled it as 'sex'.

These days, I present couples with the target diagram overleaf and get them to think about every activity that might constitute 'sex' and where to put it. In order to be clear where the boundaries lie, I also ask people to add activities that lay just over the border and which they don't consider sexual.

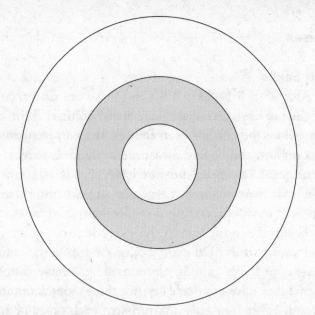

To give you some ideas, here is what constitutes sex for Luke, a forty-one-year-old heterosexual:

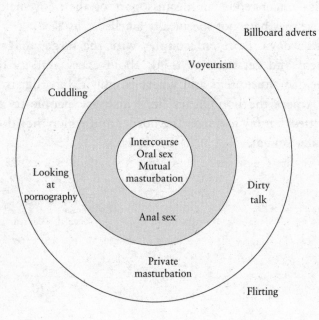

At the centre, he put: Intercourse, oral sex and mutual masturbation. In the second circle, he put anal sex – which included
occasionally penetrating his girlfriend's anus with his penis
and her putting her finger in his anus to massage his prostate
gland while she masturbated him. I asked him why he'd put
it here. He explained: 'It's not really our usual lovemaking,
more a spicy extra.' In the outer circle, he put voyeurism
(which included activities that were not specifically erotic,
but still intimate, such as watching her towel herself after a
long bath or cut her toenails), dirty talk (on the phone when
he was away on business), private masturbation, looking at
pornography (mainly on his own but sometimes with his girlfriend) and cuddling (intimate touching but not leading to
arousal). Outside the target, he put activities that might
provide a flicker of desire but did not, for him, constitute sex:
flirting (telling a colleague she looked nice at a party) and
billboard adverts (semi-naked women on posters). Remember,
this is just Luke's definition of 'sex'. There is no right or
wrong answer. It's up to you.

First Impressions Cards

Discussing something new, personal and revealing is always
going to create anxiety. Many times in my counselling room,
a client will begin to make a suggestion for improving sex but
pull back, worried about the reception from their partner.
Often, what they perceive as hostility is just their partner
thinking how to respond. To get round this problem, I developed some 'First Impressions Cards'. It allowed the partner
listening to give an instant reaction – without committing
themselves – thereby reducing the stress for the partner
proposing and improving overall communication. Once over
this initial barrier, and the fear that their partner thought

them a pervert or a prude, these couples had no problems discussing their reservations and finding a way of making something enjoyable for both of them.

So make up the cards below and put them on the table between the two of you. After the person making the suggestion has outlined the basic idea, the other picks up the most appropriate card and explains their reasoning.

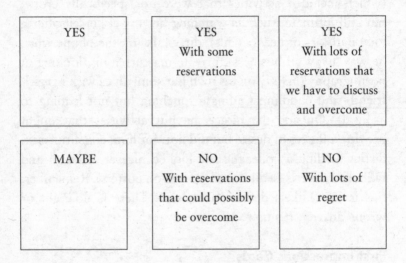

YES	YES With some reservations	YES With lots of reservations that we have to discuss and overcome
MAYBE	NO With reservations that could possibly be overcome	NO With lots of regret

At any point in the subsequent discussion and clarifications, either partner can pick up a card to express his or her state of mind.

Messages About Masculinity and Femininity

One of the constant themes of this book is the need for couples to talk more. Here is a set of prompts that I sometimes use in therapy to understand the messages that we have been given by our parents, our friends, the media and the wider society. Try discussing them with your partner and discover what promotes and what hinders good sex.

What positive messages are there about men?

What negative messages are there about men?

What positive messages are there about women?

What negative messages are there about women?

How reading this book has changed my mind about men and sex.

How reading this book has changed my mind about women and sex.

What I believed at eighteen about men and women.

What I believe today.

What I would like to believe.

Central task for Unlocking Fantasies: Getting in Touch With Your Own Sexuality

Sexuality is a powerful window into who we are. Unfortunately, we are often too frightened to take a long, honest look at ourselves – partly because we worry about not liking what we might find and partly because we worry that our partner might find this version of ourselves unacceptable. So we fall into one of two traps – either we cover our eyes and only peep through our fingers at our sexuality or, alternatively, we damp down our curiosity about our sexuality by using second-hand fantasies from pornographers. Women are more likely to fall into the first trap. Men are more likely to fall into the second trap.

This task focuses on private masturbation and suggests ways of developing personal windows into your sexuality. First, you need to honour this exercise. By this I mean setting aside enough time to get in the mood – rather than accessing porn and simply 'getting off'. (If you are a regular porn user please take a break, so that your mind is not full of second-hand images and scripts.) Maybe you would like to have a bath, put on some music or light a candle – in the words of Woody Allen – 'Don't knock masturbation, it's sex with someone I love' – and therefore it should be worth putting in a little bit of effort. Next, empty your brain of day-to-day clutter. If you find it hard to switch off, concentrate on the sensation of the air going in and out of your nose. Start to caress yourself and explore your body with your hands, partly to help yourself relax into the moment but mainly because this is the opportunity to have just the amount of foreplay you need to prepare for sexual touching. Only when you are truly ready should you fondle your genitals and build-up to masturbation. What images, shapes, pictures, ideas, stories or scenarios float into your mind? If you have tried lucid dreaming, there might be material here that you could use. Allow time for sexual thoughts to establish and develop. Enjoy yourself. Afterwards, think about what have you learned about yourself.

If you find it hard to relax, remove second-hand scenarios from romantic fiction and pornography or throw off destructive messages that masturbation is wrong, try reading the American Author Nancy Friday who interviewed hundreds of ordinary women and men about their erotic fantasies: *My Secret Garden: Women's Sexual Fantasies* (Simon and Schuster, 1973) and *Men in Love, Men's Sexual Fantasies: The Triumph of Love Over Rage* (Dell Publishing, 1980).

Prairie Voles and Becoming Sexual

Our understanding of the bond between mother and child was revolutionised in the 1950s after John Bowlby – a psychoanalyst and former head of the children's department at the Tavistock Clinic – watched an experiment with baby rhesus monkeys. Some were raised normally by their mothers, some received just food and water and a third group were given a surrogate (a soft cloth round a wire frame). Not surprisingly, the baby monkeys without any nurturing grew up to be delinquents and those with their mothers were well adjusted. Interestingly, the monkeys with the surrogate mother did worse than those which had been properly nurtured but significantly better than those which had received just food and water.

Our knowledge of what happens to the brain when the body is starved of affection has been increased by studying rats. Scientists at Columbia University have discovered that the quality of maternal care that a pup receives will influence the amount of oxytocin in the body and effectiveness of the vasopressin receptors in the brain. As we know from the prairie vole, oxytocin and vasopressin are responsible for bonding. Therefore these pups with interrupted mothering will suffer from a hormone deficiency and find it difficult to form pair bonds when they reach adulthood.

What happens to the body at puberty and how becoming sexual changes behaviour has been extensively studied in the prairie vole, too. Forty-day-old virgin female voles were paired with three different kinds of males: breeders (adults which had bonded with a mate and were taken from the female and their offspring shortly before the experiment), experienced (adults which had mated but subsequently had been housed in all-male groups) and adults (sexually inexperienced). Whichever male the virgin females met, they exhibited the same prairie vole flirting techniques: brushing, scratching and moistening their fur with their front and hind legs. However, the males' reactions differed greatly. The breeders were the most rejecting and spent 68 per cent of their time attacking, chasing or in similarly aggressive behaviour. The sexually experienced were less antagonistic but still spent 50 per cent of the experiment rejecting the young females. The adult virgin males were most welcoming and the experiment often ended up with the two prairie voles sitting side by side. When the young male was a sibling from the same litter, the two voles would just sniff and neither huddle nor be aggressive. So the incest taboo in prairie voles seems just as strong as in humans.

So what would make two virgin prairie voles bond? The first option is the sheer amount of time spent huddling together. The second option was injecting vasopressin into the young males. Even without having the chance to mate, these voles showed all the typical bonded male behaviour – like baring their teeth to stranger males and being territorial. The third option, of course, is allowing the prairie voles to mate.

The desire to reproduce in virgin female voles is induced by exposure to an unfamiliar male's scent – the prairie vole equivalent of Chanel No. 5 is urine. Over the next two days, these young lovers will probably copulate fifty times.

When scientists monitored these lovers, they discovered increased activity in three parts of the male vole's brain, which are rich with vasopressin receptors. This is what makes him contribute to nest-building, nest-guarding and other parenting skills such as huddling and retrieving pups that wander from the nest. With the female, oxytocin is the key to bonding because scientists were able to induce a partner preference in virgin voles by injecting them with this hormone.

As it turns out, the polygamous montane vole and the monogamous prairie vole have similar levels of oxytocin and vasopressin and in both species mating releases dopamine (which controls emotional responses in the body and, in particular, pleasure). However, in the prairie vole, the reward pathways lead to regions of the brain important for social behaviour while in the montane vole they do not.

Step Six:
Addressing Specific Sexual Issues

For the first five steps, my programme assumes that you and your partner get on reasonably well and have okay sex together but want a closer and more passionate connection. However, there are other couples who have specific sexual issues and need extra advice. If you fall into this category, the first five steps (and the structured programme of adding layers of sensuality to your lovemaking) will provide a good foundation for work on resolving your difficulties. This sixth step looks deeper into the most common specific sexual problems that couples bring into counselling. If you don't fall into this category, you will still find this chapter insightful and it will help you understand your sexuality better.

My Partner Has a Low Libido

When a woman gives birth to a child, she produces more oxytocin in her brain – as in the prairie vole, this is designed to encourage bonding, nurturing and nursing her child. This increased level of oxytocin will last for two years and then it will start to wane again and at this point vasopressin starts to increase and women become more sexual again. In this manner, evolution has encouraged women to want a child about every two years. Dr Gillian Hudson-Allez, a psychosexual therapist and author of the training guide for counsellors, *Sex and Sexuality* (Wiley-Blackwell, 2005), believes that once women have had as many children as they personally want their overall sexual desire drops: 'Instead of being spontaneously horny, as they might have been before they had children, they become sexually responsive. In effect, their partner has to push the right buttons for them to be sexual. They are less likely be rushing around feeling up for it.'

Dr Hudson-Allez sees another difference between men and women: 'When men have sex with a long-term partner, it is part of showing their love. So when women say "I don't want it", men feel personally rejected because it is their love that has been turned down.' This is possibly because, as we have discovered, ejaculation is the only time when men produce oxytocin. 'For women, sex becomes an optional extra as they are showing their love with all the other things they're doing in the relationship,' explains Dr Hudson-Allez.

There has also been some preliminary research about how levels of oxytocin influence whether female prairie voles are more focused on pups or their partners. Scientists at the University of California and University of Illinois injected different doses of oxytocin into newly born voles. When they were adults, they tested how much time each group of voles spent with their partner, a stranger vole and a random pup that had been introduced into their habitat. At the lower dose, the females spent most time with their partner and took longer to approach the pup. When they increased the dose, the females were quicker to retrieve the pup and no longer displayed a preference for their partner. These findings tie in with anecdotal evidence from my female clients who have told me: 'I thought I knew about love at first sight but that was before my daughter was placed in my arms. She looked up at me and I just melted' and 'The real love affair is between mother and baby.'

Whatever the impact on the human body of oxytocin, babies have a dramatic effect on our sex lives – and not just because they are exhausting and time-consuming. Bathing a baby, changing nappies, carrying it around, playing together and rocking it to sleep are all incredibly intimate acts and involve lots of skin-to-skin contact – to the point that our needs for human closeness can be fulfilled by looking after a child. No wonder some mothers say about sex: 'I could take it or leave it.' On one level, they are getting all their emotional needs met elsewhere.

Tania, twenty-eight, had two small children and a baby and her life revolved around caring for them. 'We've got three beautiful children and Benjamin is a great dad. Okay, we had a rocky patch because he doesn't see the practical things that need to be done – he'd rather be playing with his daughters than putting another load of washing on – but that's been sorted and things run smoothly enough. I've got a lot to be grateful about, but . . .' She stopped talking and I could sense this hard lump of resentment, grudge and upset.

'Your sex life is not very rewarding.' I suggested.

'Nobody with three small children expects that.' She pushed away the idea before she'd even had a chance to think about it.

'So why are you so angry?' I asked.

A torrent of complaints about housework and not being appreciated tumbled out, along with some tears.

'You don't feel special or cared for yourself,' I empathised. 'What would it feel like to be cherished and wanted?'

'Wonderful.'

'That is what good lovemaking is all about,' I explained.

In effect, Tania might have been getting her needs for physical closeness met by looking after her children but it is only part of the story. We also need adult intimacy too – where, of course, we give but we also *receive*. In effect, a rewarding sex life replenishes some of the emotional energy that we expend caring for children and helps keep us sane. In the hurly-burly of everyday family life, it is easy to overlook this important truth. Perhaps it's because babies can make mothers blind to what's going on around them.

Let me explain with a personal story about a dinner party in Central London where one of the guests had just had a baby. The baby boy couldn't have been more than a few weeks old and I could tell his mother did not really want to be there – but her husband had probably insisted. She was entirely wrapped up in caring for the baby and hardly ate at all. The hostess was rather drunk – food had been delayed because my partner and I had been held up in Friday-night traffic. During the meal, the hostess leaned across the dinner table and gave the father of the baby a passionate kiss. I was shocked but what surprised me most was that his wife had not registered what happened. She only had eyes for the sleepy baby in her arms. I understood better when – during a gap between courses – the female guests took turns holding the baby and I asked if I could hold him too. I don't know if I was picking up the feelings of the other women around the table – part of my training – or responding to something inside myself. When I felt that baby's heart beating close to mine, his surprising heaviness in my arms and the way he grasped my finger with his hand, I experienced an almost overwhelming sense of completeness. Watching the women

– who were all mothers of older children – pass round the baby and their eagerness to smell him and play with him, I had a picture of how they might have looked twenty years ago at college. However, then, they would have been passing round a joint of marijuana instead! It made me wonder if babies are actually addictive, with the power to make women blissfully unaware of everything else – even their partner's potential infidelity.

Another time when women can be less interested in sex is after a hysterectomy. Experts are divided on the reasons why. Some consider it to be part of a psychological adjustment – partly mourning for the loss of fertility and partly reassessing what it means to be a woman. Others, like Rik van Lunsen, Head of the Department of Sexology and Psychosomatic Gynaecology at the University of Amsterdam, believe that sexual 'arousability' – how likely a woman is to respond to sexual stimuli – is dependent on androgen (a naturally produced steroid) and suggests supplements post-hysterectomy. Similarly, he thinks hormone replacement therapies for menopausal and post-menopausal women can reduce the levels of androgen in the body.

There is a third reason why couples arrive in counselling with different levels of desire. Alan Riley, professor of sexual health at the University of Central Lancashire, has analysed a large number of people and their range of arousal. He plotted a graph from those with the lowest amount of desire to the highest. The majority of the population lies somewhere in the middle. However, Professor Riley noted that women score on the lower end of sexual desire and men score on the higher end. Take a typical woman in a relationship with a standard man and there will be a discrepancy of how often they want to have sex. If he is pressuring her and she is going through the motions to keep him quiet, it is possible that she will never reach the point of spontaneously desiring her partner.

Lauren, thirty-four, had, in her words, 'gone off it' – although she would consent to having sex to keep her partner happy. Brian knew that pressuring Lauren was counterproductive but kept making advances: 'Because I never know when I'm going to strike lucky.' Although Brian was getting sex – about every ten days – he was also dissatisfied: 'I don't think my wife really fancies me. It's always me who has to ask. How do you think that makes me feel about myself?' My suspicion was that Lauren found sex a duty rather than a pleasure but she had never had the breathing space for her desire to reach a sufficient level to either initiate sex or to benefit from the release of an orgasm.

So I asked Brian: 'What would happen if you didn't ask for sex?'

He looked glum: 'She'd never want it.'

'Does she now?' I asked.

'Not really. She does it for me.'

With reluctance, Brian agreed to an experiment. He would not ask for sex, drop hints or make innuendo-type remarks. Instead, he would wait until she approached him.

'I'll have blue balls by that time,' he joked.

'That's just the sort of crude remark that turns me right off,' said Lauren.

When they came back the next week, Lauren had not initiated sex. I had warned Brian this was likely and that she might take a 'holiday' from lovemaking. However, Brian was not as frustrated as I had expected:

'She might not have wanted sex, but she came and gave me a cuddle on the sofa. It was really nice and I felt so close to her.'

In all, it took two weeks before Lauren felt enough desire to ask Brian for sex. They came to that week's session with big smiles on their faces.

'I can't tell you how wonderful it was when she led me upstairs by the hand,' said Brian.

'Just before we finished, I screamed loud enough for half the street to hear,' joked Lauren.

Another example is Lynne, thirty-two, and Michael, thirty-four, who had two children aged eleven and seven. They arrived in counselling because Lynne had fallen out of love with Michael. Although they seldom argued (see my book *I Love You But I'm Not In Love With You* for more about the link between suppression of anger and a general lack of passion), it was clear that the major problem was a lack of desire. 'It's nothing personal,' Lynne told Michael. 'Brad Pitt could walk in here and I wouldn't be interested. I wondered if I might really be a lesbian, but women don't really do much for me in that way.'

Unfortunately, Michael enjoyed sex a lot: 'I really love my wife. I think she's really beautiful and I want to make love to her. What's wrong with that?' The problem had come to a head when finally Lynne had started to refuse sex and asked for a separation. Halfway through their general counselling, I put Michael and Lynne on the programme outlined in this book, banned sex (which Michael found amusing: 'It's not like I'm getting any anyway') and introduced the non-sexual touching exercises. After two weeks on the programme, they returned with a guilty secret:

'I found myself so turned on by touching Michael that I jumped him,' said Lynne.

'I told her that we shouldn't but I couldn't stop her. It was wonderful and we made love,' said Michael.

In effect, Lynne had been given enough time – without being pressured into sex – to become spontaneously aroused and experience her own desire again (rather than succumb to his).

Getting out of the high-desire versus low-desire trap

When couples have a poor or non-existent sex life, it is easy for one partner to be labelled as the 'problem'. This is especially the case when one partner – normally the man but not always – would like more sex and points the finger at the other. However, I am keen to remove the label and reframe the problem as a shared one – partly because blaming someone never helps but mainly because the picture is far more complicated. When the University of Quebec took forty couples with low sexual desire, and a control group – and gave them standard questionnaires to measure depression, anxiety and compatibility across nine indicators including household tasks, money, social activities and rearing children – they found a strong link between loss of desire and dissatisfaction with the relationship in general, but only a moderate link with anxiety and a very weak one with depression. In other words, problems outside the bedroom were being expressed inside the bedroom.

Therefore my first step in treating these couples is to broaden the high desire/low desire debate away from sex. In every area of married life, one partner has a greater motivation for doing things than the other. For example, what about arranging social activities or a day out? What about getting the children to bed? What about disciplining the children? What about visiting relatives? What about cleaning and maintaining the house? What about budgeting? In many cases, the person who is pushing for more sex is the person withholding or putting the breaks on in other areas. If this sounds familiar, listen to your partner's frustration and anger. Does it motivate you or does it make you less likely to cooperate? How does it feel to be the low-desire partner in this area? Does your veto power destroy innovation, creativity and joy in this sphere of married life? Are you doing, outside the bedroom, the very thing you're accusing your partner of doing to your sex life?

The next thing that is frustrating about the low and high desire debate is that men and women are asking each other for the same thing: closeness and intimacy. Unfortunately, they are expressing their needs in different ways. Generally, a woman will ask for more talking, more sharing of feelings and more romance. Generally, a man will simply ask for more sex. This is mainly because each gender has been socialised in different ways. Although things are changing – thank goodness – boys are still being taught to hide their feelings, solve their own problems and be strong. The only socially acceptable ways to be a man and get close to their partner is through sex. Girls, by contrast, are still taught to make connections and use sharing feelings to create bonds, and warned about men who 'want only one thing'. No wonder many couples find this subject so loaded.

Therefore, the best way out of the low/high desire trap is to understand the similarities – rather than concentrating on the differences – and for both partners to try and speak a little bit of each other's language. In other words, for the high-sexual-desire partner to spend more time talking and listening and for the low-sexual-desire partner to value sex as a way of communicating. (If you are the lower desire partner and find this idea makes you anxious, look at 'Simmering' in the exercise section.)

Male-specific Sexual Difficulties

Although in most long-term relationships, each partner has made an equal but different contribution to the general sexual unhappiness, there are some instances where one partner's specific problem undermines the couple's sexual happiness. Even under these circumstances, it is more often a shared problem – that one partner is exhibiting – rather than his or her fault. So instead of one person taking the blame, it is important to understand how sexual issues interlock and how one partner's problems can mask the other's. So please read about both the male *and* female specific sexual difficulties sections before drawing any conclusions.

Men have been brought up to be strong, self-reliant and successful on the sports field, in the boardroom and in the bedroom. If something goes wrong, the man has to pick himself up, sort it out and carry on without complaint. Any man who fails to live up to these ideals is not only weak – possibly the worst insult that you can throw at him – but also, worse still, somehow not a man at all. Okay, it is just about acceptable not to be good at sports – as long as one compensates by excelling in the business world. The one arena where it is simply not acceptable to fail is the bedroom. Men have to make the right moves, keep an erection and provide an orgasm for their partners. It is a lot of responsibility to have on your shoulders – or, more accurately, your penis – and makes sex about performing and scoring rather than pleasure and closeness. Into this anxiety-making cauldron throw a set of myths about men and sex that are not only hard to attain but also don't necessarily lead to great lovemaking (and in many cases actually undermine it). These include:

- Men know everything about sex

- Men are always ready and interested

- A real man makes the earth move for his partner

- Sex is centred on the penis

- A penis should be a foot long and hard as steel

Anxiety almost leaps off the page in this letter to my website from a thirty-year-old virgin: 'I'm not bad-looking, in fact, I have nothing to worry about there – but I despair because I've not only never had sex but I've never had a girlfriend either.' Like all men, he has to reassure me about his masculinity. 'I have a successful career and no lack of personal achievement (and am well educated with a post-grad degree). I can talk to women for hours if I'm not trying to pull but I have no confidence in approaching women I like. I become a wreck. My parents want me to find a wife but what am I supposed to do? If I do meet someone, what am I going to tell them about my history or lack of it?'

Here is another letter from a thirty-seven-year-old man: 'I am very worried that I will be a virgin for the rest of my life and that is driving me to despair! Could you offer me even the remotest possibility of any hope? Also, because I am totally inexperienced in the art of love, I don't have very much knowledge of how to be a good lover, for example, I don't know how to kiss passionately.'

The myth of men knowing everything about sex makes it simply inconceivable for these correspondents to tell a potential girlfriend about their situation and let her initiate them into the joys of lovemaking. Worse still, this ignorance about sex can put men at risk. I had a twenty-nine-year-old client – once again, with a post-graduate degree – who discovered a woman with whom he'd recently had a one-night stand was two months pregnant. 'The news gave me a nasty shock but I don't think I'm in the frame because although I didn't use a condom, I did withdraw in time,' he told me. I had to inform him that semen is present in pre-ejaculatory fluid.

However, the most pernicious myth of all is that sex is centred on the penis. It not only reinforces the idea that real sex = intercourse (and somehow anything else is second best), but also drives many of the most common sexual problems for men *and* women.

Erectile dysfunction

There is immense pressure on a man to maintain an erection not only for himself (because failure makes him less of a man) but also for his partner too, as many women and gay men take any limpness as a personal slight – as if she or he is not attractive enough. Indeed, many men think an erection equals desire – even though they can wake up with an erection (caused by the pressure of the bladder on the prostate) and that fear can trigger one too (this is how men have been forced to perform sex acts at gun point). Conversely, a soft penis does not mean that a man is not excited, as many men will lose their erection while giving oral sex (because their attention is on their partner not themselves). As I have said many times already in this book, erections come and go. Ultimately, all that losing an erection signifies is that not enough blood is flowing to the penis. This could be caused by various health conditions (such as diabetes, heart disease, multiple sclerosis and not enough testosterone), various medications (anti-depressants, beta-adrenergic blockers, sleeping pills, anti-psychotics and some cardiovascular drugs), street drugs (ecstasy, heroine and, in higher doses, cocaine, marijuana and LSD), long-term cigarette smoking and alcohol abuse. Alternatively, the lack of erection could be because the man is tired or his mind is preoccupied with other thoughts.

When psychologists at Harvard University looked at what 2,250 volunteers were thinking about during a range of pleasurable activities, they discovered that their minds wandered 70 per cent of the time and even with sex, people only concentrate 90 per cent of the time. This figure will drop considerably during times of stress – like redundancy, bereavement and financial problems. So although men might still have sexual desire, and certainly have a need to be intimate with their partner, they might not be able to maintain an erection.

'I wanted to prove so much that I could be good at something,' said Nicholas, forty-one, 'especially after younger and less experienced men started to get promoted over me, but the more I worried about performing, the worse it got. Things would start off fine, I'd be hard and ready to penetrate, but if April, my wife, isn't properly lubricated or I have trouble entering, that's it. My concentration goes and it's all over. April tries to be nice but I know she's disappointed. Hell, I'm disappointed. A complete failure.' There was something else troubling Nicholas, but it took a while for him to have enough courage to continue. 'I have these images of her been fucked hard by another man and having these orgasms that leave her panting and screaming with pleasure. They really haunt me. I don't think I can keep her if I can't satisfy her.'

How to deal with erectile dysfunction: One of the advantages of the success of Viagra and similar drugs is that what used to be called impotence is now freely discussed. The disadvantage is that both men and women are quick to label occasional problems maintaining an erection as erectile dysfunction – which can exacerbate rather than ease the problems – and many younger men are using these drugs as a sort of 'insurance policy'. The result is that none of the underlying myths about sex have been challenged and the problems medicated rather than solved. So what's the alternative?

- **Listen to your body:** You are not a sex machine and it could be that your body is trying to tell you something. For example: 'I'm angry with being taken for granted' or 'This relationship is not working for me' or 'I'm burnt out'. In many ways, a lack of erection is an early warning that something important needs to be attended to. Certainly Nicholas discovered that half the problems were in his head, not his penis: 'I was expecting far too much from myself. When I stopped and looked at my work load, the amount that I was drinking and the fact that I was angry with my wife – because she kept on throwing money around like confetti – it was not surprising that I wasn't really up for sex.'

- **Get a health check:** Speak to your doctor and be certain that you don't have any undiagnosed health problems. If you are on a medication that might be interfering with your sex life, there is probably an alternative. Be aware that most doctors, like the population at large, are often embarrassed about discussing sex and do not routinely ask about the side effects of prescription drugs on erectile function.

- **Be positive:** Celebrate the pleasures of the soft penis, it is just as sensitive as an erect one. Many men discover that they still enjoy receiving oral sex and their partners enjoy the sensation of the penis growing and stiffening in their mouth. Even if you don't become fully erect, it is still possible to masturbate or be masturbated to ejaculation. If you have been following my programme, you will also be comfortable giving and receiving sensual pleasure with your fingers and tongue. Therefore losing an erection does not mean that lovemaking has to stop, in fact, many women find it easier to have an orgasm from masturbation or oral sex than intercourse. (There is more about this later in the chapter.)

- **Stop catastrophing:** Negative statements such as 'I'm over the hill' or 'My wife will leave me' are probably not only inaccurate but also have a magnetic quality and attract other depressing thoughts. Next time your inner voice starts running you down, instead of listening, imagine taking a cricket bat and simply knocking the negative statement out of your head. Stop making repeated apologies as this will make you feel worse and it does not make your partner feel better. In fact, many women just get angrier because, they reason, if you meant the apology you would have got help earlier. (Unfortunately, as woman are socialised to ask for and give help, they find it difficult to understand how shameful it is for a man to admit to failing in something.)

- **Focus on more positive images:** Instead of focusing on losing your erection, imagine it happening and staying calm and using your fingers and tongue to pleasure your partner. Imagine a guardian angel sitting on your shoulders and whispering positive messages: 'There is help out there' or 'The programme in this book is really going to work.' Imagine the great sex you're going to have in the future – in detail. Finally, recall your other virtues: 'great dad' or 'sensitive listener'.

- **Give yourself time:** If you can step away from the tyranny that sex = intercourse and become less anxious about your erection, you will discover the truth that erections go but they also come back. There is no reason why you can't continue to enjoy sex into your seventies and beyond.

Lack of ejaculatory control

One third of men cannot control when they ejaculate. It is not just younger men but men in their forties and fifties who reach orgasm too quickly (what is known as premature or rapid ejaculation) or take too long (retarded ejaculation). For the rest, control is never perfect but, up to a point, they can choose to come up to the threshold of inevitability and retreat back. When a man has poor control and orgasms very quickly – possibly only a few thrusts after entering the vagina – it will make him anxious and miserable. Meanwhile, his partner will often suffer from lack of desire. As one woman said to me: 'Why bother, if it's all over before I get warmed up?' By contrast, men with retarded ejaculation sound like great lovers – after all, they can have intercourse for ever. However, regular bouts of thirty, forty and even sixty minutes of pounding away can leave both men and women sore and frustrated – especially if he is unable to ejaculate and provide their love-making with that sense of completeness. Fortunately, there is help available for lack of ejaculatory control and it is one of the most straightforward to solve. All you need is knowledge, attention and skills (which can be taught). First, I will deal with premature ejaculation or PE.

Listen to your body: Men with poor ejaculatory control are not focusing on the sensations in their own body enough. It is great to be a considerate lover but not to the point that you ignore the signs of impending ejaculation. So take time out to masturbate alone. The first time, there is no need to do anything different from normal – just be aware of the growing sense of arousal and tension. Be aware when you cross the point of no return – when the seminal vessels and the prostrate gland begin to contract – and ejaculation is inevitable.

Consult your doctor: Low levels of some anti-depressants have been known to slow down men's ejaculatory response and this had led to a range of drugs and creams coming on to the market. Some men would rather do without them – as the side effects can be anxiety, sore mouth, dizziness and sleep disturbance. The creams aim to numb the penis and are applied about thirty minutes before intercourse and have to be thoroughly wiped away or will reduce the sensitivity of the vagina. Although not for everyone, there is a place for medication in combination with the following exercises.

Stop/Start: This method was pioneered by Dr James Semans in the mid-fifties. This time you masturbate alone but as you become aware that you are approaching the threshold of orgasm – stop. Quickly breathe out a few times, as this will reduce the tension in your body and your level of excitement. Rest for a few seconds and when you feel under control again, resume your masturbation. Try to vary the strokes – slower and faster (and see what effect this has), alternate your grip (two fingers and thumb or whole hand) and where you stimulate (start with the tip and then move further down the penis). After a few sessions where you have learned to reach the threshold and retreat, add in an extra dimension and masturbate with massage oil or some other form of lubrication. Some men find it helpful to monitor their levels of arousal by using a traffic lights code: green (keep going); amber (caution: slow down); red (stop immediately). Aim to be able to masturbate for fifteen minutes alone before moving on to the next stage.

Recruit your partner: Explain to your partner that you will stop whenever you are in danger of reaching the threshold – and that she or he needs to be still too and not thrust up to meet you. The traffic-light system is a quick and easy way of communicating what is happening in your body. The stops will probably need to be a bit longer than when masturbating alone. Take deep breaths, relax and enjoy the pleasant sensation of being inside her or his body. Some couples will talk to each other or whisper sweet nothings. Try varying your speeds and how far in and out that you thrust – as this is how men with good ejaculatory control delay their orgasms. Accidents are common – but don't worry – it is a chance to practise using your tongue and fingers to satisfy your partner. Solid proof that ejaculation does not mean the end of lovemaking will reduce your anxiety and reassure your partner that her or his needs are not being ignored. In addition, the accident will have provided data for redefining your point of no return and improving control.

Give yourself time: Aim for about fifteen minutes of intercourse before ejaculating. It will probably take a while to reach this point. I recommend men masturbating twice or three times a week to gain control alone and then working with their partner at a similar frequency on the start/stop programme. Don't fall below twice a week as sexual frustration will hamper rather the promote control. In total, I would expect a man to take between four and six weeks to gain ejaculatory control. If this programme does not work, or you find it hard to follow, there is an alternative approach – developed by Masters and Johnson, the founders of sex therapy – called the squeeze technique (which involves squeezing the penis rather than stopping intercourse). A good sex therapist will help explain more.

Retarded ejaculation

Although most men will have occasions where they cannot reach a climax through intercourse, there are some who find it extremely difficult and rarely or never ejaculate in their partner's vagina or anus. Jonathan, thirty-eight, had had many partners over his sexual career: 'It doesn't matter what I do, for how long or how attractive I find the girl, I never cum inside her. Some of the lovemaking has been very passionate and I've sort of stopped worrying. When I know she's satisfied, I sort of stop. There have been times when I've faked it, but these days I can't see the point.'

Retarded ejaculation is more an emotional problem than a physical one and I was not surprised to learn that Jonathan had problems letting people get close and none of his relationships had lasted more than a few months. 'I can't stand feeling obligated, it's like the walls closing in on me and I go all quiet. She'll start pushing for answers, which makes things worse still, and one of us, normally me, will call it a day.'

When I started working with Jonathan, he had recently finished a short relationship where there had been a strong mutual sexual attraction. 'Almost at the beginning, she'd said that she didn't see us having a future,' he explained, 'and that sort of let me off the hook and I could relax and really enjoy the sex.' With this girlfriend, Jonathan had 'finished myself off' by masturbating after he withdrew. Up to that moment, he had only masturbated to ejaculation in private.

The main focus of our work was combating Jonathan's anxiety at the beginning of relationships by helping him to talk about his fears rather than suppress them. When one of his dates turned into a relationship, we decided to work on the retarded ejaculation too. 'We'd made love a few times and when I pulled out, she said, "Don't you want to climax?", so I masturbated myself and she held my other hand. It was really nice,' explained Jonathan.

Over the next few weeks, I encouraged Jonathan to ask his girlfriend to straddle him so that he could fondle her breasts or kiss her as he masturbated. The next stage, he would masturbate himself and re-penetrate her after he'd passed the point of no return and then climax inside her. 'To be honest, the pleasure isn't much greater for me but she enjoys it and we feel closer cuddling afterwards.' Over time, Jonathan started to relax enough to let go emotionally and reach a climax without masturbating. His retarded ejaculation was something that belonged in the past.

Female-specific Sexual Difficulties

Girls get more complicated messages from parents, schools, media and the wider society than boys. On the one hand, we encourage our daughters to excel, to get good grades, be independent and forge a successful career but on the other, the old ideas that a woman without a man should be pitied are still alive and well. In the same way that a weak man is somehow not a man, a woman without a husband or children is somehow less feminine. While men are competitive on the sports field and over who earns the most, women compete on who is the most attractive or whose children are doing best. At least men are partially in control of their arena – they can practise their ball skills or study business books. Women, however, are competing in an arena which is largely outside their control – such as their looks and their children's success (despite the promises of the beauty and diet industry, our level of attractiveness is basically fixed and much as we love our children, they are their own people, not extensions of our egos).

While sex is a source of a simple pleasure (and some frustration) for boys, sex is a minefield for girls. 'I was only twelve years old and my dad had given me money to buy a dress for a party he was giving,' explains Julia who is now thirty years old. 'I just thought it was pretty but it must have been short and revealing because I remember the looks on all the men's faces when I walked in. It was exhilarating as, previously, I'd felt ignored and powerless.' Julia's parents had split up when she was ten.

'My new-found attractiveness was also frightening, too,' she explained. 'My uncle cornered me in the kitchen and told me I was "jail bait".' Before too long, Julia's sexuality became a battlefield between her and her mother. She lost her virginity at fourteen and when her mother discovered that Julia was on the Pill, she threatened to report her to the police – for underage sex – if her daughter did not give up her boyfriend (who was a year older). By contrast, if a boy was discovered to be having sex at this age, many fathers would congratulate him.

So what are the myths about sex for women?

- Women are not as interested in sex as men and don't have the same sexual urges

- To want sex is slutty

- Good girls don't

- Bigger breasts are more feminine

- Vaginas are dirty

- Women should please men in bed

- While men have an on/off switch, women have hundreds of dials that all have to be at the right place

In my experience, a woman's level of comfort with her sexuality is directly related to how her mother felt about her own. 'My mother had an unrelenting "abstinence only" sex education policy, which, in retrospect, I think was very damaging. However, I could never confront her about it because I knew I'd upset her,' writes Stella, to my website. Despite being thirty-three, she has only had one casual and short-lived relationship. 'When I was a teenager she was always pointing out that sex outside marriage was wrong. I can't stress how strong the message was, how it stayed with me and how I now feel very scared of sex. After I left home at eighteen, I was extremely shocked that other people my own age were having sex and their parents didn't mind! These days I don't rationally believe that sex outside marriage is wrong, quite the reverse, but I can't get my mum's warnings out of my head.'

While boys handle their penises on a daily basis (when urinating), girls are not encouraged to look at their vaginas. Boys have hundreds of names for their penises but girls are given no vocabulary at all. Perhaps it is not surprising that many grown women refer to their vagina as 'down there' and make a sour face. Ultimately, if a mother is not at peace with her genitals, it is unlikely that her daughter will be comfortable exploring her vagina, discovering her clitoris and the pleasures involved. When I have suggested to some female clients that they could take a hand mirror and look at their genitals, I might as well have suggested that they dance naked through the aisles of their local supermarket. Ultimately, for these women, it is okay for their husband to explore their vagina with his tongue or fingers, but not for them to do so. It is hard to think of anything sadder than someone else being allowed pleasure from your body but denying it yourself.

Female anorgasmia

In their most recent sexual encounter 85 per cent of men report that their partner achieved orgasm (in research for the National Survey of Sexual Health and Behaviour). When women were asked the same question only 64 per cent said that they did. Why is there such an orgasm gap? I'm afraid that we're back to that myth that is undermining good love-making: sex = intercourse. While men are more likely to orgasm when sex includes vaginal intercourse, women are more likely to orgasm when a variety of sexual acts are included (such as masturbation and oral sex). Unfortunately, this basic fact is not widely known. Throw in a lack of knowledge about woman's genitals – from both women and men – and we have the recipe for a lot of unhappiness and many women being unfairly labelled as sexually dysfunctional.

Anorgasmia is when someone – and it can be men too – cannot achieve an orgasm. Sometimes it is down to something medical (such as diabetes, multiple sclerosis or some pelvic trauma from falling on a climbing frame or gymnastics beam) or a side effect of drugs (anti-depressants and selective serotonin reuptake inhibitors or heroin addiction) but, most commonly, the problem is a woman's lack of knowledge or her partner's technique.

The clitoris has more nerve endings than any other structure in the human body – somewhere between six and eight thousand. This is around four times more than the male penis. Not surprisingly, the clitoris provides the most intense pleasures – so much so that many women prefer to masturbate to the right or the left rather than directly.

Unfortunately, the clitoris rarely gets stimulated in sexual intercourse. Sometimes, the penis entering and withdrawing the vagina tugs at the vaginal lips which are attached to the hood of the clitoris and provides indirect stimulation. The clitoris can also be stimulated by rubbing against the man's pelvis – especially when the woman is on top and leaning forward enough. However, it is difficult to maintain good enough contact during intercourse. The advice from sex therapists is that it is much easier to use fingers. Ultimately, it is not important whether a woman reaches a climax through intercourse alone, intercourse and masturbation combined or through oral sex or masturbation. There is simply no hierarchy of orgasm. What counts is that she feels good and the couple feel close and satisfied.

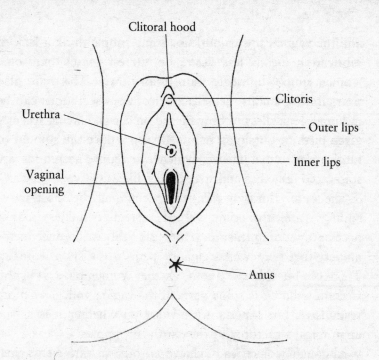

Clitoral hood

Clitoris

Urethra

Outer lips

Inner lips

Vaginal opening

Anus

When I quiz couples about their sex lives and ask if the woman has an orgasm (as part of a standard assessment), there can be some confusion. While male ejaculation is obvious, a woman's climax is largely invisible. So how do you know if you've had one or not? The best way to describe the experience is that an orgasm is a bit like a sneeze – a build up of tension and then a release. In most cases, when I offer this explanation, a woman will relax and nod. Yes, she has had an orgasm. Unfortunately, all the clichés of romantic novels – where the whole body shakes or the world is knocked off its regular orbit – can lead some women to question the response in their own bodies.

There is also as much misinformation about vaginal lubrication as there is for male erection. During lovemaking, extra blood flows to the vagina causing it to expand and lengthen and the vaginal lips to puff up. Some people think a lack of lubrication means less desire or interest in sex but some women simply lubricate more than others. There are also times in a woman's menstrual cycle when secretions can be minimal, regardless of how turned on she is. Having recently given birth or nursing a baby will also reduce the amount of lubrication. Other factors which can reduce secretions are some cold remedies and street drugs like ecstasy.

The outer third of the vagina contains the most nerve endings – after this point, women can register fullness but not necessarily more pleasure. (Hopefully, this will reduce men's anxiety that they need a gigantic penis to satisfy a woman.) There is a huge debate about whether women have a G-spot. Certainly there are some parts of the vagina which are more responsive, but experts are divided on whether it is a true anatomical structure like the clitoris or nipple.

Although women can achieve an orgasm through vaginal penetration alone, the best way is by stimulating the clitoris with light rubbing, in rocking or circular motions. The lighter and more lubricated the touch the better – this is one of the reasons why a talented tongue works wonders. While men don't need further stimulation past their point of no return, women require consistent and continued attention until the orgasm is complete. Some woman can be very still and quiet just before an orgasm – almost as if listening and waiting for its approach. Unfortunately, many men think their partner has lost interest and stop, thereby aborting the orgasm. The advice to men from sex therapists is to keep going and to women to mentally accept the oncoming orgasm. Prior to climaxing, the clitoris can retreat behind the clitoral hood. Don't go looking for it, just keep stimulating the general area. Communication is very important at this point as every woman is different – some like their partner to slow down and be a little gentler but others want him or her just to keep going.

In most cases, where women fear that they cannot have an orgasm, I find that more knowledge, helping their partner to improve his ejaculatory control (so intercourse lasts longer), or introducing other forms of lovemaking beyond intercourse, will resolve the problem. If this is not the case for you, I would suggest getting a referral to a sex therapist through your doctor.

More commonly, I see women who do have orgasms but only occasionally. A typical example is Carol, in her mid-fifties, who has been married for over thirty years to Declan, fifty-nine: 'I always say that sex, for me, is not about having an orgasm because I enjoy the closeness and I like giving Declan pleasure, but sometimes I do wonder . . .' She stopped and sighed: 'What about me?' In the early part of their marriage, Carol had achieved orgasm through intercourse but not in the past twenty years. 'Something changed, I don't know what,' she explained. Fortunately, she had recently started reading self-help books and had gained a better understanding of her body. When Declan's job took him abroad for three months at a stretch, she bought a vibrator and found that it reliably gave her an orgasm. Although they used the vibrator together, when Declan returned home, it did not become a regular part of their lovemaking.

When we reached the Fortnight of Variety in my programme, Declan shadowed the way Carol played with her genitals but was unable to give her an orgasm. When I questioned them further, I discovered that there were three problems. Carol felt she *had* to orgasm to complete the exercise.

'What I've liked about the previous exercises is that there is no planned destination,' she said. 'I would relax and enjoy the moment.'

I reassured her that there was no requirement to orgasm but as we talked more, it became clear that being unable to give Carol an orgasm was a source of sadness for Declan.

'I'm worried that I might hurt her, so I think I'm too tentative,' he explained.

'So what do you think is the difference between the vibrator and Declan's fingers?' I asked.

Fortunately, Carol had been thinking about this question herself and already knew the answer: 'A greater area and greater pressure. Also, with the vibrator, I'm not worried about wearing Declan out.'

'How long did he masturbate you for?' I asked.

'About five minutes,' they replied and I gave them a quizzical look.

Carol laughed. 'Yes, I suppose a penis can wear out in five minutes but not fingers.'

When we had looked at their preferred types of lovemaking (and did the questionnaire together), Carol had been surprised to discover that she enjoyed trance.

'It takes time to fall into trance – certainly more than five minutes,' I explained, 'and repetitive patterning is important. By this, I mean making the same type of move over and over – perhaps varying the pressure or the area covered but only very slightly.'

As we talked more about masturbation, it became clear that Carol enjoyed plenty of different types of touching in the first stages but as the orgasm approached, and she fell into a trance, that would be the moment to switch to patterning. To achieve the added area to match the vibrator, Declan would experiment – in the variety phase of masturbating – with using two or three fingers. To achieve more pressure, Declan would explore different depths of penetration (although

Carol could use her hand to encourage him to push down harder or lift his fingers back if his touch was too firm.) I also encouraged him to be much closer when he watched her masturbate at the beginning of the exercise, so that he could truly see and understand her technique.

To keep the exercise balanced, I wondered if Declan would enjoy more variety of touch (different grips and speeds) when Carol masturbated him. In this way, she could torment him by stopping and starting and not giving him the patterned touch which prompts ejaculation until she chose the moment.

The next week, they were happy to report that not only had Declan given Carol an orgasm but also, by delaying Declan's orgasm and really torturing him, she had taken his enjoyment of sex to a new level too.

Vaginismus

This is the technical term for a woman's inability to engage in any form of vaginal penetration – not just sexual intercourse. Some women cannot insert a tampon or have a full gynaecological examination either. A bit like our eyes blinking when something approaches, the vagina contracts and penetration is painful or impossible. In most cases, the problem is psychological but it is worth checking that there is no infection which might be causing irritation or inflammation.

Vaginismus is most likely to effect young women – although some wait many years before seeking help. It is caused by the usual combination of problems: lack of knowledge, the myth that sex = intercourse, and poor male technique. I will tackle these one by one.

Although we think of the vagina as a hole, it is more a potential space than a real one. Let me explain more. When not aroused, the vaginal walls are relaxed and touch each other. However, when the vagina is sexually excited, the walls expand and can easily accommodate a penis. Unfortunately, an inexperienced man – often worried that he will not able to sustain his erection – will blunder towards the vagina, not giving his partner enough time to relax and become aroused. Sadly, because many people believe sex = intercourse, after a couple of painful prods, lovemaking is abandoned altogether. Normally, the woman feels shame and the man is angry – thereby increasing the anxiety levels for the next time the couple makes love. Anxiety and tension make vaginismus worse and hardens the problem from a temporary step-back into an impenetrable wall between the couple.

When Carrie was seventeen and in her first relationship (with a boy the same age), they had nowhere to go and make love. 'We had a couple of attempts on my parents' sofa but I was always worried they would come home and his parents never went out,' she explained. Carrie's mother had never discussed sex: 'She asked if I'd covered the basics at school and I nodded. I don't know who was more embarrassed, her or me, and the subject was thankfully closed.' Although her mother was not explicitly 'anti-sex', she found any discussion of emotions uncomfortable, so discussing something as personal as her daughter's body or giving her permission to explore it was simply impossible. 'I don't know if it was fear, anxiety or what, but that first time I just couldn't relax enough for him to enter me,' said Carrie, 'but the weirdest part is that my boyfriend and I didn't talk about it. He just put himself away and that was that. We tried a couple more times but it was no better.'

Carrie went on to have two more relationships that were sexual but involved no penetrative sex. At twenty-six, she married an old university friend: 'We talked about having a baby, which was strange, because goodness knows how that was going to happen – but we never discussed my problem. He was a nice guy, who put me on a pedestal, but I had no respect for him.' It was not until Carrie was thirty-one, and divorced, that she started a short six-month relationship that turned out to be incredibly sexual. 'I don't know if it was because I was older and more confident, the overwhelming attraction I felt for him or that he was more experienced and knew how to turn me on, but I had no problem at all. Sex was a revelation, I finally understood what everybody was talking about.' Unfortunately, this boyfriend moved abroad and the relationship ended. It was not until Carrie had a series of sexually rewarding, but emotionally empty, relationships – and she came to see me to understand why it was she couldn't find love – that she talked to anyone about her history of vaginismus. It turned out that Carrie had a fear of intimacy – a hangover from her repressed childhood. We also worked on destroying the myth that nice girls don't enjoy sex and, halfway through her counselling, she met a man that she both respected and wanted to go to bed with. Fortunately, she had gained enough confidence to discuss her fears with her boyfriend: 'We took things really slowly. Lots of kisses, cuddles and stroking until I was almost begging him to penetrate me.'

If you are in a long-term relationship and find intercourse painful or impossible, sex therapists have a programme to help. This includes the touching exercises in this book, helping you and your partner to talk more openly about sex and experimenting with a series of dilators which get progressively larger.

Sexual Problems Are Shared Problems

As I've already explained, people are quick to label themselves as having 'a problem' – even though sexual difficulties have their roots in a variety of interlocking places. Certainly one partner might be exhibiting the problem but, taking Carrie and her vaginismus as an example, how much of the dysfunction was down to her inability to relax and how much to her early partners' clumsiness and lack of knowledge? Frequently, sex therapists discover that a woman might come into therapy with anorgasmia but her partner has poor ejaculatory control too. I had a couple where the man had retarded ejaculation but his wife had a disgust of semen. If he came anywhere close to climaxing through masturbation, she swathed his penis in tissues. Unsurprisingly, he would quickly lose interest.

Who has the sexual problem is a bit like the old philosophical debate: which came first, the chicken or the egg? Ultimately, it does not matter who exhibits the problem. It is the relationship as a whole, not one half that needs help. Taking away the idea of 'blame' makes it easier to work together as a team and improve lovemaking. And the good news is that the specific sexual problems outlined in this chapter are easy to treat and the success rates are high.

My Partner is Using Pornography

Men and women are sexually stimulated by different things. Men are particularly visually orientated and even in their fantasies concentrate more on body parts and intercourse. In male monkeys, the level of testosterone is boosted when they see a sexually available female or watch another pair of monkeys copulate. Meanwhile, brain scans of the human male show more activity in the regions associated with visual processing. The same scans in female brains reveals more activity in the parts associated with emotion and the retrieval of memories. Therefore, it is not surprising that men and women have very different attitudes to pornography.

Gemma and Mark – in their twenties – came into counselling after she caught him looking at Internet pornography. 'It's not just that I know he's comparing to me to those horrible women,' said Gemma, 'but that they're stuck in his head while he's making love to me.' Mark had also admitted that he often masturbated alone. Gemma felt betrayed by this too: 'We have a very active sex life, at least three times a week, so why does he have to sneak off into a corner? If he felt turned on, he could have made love to me.' She would have been horrified at another of Kahr's findings: 90 per cent of men and 86 per cent of woman masturbate regularly alone. Gemma claimed that she never thought of anybody beyond Mark.

The arguments about pornography had escalated and Mark had agreed not to go online. 'I want to keep the peace and show Gemma that she's what matters to me, but work is really difficult without the Internet because I need to order supplies for my business,' said Mark.

'You should have thought about that before looking at filth,' replied Gemma.

'Some of my work supplies are really specialist and difficult to track down by phone.'

'You're just making excuses,' said Gemma and she turned to me. 'I think he's addicted to porn.'

Is there such a thing as sex addiction?

When someone is labelled a sex addict, we immediately picture a Hollywood star who has had a string of affairs or been caught with a prostitute. One half of the media will scoff – 'It's just an excuse' or 'He's trying to get sympathy' or 'He won't take responsibility for what he's done.' The other half gets a second-hand thrill from recounting all the sordid details. The picture is further complicated because there is no agreed medical or legal definition for sex addiction. So can you be addicted to sex?

Therapists are certainly seeing a growing number of men whose lives have spun out of control because they can't stop visiting prostitutes – even though they have promised their wives over and over again – or have run up bills of thousands of pounds on adult telephone chatlines or regularly spend the *whole* night watching Internet pornography (despite having to go off to work in the morning). It is not just the behaviour that is so destructive but the context. I've worked with a man who missed his brother's funeral because he was having sex with a prostitute and another who would masturbate seven times a day in the office toilet. He had been caught once and given an official warning but despite his job being on the line, he had not stopped. These stories, and countless more, have provided the frame work for deciding if someone is abusing sex or not:

- The behaviour is compulsive.

- It interferes with normal living and causes severe stress on family, friends and problems at work.

- Sex is used to block out feelings, self-medicate or as a 'reward' for getting through something stressful or painful – even though, afterwards, the 'addict' feels guilt and disgust. Unfortunately, shame just triggers another visit to a prostitute or a marathon porn session.

- Although someone abusing sex will often stop for a while, they find it hard to maintain abstinence in the long term. In the pre-Internet era, for example, men would throw away their magazine and videos but would gradually start collecting again. Today these men will willingly allow their partner to control the password to the family computer but later go out and buy a secret laptop and set up a private Internet account.

- There is often denial about the full extent of usage and dependency. So when an addict is faced with how many hours have been consumed by his addiction or the size of the bill, he finds it hard to believe.

There are lots of myths about sex addiction:

- **It is only men who abuse sex.** I have met women who compulsively cruise adult dating sites – often when drunk – and invite strangers round to their home, even though many of their 'dates' become verbally abusive and some turn violent after having sex. Quit Porn Addiction, a UK counselling service, report that one in three of their clients are women struggling with their own use of pornography.

- **It is fun.** The sex is surprisingly joyless and the regret is not just limited to the morning after. Some men report throwing up before meeting a prostitute but feel 'obliged' to go through with the sex after having spent hours choosing and arranging the session.

- **It is linked to a high-sex drive.** This is like saying alcoholics are thirstier than the general population. In many ways, it is not about sex at all but a way of anaesthetising oneself from pain (even though it will cause more pain and set up even more destructive behaviour).

- **It is something that you're saddled with for life.** Although some men have been consuming large amounts of pornography since they were teenagers, for many it is associated with a particular stage in their lives (such as their wife becoming pregnant or getting promoted). Obviously, the longer and more ingrained, the harder it is to cure. Like all addictions, the success of treatment depends on the degree of commitment to change.

How do people start abusing sex?

For many men, their relationship with pornography is reasonably healthy. It can be a source of information, when they are young and inexperienced (and plug some of the holes in the purely biological approach to sex education in schools) and a solace when they are between girlfriends or boyfriends. For young women, brought up to believe that watching pornography is hip and liberated, it can provide a distraction when they are feeling anxious or bored and a sense of power that they don't have in real life. In the same way that it's perfectly possible to enjoy a drink without becoming an alcoholic, you can use pornography without becoming a sex addict. However, for some people, their relationship with porn is more complicated.

Shane is in his mid-forties and discovered his father's collection of top-shelf publications when he was thirteen: 'It was a like a kid from the countryside going up to London. My eyes were on stalks. All these beautiful girls, all laid on these pages for my pleasure. It was complete sensory overload. I looked down and realised that I'd ejaculated.' It was Shane's first orgasm and, at the time, he had no idea what his body had just done. 'I'd squirrel away one of my father's stack of magazines and look at it at my leisure.' Over time, Shane would spend longer and longer flicking through the pages. 'I'd be looking for just the right image but if I found something good after just a few minutes, I wouldn't finish masturbating – because that would spoil things. I'd slow down and keep looking. Sometimes an hour or maybe two would go by. It seemed impossible but I'd hear my mother or father returning and have to stuff the magazines back.' The atmosphere in the house was becoming increasingly fraught and his parents' fights had turned nasty. 'My brother and I would sit at the top of the stairs and listen to the insults. One night my mother came up with a sandwich in the middle of the night – which, looking back, seems a bit strange because I wasn't hungry but I ate it. That was one of the better times; most nights we were left to our own devices.'

'Did you and your brother support each other?' I asked.

'No, we were both in our own little world coping as best as we could.'

With no reassurance, no cuddles from either parent and no opportunity to talk – as the rows were a 'non subject' the next morning – Shane took refuge and comfort in his father's porn collection. 'It gave me a warm, fuzzy feeling,' he explained.

During his twenties and thirties, Shane had a string of girlfriends – some more important than others – and his porn use subsided. However, aged forty, he ended his most serious relationship to date and shortly afterwards his mother died. Unable to cope with so much loss, he escaped into porn again: 'For a while, I could forget how sad and empty I felt.' However, there had been a big change since his childhood: the Internet. While previously he had to cope with the shame of buying soft pornography in a newsagent's or the risk of being seen by someone he knew coming out of a licensed sex shop, the Internet was entirely anonymous. Not only was there unlimited pornography, available twenty-four-seven, but the sites he visited were littered with advertisements for prostitutes. 'I thought "My business is going well, I can afford to pay for sex. I need never be alone when I need company." Unfortunately, I had no idea about the etiquette or what to do in a brothel. After I had sex with the first prostitute, who was incredibly beautiful, I just burst into tears. It was like a dam bursting from all that pent-up pain. She must have been kind because we made love again. I didn't know that was against the rules. Of course, I tried to see her again but that wasn't allowed either.' Over the next five years, Shane began to use prostitutes regularly, sometimes as often as three times a week. 'There is this moment of intimacy but it's only fleeting and ultimately, when you're standing outside on the street, you know it was all an illusion.'

Shane would tell himself that he was harming nobody. 'It's not like I had a wife or anybody I was betraying. I was single and only answerable to myself.' Certainly the stakes appeared much lower than for married men whose marriages are put into jeopardy by repeatedly visiting prostitutes. However, Shane *was* harming himself. While 'self-medicating' with prostitutes, he was not dealing with his bereavement and the complicated feelings associated with his mother (whom he both loved and felt angry about) or making new relationships (despite his greatest goal being to get married and have children). Worse still, he was switching off his natural empathy for other people when having sex with prostitutes – otherwise he would have to consider what it was like for the women to 'service' so many men or issues such as forced prostitution and human trafficking.

When looking back at his other relationships with women during this period, Shane admitted: 'I was thinking with my dick when I was on a date. "When am I going to get sex?" or "How could I persuade her into bed? An expensive meal maybe, and back to my place for a nightcap and, if not intercourse, perhaps a handjob." Sometimes, I'd think "I don't fancy her enough for all that effort, all that talking, I could just phone up and order sex".'

'How do you think these women felt being pestered for sex?' I asked.

'Not very good.' He looked at me bleakly. 'If I truly want to be married and start a family, I'm not doing myself any favours.'

Meanwhile, Shane's use of prostitutes was having a profound impact on his taste in women. 'I always book Asians and that's what I put into search engines when I'm looking for porn. So I've started dating only Thai, Chinese and Japanese women. The rest simply didn't do anything for me.'

'So your pool of potential dates became smaller and you crossed off plenty of women who could have made perfectly good partners,' I commented.

'I'd get a high sitting with these beautiful young women,' explained Shane, and his eyes had a far way look, 'except there'd always be something wrong with them, or they wouldn't be with me.'

'Hang on. Explain that statement.'

'I'm not stupid, I'm closer to fifty than forty and a little over-weight. So I'm not their dream date. If their English was better or they were more educated, they wouldn't be with me.'

'So not only are they "damaged goods" but they're doing nothing for your self-esteem either.'

As we reviewed his recent relationships, a pattern began to emerge. 'They complain that I'm only after sex and I worry that they're only after my money – there's always a bill for college that needs paying or they're behind with rent.'

I was struck by how the sexual/financial transaction of prostitution was mirrored in his dating relationships. 'So you both end up feeling used?' I asked.

The realisation that his prostitution and pornography habit was not just a coping mechanism for being single but for keeping him single made Shane stop hiring prostitutes and, later, using pornography. (There is more information about his treatment in the exercise section.)

I have told Shane's story in detail, rather than a more extreme example, because many men will be able to relate to it and because it illustrates the three main contributing factors for sex addiction:

1. **Childhood sexual abuse.** (Showing pornography to a minor is illegal and although Shane's father didn't want him to look at his collection, leaving them somewhere his son could find them was reprehensible. Most addicts, however, have suffered something much worse.)

2. **Trigger circumstances.** (The loss of Shane's mother and splitting with his girlfriend turned his manageable, but still questionable, relationship with pornography into a problem relationship with prostitutes.)

3. **Greater opportunity.** (In the same way that crack cocaine has dramatically increased the number of addicts – who were possibly using other drugs recreationally without getting into serious trouble – sex addiction experts are reporting that the Internet, and being only a couple of clicks away from a prostitute, is causing men without the normal underlying factors of childhood abuse or any serious triggers, such as job loss, a serious car accident, marital breakdown etc., to get into difficulties with pornography.)

Our attitudes to addiction have undergone a revolution and we are now more likely to see it as an illness than as a character failure. However, when it comes to sex addiction, our attitudes are lagging behind. 'We're still stuck in the seventies and although we no longer think of an alcoholic being a tramp on a park bench, we still picture sex addicts as perverts in dirty raincoats,' says Paula Hall, who is a Sexual and Relationship Psychotherapist and leads a sex addict recovery group. 'The reality is that sex addicts come from all walks of life – including successful "go-getting" businessmen.' Paula thinks that the parallels between our use of alcohol and sex are helpful. 'In our culture, we're not generally anti-drink and we don't think a return to prohibition is the answer. In the same way, we don't have problems with sex and we don't think abstinence works either. However, while we're more forgiving of alcoholics – because "there but by the grace of God go I" or we've got friends that we suspect are problem drinkers – we still have a closed mind to sex addiction. While, in reality, our relationship to both these drugs is quite similar.'

So what are the parallels? With alcohol, most people are 'social' users who enjoy a drink without any problems.

Similarly, most people are 'social' users of sex and do not have intercourse with inappropriate people, put their health or job at risk or spend hours looking at Internet pornography. However, in the same way that there 'at risk' drinkers – who often don't know when to stop – there are 'at risk' users of sex. There are three key questions to decide whether or not you fall into this category. Do you spend eleven hours or more a week looking at pornography? (Shows compulsion.) If you can't get access to your chosen form of sexual stimulation, does your mood change? (Indicates self-medication.) Do you become irritable, moody or feel unwell? (Suggests withdrawal symptoms.) The next category is 'binge' users, who can go weeks and months without abusing sex but then go off the rails – often in a spectacular way. Finally, there are 'addicts' who regularly use sex or pornography to regulate their moods and help them cope with stress (even though their usage causes more stress).

What about the partners of people abusing sex?

It goes without saying that it is profoundly upsetting to discover that your partner has been visiting prostitutes, watching large amounts of Internet pornography or using adult dating services. In some ways, the pain is similar to infidelity. However, there are many extra levels of shock ('Did he use a condom and am I at risk from sexually transmitted diseases?') and the shame is greater ('What would my friends think? Would anybody understand?'). The offending behaviour is also harder to understand (at least, with an affair, there is the 'excuse' of love or being flattered by attention) and it is more challenging, too (as it can raise questions about the tastes and sexual interests of the men concerned). Worse still, men who abuse pornography and use prostitutes are even more likely to lie or minimise the extent of their behaviour – as their shame and shock is greater too, and they fear a complete disclosure might end their marriage. Therefore, the truth is even more likely to come out in stages than with infidelity.

'It's not like I'm a prude,' said Cynthia, thirty-one, after she discovered her husband had been visiting prostitutes again, 'if he'd told me what he wanted, we could have talked about it. Except he has to lie, go behind my back and spend money we don't have.' Her husband, Martin, thirty, was full of remorse:

'I really love her and wouldn't do anything to hurt her,' he told me.

'So why do it?' Cynthia chipped in.

'I have these fantasies, they just build and build until I have to do something about them. Not that anything lives up to what I expect. I promise myself I'll never do it again but a new fantasy, a new sexual peak looms, and I just have to go after it.'

After the most recent transgression, Cynthia had started compulsively checking the computer and bank statements, and phoning to ensure Martin was where he said he would be. Other common reactions to someone discovering a partner is abusing sex include:

- Reawakening of old wounds in the relationship. (Cynthia's and Martin's battles over spending priorities came back up to the surface.)

- Triggering partner's past traumas. (These can be everything from childhood sexual abuse through to something completely disassociated with sex – like a bereavement or a car crash.)

- Damaging the sex life of the couple. (Cynthia felt too disgusted to be sexually intimate with Martin and he felt too ashamed to ask.)

- Feelings of hopelessness, depression and numbness. (Cynthia that felt nothing she did had any impact on Martin's behaviour.)

In the same way that a lack of knowledge and myths in the media about sex addiction make it harder for men to ask for help, their partners have unhelpful beliefs that hold back recovery too:

- **It's all my fault.** The partner believes that if she had been, for example, sexier, more sexually liberated or more understanding – the list is endless – she could have headed off the crisis. This is a natural reaction to the helplessness many women feel after discovery. They hope that by taking all the blame, they are back in control. After all, this false reasoning goes, if I change, he'll change and everything will be okay. With most relationship problems, this can indeed be a way forward. However, if your partner is truly a sex addict, your actions will have little or no effect on his behaviour. Even if your partner is only abusing pornography, he has to take responsibility for his behaviour.

- **If he looks at porn, he doesn't love me.** This kind of 'all or nothing' or 'black and white' thinking ups the stakes and does not take into consideration the complexity of human feelings.

- **I'm not good enough.** Personalising everything is another way of trying to take control again – although in a self-destructive way. A man's use of pornography probably says more about his childhood and his inability to deal with feelings of stress and anxiety than it does about his partner.

- **All men are animals.** These over-generalisations and the magnification of the problem undermine coping skills and encourage panicked rather than thought-through reactions.

- **He looked at the waitress, he must have fancied her.** Jumping to conclusions or drawing on one area of your life together to make a cast-iron case in another – for example, 'He's tired and irritable, so he must be lying again' – makes recovery harder and discounts any remaining positives left in a relationship.

What to do if you discover your partner is abusing pornography or using prostitutes

Although every situation is different, there are some common strategies for moving forward either together or apart:

1. Don't make any long-term decisions while you're still in shock. (Especially about who to tell and whether to stay or go.)

2. Find out what really has been happening in your relationship. (Keep calm and try not to condemn too much, as shame will make your partner clam up and keep back information. Remember, it will probably take time to

get a full disclosure, so keep the lines of communication open.)

3. Take care of yourself. (Think carefully about digging for specific or graphic details as these could put pictures into your head which might hamper your recovery. When you feel compelled to find something out, step back and ask yourself why. Are you trying to punish yourself? Are you looking for a magic solution that will take everything back to how it was? How realistic is this?)

4. Read books and consult websites from appropriate organisations like Sex Addicts Anonymous and Sex and Love Addicts Anonymous. (Seek to understand the difference between using, abusing and becoming addicted to pornography, adult chatlines, etc. It is important not to minimise your discovery but exaggerating the evidence is equally unhelpful.)

5. Decision time for your relationship will be later than you expect. (This should come only when you truly know what you're committing to or what you're walking away from. In this way, you will make an informed decision and one to which you can stick.)

6. Seek professional help. (If your partner's behaviour is compulsive, he should be in some sort of treatment programme but you will also need support either from your own therapist or together as a couple. For more minor cases of using or abusing pornography, there are ideas in the exercise section.)

7. Do not expect too much change too quickly. (It will have taken years for your partner's problems to take hold, so do not expect the damage to be righted overnight.)

Sex and the Aftermath of an Affair

In the largest survey of its kind, 'Sex in America', one in three women and one in seven men reported that they have little interest in lovemaking. On the one hand, that's fine. Nobody should have sex they don't want. However, being in a low-sex or no sex-marriage – in sexual therapy, low sex means making love only every other week and no sex, less than ten times a year – has consequences. What about the desires and rights of their partners? Because, equally, nobody should do without the sex that they *do* want.

The result is often an unspoken fight with the person who wants little or no sex also wanting his or her partner to accept their choice and to remain loving, generous and committed to the relationship. Meanwhile, the person who wants sex also wants to be in a loving and committed relationship. Therefore he or she has two choices: to keep asking for sex (which can easily become pestering and create a bad atmosphere) or to hope that his or her desire goes away (which is unlikely).

Unfortunately, most couples with this dilemma do not ask for help. (It is hard enough to admit to each other that they have a problem, let alone speak to a third party.) Instead, they stumble along hoping the issue will solve itself. Maybe a romantic holiday will do the trick or the children will be that little bit older and they will have time for each other again. In the meantime, the partner wanting sex is increasingly vulnerable to having an affair or joining an adult dating site (in the hope that he or she can stay married but have casual sex on the side). Although someone embarking on an affair or arranging a sexual liaison doesn't expect to be discovered, it is almost inevitable. Modern technology not only facilitates infidelity but also leaves a digital trail of emails, texts, credit card bills and computer history files.

Luckily, there is an upside to an affair being uncovered – which is just as well, considering the pain, heartache and guilt involved. So what is this positive? It is no longer possible to ignore the underlying sexual issues and, sometimes for the first time in their relationship, couples begin to talk and resolve their differences.

The journey from discovery to recovery

It is possible to emerge out the other side of an affair with a stronger and better relationship (as I write in my book *How Can I Ever Trust You Again?*). However, there are two types of couples who find it harder to reach recovery. The first are those in long-term low or no-sex relationships (rather than in one of the temporary lulls in sexual activity that all couples go through because of stress, money worries or small children). The second are those who get stuck somewhere along the recovery process. The root of their problem might not necessarily be sex, but I've had quite a lot of success treating these couples by looking at their problems through a sexual focus.

The journey from discovery to recovery involves seven steps: Shock and Disbelief, Intense Questioning, Decision Time, Hope, Attempted Normality, Despair – Bodies Float to the Surface, Intense Learning. So how could improving your sex life speed up this process?

Shock and Disbelief: After ten years of marriage, Suzanne's husband Josh told her he didn't feel that he loved her any more and put most of the blame on their poor sex life. 'This had been an issue since we married when my husband lost interest – excluding holidays, when things are great,' Suzanne explained at our first history-taking session. 'I tried to explore the matter with him without success on numerous occasions and got to a position where I ultimately accepted that he had a very low sex drive and that I should love him regardless. I felt my husband had similarly accepted my flaws. I was aware that we were having a difficult time – no more so than previous times, and we had a special trip coming up that I hoped would help us reconnect.' Suzanne went into shock when her husband asked for 'space' and a few days later told her their marriage had 'run its course' and subsequently moved out.

Intense Questioning: After a few days, and sometimes a few weeks, the shock and numbness begin to wear off and are replaced by a thousand and one questions. In the case of Suzanne and Josh, I'd been suspicious when Josh had refused to attend counselling too. Apparently, he was 'too angry' and 'there wasn't any point'. In my experience, most people who fall out of love or have become best friends rather than partners, as Josh claimed, are happy to come to counselling either as a favour to their partner or as a way of easing themselves gracefully out of the relationship.

When Suzanne started asking 'how', 'when', 'why', Josh's answers became increasingly evasive. Finally, she hacked into his email account: 'I'd had concerns about him being overly friendly with a woman on a networking site and I found all these explicit messages to her. It was heart-breaking.'

At this point in the journey from discovery to recovery, there is a lot of blame flying around. Suzanne blamed Josh for ruining their marriage with someone 'he has only known two minutes' and Josh was blaming Suzanne for being angry and distant. No wonder, as Suzanne said, 'our whole relationship seems like a lie' and in many ways, it had been built on two lies: 'Everything is okay' and 'It doesn't matter that we're not only having no sex, but are also not talking about it either.'

Tempting as it might be to get sucked into the blame game, it is better to step back and ask yourself: why was your relationship so vulnerable (to the point that it could be undermined by a few emails); what changes would you like to make to your relationship and, in particular, your sex life?

Talking about sex is vital at this stage in the recovery process. First it challenges, your partner's preconceptions about your attitude to sex. When Duncan, forty-nine, was caught out by an explicit text message, he got a shock: 'I honestly thought my wife, Elizabeth, wouldn't mind. She wasn't really interested in sex, that it was something she did for me rather than for herself, but I discovered that I'd got her all wrong.' Duncan's affair was a turning point for Elizabeth. She re-evaluated her relationship and, through counselling, changed the face she presented to the world. 'I was always cool, calm and in control. If you didn't like it, that was your problem not mine. So Duncan thinking I wouldn't care about him cheating on me with this other woman stopped me up short. Of course I minded. I minded a lot, but how was he going to know if I kept my feelings to myself? The truth was I enjoy sex but I can't just turn myself on, the way that Duncan can.' Immediately, the problem had changed from Elizabeth doesn't like sex (which seemed an insurmountable obstacle) to Elizabeth needs longer to be turned on (which is easily fixed).

Second, talking about sex demonstrates that you recognise that your relationship is in trouble and that something needs to be done.

Tina, forty-one, came to see me as a last resort. Six months previously, her husband Bob had told her that he had no more love to give and wanted a temporary separation. Tina thought he was having a mid-life crisis or a breakdown – as he had a high-powered but stressful job. 'He'd either be withdrawn or angry and accusing me of not supporting him – which couldn't be further from the truth. I've always been very proud of his success,' said Tina. Although Tina did everything she could to discourage him, Bob took a flat in town during the week and came back home to the countryside on weekends to see Tina and their two children. Before long, Tina discovered that Bob had signed up to a dating site and was seeing other women. During our first session, Tina told me everything about his job, his mother, their children, their special bond. However, there was one subject missing: sex. So, finally, I interrupted her flow and asked about it. She explained that their sex life had taken a terrible knock after a car accident (which caused his temporary impotence) and over time it had dwindled to virtually nothing.

'Why do you think that's important?' she asked.

'What do you think it must be like to be a forty-year-old man and think you'll never have sex again?'

'It's not that brilliant being a forty-something woman, either.'

'You need to tell him that you want a better sex life too,' I told her.

At our next session, Tina reported: 'I went away determined to bring up the topic of sex but there never seemed the right moment to talk. It was tough – and I had to hold on to the breakfast bar in the kitchen to steady myself – but I told him that I was dissatisfied with our sex life too and wanted something better. The look on his face was priceless.' Nothing that Tina said previously – about the financial implications or the effect on their children of divorce – had had the slightest impact on Bob. He would just reply: 'But I've moved on.'

However, after they talked more about their mutual disappointment over their sex life, Bob put their divorce on hold and they came for counselling together. (For more advice on talking about sex, see Sexual Jeopardy in the exercise section for some prompt questions.)

Decision Time: Once the majority of the facts about an affair have been discovered, it is time to assess the damage to your relationship. There are eight types of affairs and the chances of rescuing your relationship is largely dependent on which kind your partner has had. So let's look at these different types and what underlying sexual problems they might reveal:

1. **Accidental.** When discovered, these people claim not to have been looking for an affair but a friendship has crossed the line. The 'friends' bonded by sharing inappropriate details about their relationships – and in particular the state of their sex lives. Sometimes the betrayal stops short of becoming physical but, either way, it is deeply hurtful and should be taken seriously. An accidental affair suggests that your sex life has been going through a bad patch – for example, the birth of a child, redundancy or the death of a parent – rather than serious long-term problems.

2. **Cry for help.** These people are quickly discovered – because they leave clues lying around – or because they

confess all. These affairs are casual, short-lived and the discovered partner claims 'it didn't mean anything'. A cry for help affair suggests that something is wrong with your sex life but there is still time to head it off before the problem becomes serious.

3. **Self-Medication.** These people are unhappy or verging on depressed – and probably have been for several years – so that only the boost of being adored or the excitement of infidelity can compensate for low self-esteem or keep their life on a reasonably even keel. A self-medication affair suggests a long-term ingrained sex problem – most probably low or no sex. Alternatively, the sex might be regular, functional, but deeply dull.

4. **Tripod.** These affairs are long-term, committed and the discovered has talked about leaving their official partner. This is the classic triangle of a husband, wife and mistress or a woman 'torn between two lovers'. At the centre of the tripod is someone who finds intimacy difficult, so he or she 'spreads' the load – normally by having a friendly, largely sexless relationship with their long-term partner and a passionate one with their affair partner. The task is to be sexual and intimate with the same person rather than splitting them into Madonna and Whore or Nice Guy and Stud. Unfortunately, to the person having the affair, leaving their partner and setting up home with their lover seems the obvious answer. In my experience, they normally end up turning their lover into a friend and become passionate with someone new (or even embark on an 'affair' with their ex).

5. **Don Juan or Donna Juanita.** These people have multiple affairs, often overlapping, or lots of casual sex. It is like they have a huge empty void and need endless sex to fill it up. A Don Juan/Donna Juanita has similar issues with intimacy as in the tripod affair but instead of one partner, it has many. These people are probably abusing sex to make themselves feel better. So although this might appear to be a sexual problem, it is sometimes an addiction issue.

6. **Exploratory.** Everybody wonders what life might have been like if, for example, they didn't get married at eighteen, had not split from their first love or made any number of different choices. Some people don't just wonder, they trace their first love, experiment with a same-sex relationship or have a wild fling. Sometimes, people who have an exploratory affair return to their relationship chastened, but more often it lights the fuse for something even more damaging. An exploratory affair suggests something is deeply wrong with a relationship and the love life in particular – as many people use this type of affair to experiment with different kinds of sex or to try on a different sexual persona. For example, I've heard justifications like 'I wanted to find out if it all still worked' and 'I knew there was a passionate woman hidden inside the dutiful wife and mother.' Even if the person having an exploratory affair or casual sex does decide to stay in their relationship, he or she seldom communicates any new-found sexual needs and, worse still, starts resenting his or her partner for not fulfilling them.

7. **Retaliatory.** As the name suggests, this affair is about getting revenge on an unfaithful partner by being

unfaithful yourself. A retaliatory affair turns a difficult situation into a toxic one and makes it harder for a couple to cooperate and resolve their sexual problems. Sometimes I meet people who have retaliatory sex to make their partner jealous – in the hope that this will rekindle his or her interest. More often, it is a straightforward desire to prove that they are attractive or to bolster their flagging self-esteem.

8. **Exit.** Break-ups are painful, hard and deeply unpleasant. Many people will embark on an exit affair to provide a boost to their self-confidence, gain some emotional support and to send their partner a clear message. An exit affair might seem like the end of the road for a marriage but these rebound relationships nearly always split up – partly because the new partners find it hard to trust each other (after all, the relationship was built on deceit) but mainly because once the dust has settled they often have little in common. (However, there is an exception. Exit affairs with childhood sweethearts or past lovers tend to be more durable.) If your relationship crumbled through low-sex or no sex-issues, tell your partner about the sort of sex life you'd like and show him or her this book.

Hope: Once couples have recovered from the initial trauma of discovering infidelity or being discovered, and taken stock of their relationship, many will decide to try again. With the flood of relief and the hope that things can be better comes a boost to their sex life. 'It felt really primeval,' says June, sixty-one, 'like I was reclaiming my man. It was passionate, needy and a little dark.' Her husband, Trevor, sixty, added: 'It was totally unexpected, June was doing things that she's hardly done before – like oral sex. It was a real roller coaster.'

Instead of occasional or same time of day/same way sex, the lovemaking during the hope stage is plentiful and adventurous. Unfortunately, relief can easily tip over into something quite dark, with the partner who discovered the infidelity becoming obsessed with details of the sexual transgressions. Bertie had been married for sixteen years and had two pre-teenage children when his wife admitted to a 'fumble' with a work colleague. At first, he was relieved that she broke off the affair and found another job. Unfortunately, he would get flashbacks while they had sex: 'She did this sexual act with him, this is what he must have seen.'

Attempted Normality: It might seem that the majority of the problems are all in the past. However, the discoverer of infidelity is still having bouts of despair or depression and the partner who was discovered is feeling guilty and checked-up on. Sadly, instead of talking, many couples keep their misgivings to themselves and plough on regardless. So while on the surface everything seems normal, underneath there are still unresolved issues.

For many couples, the initial burst of 'making-up' sex has diminished and the affair partner is still a presence – albeit metaphorically – in their bedroom. 'I found myself trying to compete and to be better than her – behaving like someone on those porn films,' said June. 'I hate myself but I can't stop.'

Trevor felt under pressure to perform too. 'There was one time, when I was tired, that I couldn't stay hard and June got all upset.'

June looked up from her pile of tissues: 'That's not how you were with her.'

If these issues are not addressed, each party will withdraw to their separate halves of the bed and begin to believe their sexual problems are insurmountable. (Fortunately, it wasn't too late for June and Trevor and there will be more about their journey later in the chapter.) Sometimes, when taking a sexual history of a couple at the beginning of their counselling, I find that affairs which have long since ended are still casting a shadow today. In an effect, the couple has been trapped in 'Attempted Normality' for years.

Despair – bodies float to the surface: A crisis brings both danger and opportunity and nowhere in the recovery process are these two outcomes more finely balanced than at this stage. In most relationships, couples know the underlying problems – she earns more than he does or he has an interfering mother – but they step round them and keep everything nice. While non-infidelity couples agree to differ about long-running issues, couples recovering from affairs are so determined to avoid the possibility of it happening again that they work harder, dig deeper and bring all the problems up to the surface. In the sexual arena, these can be long-term issues – such as frequency of lovemaking, pornography, who initiates sex or dressing up. Generally, both partners are only too aware of the problems but have chosen to ignore them. However, the crisis of infidelity can encourage one partner to reveal a secret from their past. These can include physical abuse from previous partners, babies born out of wedlock, abortions and, in particular, childhood sexual abuse. However painful it is to confront these issues, I am always cautiously optimistic as, at last, there is an opportunity to lay the ghosts to rest. (There is more about the impact of previous sexual abuse later in the chapter.)

Intense Learning: In the 'Attempted Normality' stage, all the problems were hidden or had not been properly addressed. Alternatively, the partner who had been unfaithful might have been holding back important information about the affair. By 'Intense Learning', both partners are in possession of all the facts and are ready to work on their relationship (rather than paper over the cracks or agree to 'try harder'). By the time Heather, fifty-six, got to the bottom of her husband Gareth's infidelity, she discovered two affairs – one more serious than the other: 'What I can't understand is how he claims that he loved both me and this other woman at the same time,' she said. It was more than an academic question. With Heather doubting he had been honest about his feelings during the affair, she doubted that he loved her today – and this was making her hold back both sexually and emotionally.

So I asked each of them to think about the ingredients for love. Gareth listed some qualities that could be shared with more than one person at a time: 'affection, respect, attraction, shared beliefs, mental rapport, physical attraction, joy, respect'. He also came up with some which needed to be exclusive: 'being faithful, integrity and trust'. Meanwhile, Heather duplicated many of Gareth's words but added: 'forgiveness, a soft place to land when in trouble, accepting partner's failings, sexual satisfaction, honesty and happiness'. The first few qualities suggested that she might be further along the healing process than she imagined.

From completing this exercise with many clients over the past few years, I would define love as three qualities: *Commitment*, *Intimacy* and *Passion*. Drawing on this definition, I challenged Gareth:

'It seems to me that you loved neither Heather nor this other woman. You might have felt passion for your mistress but weren't committed – or you would have set up home together. You might have been committed to Heather in a "paying the bills, eating Sunday lunch with the family" sort of way, but you weren't truly intimate. How can you be if you've been holding back so much?'

One of the triggers for the affair had been that Gareth lost his job after twenty years' loyal service with the same company and had been so depressed that it took him months to access the counselling and job-seeking services that had been part of his severance package. 'You couldn't open up to Heather about how much you were hurting or how betrayed you felt?'

Gareth looked down at his shoes.

'You might have told the other woman about that pain, but you weren't truly intimate because you were seeing yet another woman at the same time,' Heather pointed out.

Finally, Gareth turned to me: 'Using your definition of love and even my own, you're right. I wasn't truly in love with either Heather or this other woman.'

'However, over the last few weeks, you've told Heather everything.'

'About 98 per cent, I think,' Heather chipped in, 'and it's taken two years to get here.'

'But you've finally laid the basis to be intimate again and your sex life has improved beyond all recognition. It seems to me you're ready to love Heather again.'

From this conversation, Heather and Gareth each had a goal for Intense Learning. For Gareth, how could he demonstrate his commitment? (Especially as he often appeared more committed to the demands of his new job than to rebuilding his relationship with Heather.) For Heather, could she ask for what she needed and not settle for second best? (Especially as she considered 'sexual satisfaction' an important ingredient for love, but had not said anything when Gareth could not bear to be touched by her, during the period where she later discovered he was having the affair.)

Overcoming a roadblock to recovery

Sometimes when couples have talked and talked about what happened and intellectually feel over the affair but are still stuck emotionally, I find it helps to put them through this programme of graduated sensuality – even if a low- or no-sex situation was not one of the main causes of the affair. There are three ways it can help:

1. **Promoting honesty:** When couples put reaching an orgasm to one side, it frees them up to really enjoy touching, kissing and holding each other. Instead of foreplay lasting a matter of a minutes, couples begin to relax, the defences are lowered, and something inside clicks back into place. Over and over again, they report feeling closer than they have been in years. With this renewed sense of intimacy, many discovered partners will reveal details about the affair that they previously withheld. 'It took me a while to reveal the full extent of my infidelity while I was on business abroad,' explained Trevor (whom we met earlier in this chapter). 'Even when we renewed our vows in front of all our friends and family in the roof garden of a five-star hotel, I held details back because I was frightened that if I told the truth I'd lose June.' However, the graduated sensual touching exercises opened up a new level of honesty where Trevor felt both close enough to trust June and ready to admit to himself that his secret was maintaining the wall between them. 'I told June that there had been two one-night stands as well as

the affair,' explained Trevor, 'I got talking to these women in the hotel bar. I knew deep down that they were prostitutes but I pretended to myself they weren't because it was nice to talk to someone who wasn't a work colleague. Of course, we ended up in my room and afterwards I gave them money.' Immediately after the confession, June was angry and withdrawn but once the shock had subsided, she had a slightly different take: 'I was really glad he told me of his own free will – beforehand I'd got information from cross-questioning or had prised it out. I feel better in myself too. When you know there's something more but your partner keeps denying it, you start to doubt your own judgement. It was driving me crazy.' June did not feel like being touched for a couple of weeks but they soon returned to the programme and their intimacy had a new level of intensity. 'I wouldn't wish what I've been through on my worst enemy,' said June, 'but Trevor's infidelity has made me realise that we were just chugging along and not really communicating properly. However, nowadays, we're not only talking more but are also having the sort of sex we haven't had in years.'

2. **Providing structure:** Many couples find themselves going round and round the same painful material over and over again – sometimes six months after discovery. In some cases, there are still important details to be revealed but more often, the partner who discovered the affair (the Discoverer) is depressed, feeling alone and needs reassurance that their partner (the Discovered) really does care. So the Discoverer reopens the same old discussion partly because talking about his or her pain is the most obvious way of releasing those feelings but mainly because after

both parties have got upset, argued and made up, he or she hears the comforting words: 'I'm sorry', 'I love you', 'I won't do it again', and the couple have a cuddle.

After years of thinking it would be better if the Discoverer asked to be held rather than ask about some minor detail of infidelity, I started putting stuck couples on this programme. I found that each week's exercises – and the talking they promote afterwards – provided a structure which made the Discoverer feel that something was being done to repair the relationship (and the affair was not just being quietly dropped) and the Discovered feel that the past was not swallowing up any possible future together.

Even though all the main details of her husband's infidelity had been uncovered twelve months previously, Dee, fifty-eight, was still plagued by the details she knew and questions she couldn't answer. 'I will wake up at four in the morning and I can't get back to sleep, so I'll go down and start writing everything down to get it out of my head. All this time later, I'm still plagued by their "special relationship" and their "special attraction" and how they went to bed together only an hour after they first met. It's like a dull toothache that never goes away but flares up into something nasty, biting and painful.' Her husband, Roland, fifty-seven, explained: 'I can leave her with a cup of tea in bed, bright and full of beans, but two hours later I'll get a text telling me she wants to pack her bags and run away.'

So I asked to read her diaries and, along to the next session, she brought about a month's worth of entries in an exercise book. Many entries were eight or ten pages long and full of painful details repeated over and over again: "She's ten years younger", "He never had erectile problems and never required lubricant" and "Did he start wearing boxer shorts to please her, even though I'd already asked him to change to something more flattering?" It was clear that being in Dee's head was both exhausting and depressing. After talking about the diaries, Dee decided that she would change her approach. When a thought popped into her head about the affair, she would try and throw it away – rather than plant it, water it and let it grow into a jungle. At the same time, I introduced the structure of the Month of Sensuality – so that instead of talking about the affair they started touching each other. The two-pronged approach really worked. Dee stopped obsessing, the touching prompted discussions about their sexuality together (rather than Roland's with his mistress), and the occasional thought that would not wither and die, they talked about.

3. **Setting goals.** Many people have affairs either because they have lost hope that their relationship can change or because they feel ignored and side-lined. Although they want to believe their partner that 'Things will be better' or 'We'll make it work', the fear remains: 'Once he or she's got me back, everything will slip back to how it was before.' Worse still, many couples have made similar pledges before and nothing fundamentally changed. So why should it this time? Meanwhile, the affair partner is holding out the prospect of 'real' change and a 'new start' – whether this will be a change for the better remains to be seen. So how do you combat inertia from the past and the lure of a possible new relationship? Lots of Discoverers use the stick approach – chastising the Discovered for the

potential harm to their children, their finances and themselves. These arguments are perfectly valid but it is hardly an inspiring banner to march under. Instead of the stick approach, try offering a carrot. And what better carrot is there than reinventing your sex life? Even better, rather than vague promises to try harder, this programme provides concrete steps for moving forward. (There is also more about how to bring lasting change to your relationship in another of my books: *Help Your Partner Say 'Yes': Seven steps to achieving better cooperation and communication.*)

Dealing With Sexual Jealousy

Jealousy is a very understandable emotion – particularly after an affair – but it is also incredibly destructive. Bertie, whom we met earlier in this chapter, discovered that rather than a brief sexual fumble, his wife had a four-month affair and her lover had taken explicit photos of her: 'My wife has been my only sexual partner and to that end I saw her as wholesome. The thought of her sexual exploits makes me physically flinch; I find it totally disgusting and that makes it hard to have close contact with her.' He genuinely felt that he could never come to terms with what she had done. So what can be done when you are so jealous that it makes it impossible to heal?

Understand the jealousy
At the heart of jealousy is fear. Someone is going to take something precious from us – and we are not going to be able to cope with pain. In fact, the hurt is so overwhelming that, for many people like Bertie, the only option is to withdraw

love or leave altogether. They imagine that choosing to end the relationship rather than waiting for their partner to leave, and thereby taking control, somehow lessens the pain. However, after spending twenty-five years helping couples cope with the aftermath of relationship break-up, I would say it makes not a jot of difference whether someone leaves or is left, the hurt is equal and, counter-intuitively, the person who sticks at the relationship, rather than the leaver, normally makes the best long-term recovery. This is because stickers are less likely to jump into a new relationship and make the same mistakes all over again. Ultimately, trying to run away from jealousy does not work. Fortunately, there is an alternative: understanding.

If jealousy is a problem in your relationship, ask yourself: Why am I so frightened of loss? Why do I think I will not be able to cope? What happened in my childhood that might explain my extreme reactions?

The next component of jealousy is low self-esteem. Deep inside, Bertie believed that since his wife had the opportunity to compare his lovemaking skills with those of another man, he would automatically be found wanting. However, it is perfectly possible that Bertie's wife would discover that, like most affair sex, it was lustful but empty and that she much preferred the caring and committed lovemaking on offer at home.

If low self-esteem is an issue, ask yourself: Why do I have such a low opinion of myself? Is there a small voice inside my head running me down or do the messages come from other people? How could I challenge these destructive voices and these negative messages? (There is more help in another of my books: *Learn to Love Yourself Enough: Seven steps to improving your self-esteem and your relationships*.)

Take a fresh look at your attitudes

Underpinning a lot of jealousy is the notion that our partner *belongs* to us. The idea is reinforced by marriage ceremonies 'Do you take this man . . .' and 'Who gives this woman . . .' and popular songs and movies. However, people are not possessions. We might give ourselves sexually to our partner but they don't 'own' us – because that is a heartbeat away from controlling, knowing what's best for us and, in the worst cases, domestic violence. Owning is the opposite of loving.

There was something else lurking behind Bertie's jealousy; he was as much upset that his 'wholesome image' of his wife had been destroyed as by what she'd actually done. I can understand his shock. His wife was not like the image that he'd carefully constructed and nurtured over the years. From my therapist's perspective, she's actually become a whole lot more interesting. She had the courage to pose for revealing photos and she was on the threshold of breaking out of the 'nice girl'/'wife and mother' stereotype and starting to explore her full sexuality. Of course, that's terribly frightening as we all like to corral our partners into a safe corner and for them to be just how we imagine – rather than accept their true complexity. During my journalism career, I interviewed many authors and was intrigued to find that most of their families do not read their books (or only with great reluctance). I think it is because writing reveals a lot about the writer and many partners are uncomfortable about the distance between how they like to see their partner and the person revealed in the work.

Ultimately, one of the challenges of recovering from infidelity is taking back our cherished but probably one-dimensional view of our partner and updating it with something more multifaceted. However, there is a consolation prize. This sense that we can never truly know our partner and that there is always more to discover promotes intrigue, passion and a more rewarding sex life.

Talk about the flashbacks away from the bedroom

It is not necessary to explain every horrible twist of your jealous imagination but if you say nothing about your behaviour and the reasons behind it, your partner can easily draw the wrong conclusions. When Miriam, forty-eight, discovered her husband's affair and some very graphic texts describing their lovemaking, she was consumed by jealousy: 'This woman kept on going on about what a wonderful kisser he was and how his "urgent tongue conquered her resistance". It made me feel physically sick and just the thought of him kissing me made my flesh crawl. So if he made to kiss me, I'd turn my head.' Unfortunately, she did not explain how kissing triggered vivid pictures of her husband with the other woman. Later in counselling, her husband revealed that he had interpreted the lack of kisses as Miriam finding him disgusting. She quickly clarified that she found the images of the infidelity, not him, disgusting and the atmosphere in the counselling room changed dramatically. In most cases, I find people have constructed a far worse reason for their partner's coldness than the real one. Explaining triggers for jealous feelings, what I call 'showing where the bodies are buried', will not only clear up any misunderstanding but will also recruit your partner to be a helpmate for resolving the problems – instead of the enemy and the source of the pain.

Unfortunately, most couples start to talk about the jealousy after it has ruined a round of lovemaking. This may be the worst possible moment. Instead of discussion being informed by rational thought, it is hijacked by hurt, rejection and anger. So follow my golden rule and discuss sexual jealousy away from the bedroom and never after consuming alcohol.

Find good images to replace the bad ones

Instead of allowing the jealous flashback to take root and sour your day, try replacing it with a positive one. This might be a picture of yourself in a favourite or beautiful place or a happy memory from your relationship. Alternatively, try superimposing the painful or tainted image with something new that belongs to just you and your partner.

Gareth and Heather, whom we met earlier in the chapter, seemed to have recovered their sexual vibrancy until what Heather called 'a very loving and generous gesture' brought Gareth's infidelity into their bedroom. 'We'd been making love,' she explained, 'but Gareth was tired and couldn't sustain his erection. In the past, that would have been it and we'd have stopped, but instead he helped me reach a climax with his fingers. A dark voice inside my head wondered why, after all these years, he'd done it, but I pushed the idea away and enjoyed the moment.' Unfortunately, the idea that he had learned this trick from his affair partner had taken root and the next morning, during a coffee break from working on the garden together, she asked if this was true. Fortunately, Gareth was straight with Heather and explained that his mistress had often wanted him to make love for a second time but he had been unable to and instead had masturbated her.

So instead of letting masturbation belong to the affair, I suggested they put a twist on this form of lovemaking and reclaim it for themselves – by doing something that neither they nor Gareth and the affair partner had done before. Ultimately, the answer came out of kissing, cuddling and sensual touching. 'We started fondling each other,' explained

Gareth, 'and it got more and more intense until I was masturbating Heather and she was masturbating me at the same time. Normally we'd have stopped and had intercourse but it felt so good that we continued and came within about a minute of each other.' They had replaced a bad image with a good one.

Recovering From Sexual Abuse

Touch is one of the most powerful forms of communication. Sometimes, it brings us closer to our partner than hours of talking. Holding our partner tight can make him or her feel safer and more likely to open up than anything else. No wonder working on your love life can release long-buried secrets. The most common one is that someone was sexually abused as a child or a teenager.

Lynne, whom we met earlier in this chapter, revealed that a group of boys whom she'd hung out with as a fifteen-year-old had taken advantage of her. 'I was a cocky kid. Always mouthing off about this or that and I suppose I came across as more knowledgeable and experienced about sex than I really was. I wanted to impress the boys, I wanted to be liked, and one boy dared me to come into the park toilets with him.' Lynne started to cry.

My approach when people reveal abuse is not to push for details or encourage them to 'relive' the experience in the hope of exorcising the pain (as this seems needlessly painful and I don't think it really helps). Instead, I allow them enough time to tell me what they choose.

'The other boys followed us in, but it was mainly one boy.'

However, in order to understand the impact on today – and their sex lives in particular – I will ask for 'the headlines'.

'What did he do?'

'He tried to rape me but I struggled, made a lot of noise and they got frightened and ran away.'

'Did you tell anybody?'

'Nobody until this week. We'd made love and I was lying in Michael's arms and it sort of tumbled out.'

The abuse triangle

Abuse brings up all sorts of powerful feelings. Sometimes, in my counselling room, it feels like the emotions are bouncing off the walls or closing in on us. This is probably because abusers ignore boundaries (between what is acceptable behaviour and what is not) or overwhelm the protective barriers of victims. Therefore, the painful feelings know no boundaries either and can easily get attached somewhere they don't belong. The best way to understand this phenomenon is to think of a triangle.

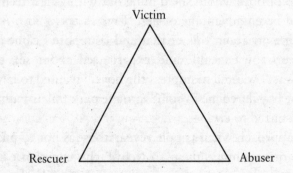

When Lynne confided in Michael, he had became the rescuer. 'I told her that there was nothing to be ashamed about and it wasn't her fault,' he said. So far, so good. However, the abuse triangle is never very stable. The couple lived in a small town and Michael knew Lynne's abuser.

'I got really angry about what he'd done to Lynne and wanted to go round and punch his lights out,' he told me.

At this point, everybody on the triangle switched places. Michael became the 'abuser' (vigilante violence is never the answer). Lynne got terribly agitated because she was worried everything would come out and had sprung to her abuser's defence. In other words, she had become the 'rescuer' and her abuser had become the 'victim'.

In other cases, the abuse triangle can be even more insidious. I had worked with Rosemary, forty-eight, and her partner in the aftermath of his affair and guided them through the seven steps towards a renewed relationship, but something was holding her back: 'Thomas and I have a much better sex life. We talk more than ever before. I've had a promotion. Life should be good, but it's like I'm wearing a black cloak.'

'What kind of cloak?' I asked. 'A fashionable little poncho?'

'No, floor-to-ceiling with a hood.'

I have to admit that I was puzzled. I would not have expected something so all-enveloping at this stage. So we tried replacing negative images with positives ones but with only limited success. When Rosemary had found out about Thomas's infidelity, she had leaned heavily on her friends but, over time, became embarrassed about the amount of support she'd needed and just how much they knew about her (especially her weaknesses) and had withdrawn. Hoping that sharing with friends again would make the cloak a little lighter, I encouraged her to take up an invitation from one of them to go out for a drink.

The next week, she told me about her night out and how she found herself talking about something that she'd basically forgotten. 'It was not like a suddenly remembered memory, but I'd put this incident in a box, buried it and told myself "It's all the in the past" and "Get on with your life",' she explained.

'On the one hand, you'd buried this box so well that it had ceased to exist. Yet on the other hand, you knew the secret coordinates.' I checked out that I'd heard her correctly.

Rosemary nodded and went on to tell about her protected and happy childhood. 'My best friend had an older brother who was a bit of a rogue. I knew he was trouble but I ignored my gut instincts. I suppose I thought I was invincible.' At eighteen, Rosemary had been out for a drink with a gang of friends and had bumped into this man. He joined the group and at the end of the evening offered to give Rosemary a lift home. She could have phoned her dad or taken the bus home but she accepted. 'I found him rather exciting and danger-ous.' However, she got more than she bargained for. 'He stopped the car in the middle of nowhere and switched off the engine. "You've got two choices: You can either go down on this," he said, and he pointed to a bulge in his trousers, "or get out of the car and find your own way home." I thought of all the fuss from Dad about "putting myself at risk" and "being stupid" and I didn't want to upset everybody so instead of getting out, I took the other option. The next morn-ing, I told myself "nobody got hurt" and "I'm stronger than this" and I went in to college as if nothing had happened.'

However, something had happened. 'Over the years, I've become quite hard. If they want somebody fired, they always ask me. I'm rational, unemotional and get the job done. Deep down, I suppose I thought that if I can deal with that abuse – no problem – surely they can cope with being fired. So many times I've told colleagues to pull themselves together and stop bringing their private stuff to work. I've been a complete bitch.' In effect, Rosemary had been perilously close to abusing her colleagues. Certainly, I considered her lack of regard for her needs as abusive towards herself. 'When I discovered Thomas's affair, I didn't even go in late. I could cope. No sick days for me. Nothing would hurt me, how stupid. Because I made myself ill and ended up in hospital due to the stress.'

What to do if your partner reveals abuse. Although most of the help, quite rightly, is focused on the 'victim' of the abuse, it is equally important that their partner gets support too. It is horrible to discover that someone you love has been through these terrible experiences and the story can hang like a cloud over your relationship. In some cases, the partner finds their loving sex has been tainted by the past abusive sex or feels like the abuser for suggesting anything more than a kiss and a cuddle. (Remember, the abuse triangle is never solid and all the positions can change very easily.) If this sounds familiar, here are some guidelines for coping in the aftermath of your partner's disclosure:

- **Report your anger rather than act it out.** By this I mean tell your partner: 'I feel angry about . . .' but don't seek revenge on your partner's behalf. At the other extreme, don't keep your feelings bottled up as this could be perceived as being angry with your partner or rejecting him or her.

- **Take your lead from your partner.** Go along with your partner's approach to dealing with the problem. It is terribly important for 'victims' of abuse to be in charge – after all, they certainly were not when the abuse happened. So if he or she wants to report the abuser to the police or to confront the relevant family member or to let the matter drop, that's up to him or her. It's fine to give your opinion and help your partner think through the consequences but the decision is not yours to make. Your job is, ultimately, to support your partner.

- **Be patient and ready to listen.** It will take your partner time to unload all the pain and talking will bring up fresh memories. The journey can take years rather than weeks and months, especially as some 'victims' will not seek legal redress until after their parents have died (because they would be, in some way, 'letting them down' or 'the shame will kill them' or they don't want their mother or father to be upset for not 'protecting them' from the abuser).

How to move forward. This is a huge subject, and there are many excellent books on recovering from sexual abuse, so I will focus down on reducing the impact of the disclosure on your relationship and your lovemaking.

- **Deal with the blame.** Many victims feel that they were in some way to blame. Lynne was angry with herself for being 'a gobby know-it-all' and that in some way 'I had it coming to me.' Rosemary felt it was her fault for accepting the lift. This is nonsense. In many cases, abusers are adults in positions of power and the victim has little or no control. Even when the abuser is a near contemporary, the victim does not have second sight and the ability to read or be responsible for the secret intentions of the abuser. Be aware that many abusers rationalise themselves into the 'victim' role by blaming the object of their abuse

– 'She egged me on' or 'He wanted it.' (We're back to the abuse triangle being profoundly unstable.) Sadly, many victims take these groundless accusations as the truth. Fortunately, talking about what happened exposes all the negative self-talk associated with abuse and any double-think from the abusers which has been internalised. Slowly, over time, it is possible to have a more balanced view and to put blame where it really truly belongs.

- **Frame the problems in the 'now'.** It is always better to focus on how the abuse is still affecting you today than wishing you could change what happened yesterday. Neil, forty-three, had been repeatedly forced to have sex by his long-term foster-father (who had abused most of the children in his care). He came into counselling with his second wife, Alison, not because of sexual problems – their love-making was the glue for their relationship – but because of repeated rows and his 'moodiness'. Neil had disclosed the abuse early in their relationship: 'I don't know why, because I never told my first wife, but perhaps I thought Alison would understand, perhaps I knew keeping it secret ruined my first marriage.' However, he had not told her much more than those headlines so she did not understand the full impact on him today. Over six months of counselling, he explained that he got angry when Alison shut the door – not because he was being 'difficult' as she imagined – but because Neil's abuser shut the bedroom door so his foster-mother could not hear what was happening upstairs. He explained that he did not have an irrational fear of bananas, as Alison had thought. If he had 'misbehaved' as a kid, he would be sent up to bed with no tea but with a banana for energy and this would be the time when his foster-father was most likely to strike. Once Alison understood the overhang from Neil's past abuse, many of the triggers for their current arguments disappeared.

- **Take control.** Look at how past abuse affects your sex life today. Unsurprisingly, Rosemary was not particularly keen on giving oral sex: 'I do it because Thomas enjoys it and I want to give him pleasure.' This is hardly the foundation for passionate lovemaking. So I broke down the ingredients that brought back the strongest memories for Rosemary: 'If Thomas holds my head, that puts me straight back in the car.' Thomas had not been aware of this hangover and readily agreed not to touch her head if she performed oral sex on him.

  Next, I helped Rosemary take control and set the pace of how fast oral sex progressed. What would happen if she licked around the penis, tantalising all the most sensitive points (like underneath the head) and slowly building up the sexual tension, until finally *she* chose the moment to put Thomas's penis into her mouth? In this way, she would be actively *giving* Thomas oral sex and would be completely in control. The couple tried this experiment and Rosemary found she could detach this aspect of making love from her past trauma.

- **Become a survivor.** When abuse is buried or forgotten, it is not possible to challenge all the distorted thinking or ease the pain. Under these circumstances, the person who suffered the abuse will feel like a 'victim'. However, once he or she accepts that this abuse really did happen (rather than pretending or wishing it did not), he or she can begin to understand both the ways that the abuse has affected them *and* how they have overcome or transcended the trauma. Sometimes, people even discover it has made them stronger or more sensitive to other people's distress. In this way, they move from being a 'victim' through to being a 'survivor'. Ultimately, this is a better place to be but it takes time and hard work to achieve this goal.

Summary

- When our partner has a low level of desire, it is easy to think there is something wrong with either ourselves or with them. However, sex is complex and the answers are seldom that simple.

- The way that men and women have been socialised (and to a lesser extent our biology) leads to different approaches to sex, which makes it harder to understand each other's viewpoint and creates a barrier to good lovemaking.

- Most sexual problems have their roots in the myth that sex must include intercourse.

- Men and women have very different attitudes to pornography and every couple has to decide for themselves what is acceptable and what is not. Unfortunately, when men are depressed or low, they often use porn to 'medicate' their feelings and in the long-run this can lead to serious relationship problems.

- Affairs put the spotlight on a couple's sex life and break through cosy conspiracies like 'It's not that important' or 'We're too tired' and help them reinvent how they make love.

- Ultimately, all it takes to have a better sex life is knowledge and a vocabulary to discuss what turns you on with your partner – two things which I hope this book has given you.

Exercises

Simmering
Many people are so cut off from their sexuality that they miss the everyday triggers for feeling desire. The following exercise will not only help you recognise the sparks but will also help fan them into flames:

- When you see someone attractive on the street, give yourself permission to enjoy their beauty, the way they move or how they make you feel. Alternatively, if you prefer, it could be a character in a movie or celebrity. (Don't feel guilty about getting turned on by someone other than your partner. People with good levels of desire naturally allow the inspiration all around them to help their passion simmer.)

- Take a moment out of your day to dream about what you'd like this beautiful person to do to or with you. Picture everything in detail, their hands touching you, their mouth begging to be kissed. Allow the images to simmer in your head.

- Later, in a quiet moment, bring the images back and watch your private erotic movie again.

- The third time round, superimpose your partner's head on to the stranger or celebrity and imagine him or her making love to you. Once again, let the images simmer and the desire begin to bubble up. You are a sexual being and have the right to enjoy these feelings.

- At the end of the day, when you greet your partner, allow a frame or a couple of images from your exotic movie to play in your head. This will guarantee a smile on your face, something more than a cold peck on the cheek and, most importantly, set up a good evening together.

- At the end of the week, look back at all the sexual impulses and celebrate them. Have there been more than you expected? Have there been triggers in the past but you were not paying enough attention?

How To Stop a Porn Habit From Getting Out of Control
Internet porn has the potential to be highly addictive, so if you're concerned about the amount of time consumed by pornography, the effect on your relationship or your own self-esteem, take control with the following steps:

1. **Don't go cold turkey.** Probably you have vowed never to use porn again and maybe even stopped for a while, but slowly have slipped back into using again. This is because stopping alone is not enough, you need to understand what unpins your porn usage.

2. **Monitor your consumption.** These are the key things:

- What are the triggers?

- How do you feel when using pornography?

- How much time has passed?

- How do you feel afterwards?

(When I did this exercise with Shane he found his triggers were: 'feeling sorry for myself', 'I deserve this for working hard', 'loneliness', 'an aching feeling inside' and 'celebration after hearing some good news'. The feelings whilst consuming were 'trance' and 'out of body' and 'paralysis' – all signs that he was using pornography to self-medicate. Shane reported that he was using for pornography about five or six hours a week and afterwards felt 'resignation', 'shame' and 'pathetic'.)

3. **Tackle the triggers.** Think about alternatives for dealing with triggers rather than going on to the Internet. If you are feeling stressed and need to unwind, what about phoning a friend or talking to your partner about what happened? If there are particular danger points – like Friday night – plan ahead and find other ways of occupying yourself. What other diversion tactics could you use?

4. **Live the feelings.** When it comes to difficult feelings – like sadness, feeling sorry for yourself and loneliness, there are three ways to cope. The first is blocking them out (which you have been doing with pornography). The second is diverting your feelings (for example, switching on the TV and distracting yourself). The third is to look the feelings directly in the eye. By this I mean acknowledging them (I'm feeling . . .), accepting them (Everybody feels . . . from time to time) rather than trying to rationalise them away or ignoring them. Next, allow yourself to experience the relevant emotion (just sit quietly and see if you can bear it). In my experience, feelings are magnified by blocking them out. When they are 'lived' they are normally unpleasant but not as scary as you might imagine. (Shane was amazed to discover

that rather than plunging into depression, as he feared, the down feelings quickly passed. There was another bonus, no more morning-after regrets from a night of Internet pornography.)

5. **Listen to the feelings and make the changes.** Our feelings normally have something important to tell us. (For example, Shane's were telling him that he needed to spend less time at work and more socialising so that he could find a partner.) Unfortunately, we don't always like the message and rationalise it away ('I've got to work hard or my business will suffer'). Sometimes the message is inconvenient, frightening or threatens to turn our life upside down. ('I'm bored and unfulfilled by my sex life with my partner, but if I say anything, he or she will be upset and angry.'). It is as if you are a square-shaped peg trying to fit into a round-shaped hole (and self-medicating to cope with the pain). What would be better: face the problem head-on and change, or keep blanking out the feelings and maintain the status quo?

6. **Be realistic.** If the problems are deep-rooted – for example, abuse when you were a child – it might be too painful to listen to your feelings without professional support. If you have been using pornography in a compulsive manner for a long time, your life has become chaotic or your behaviour destructive, you should also consider entering a seven-step programme or joining a support group.

What is a Healthy Sexuality?

Whether you are struggling with a porn habit and considering where the boundary between acceptable and unacceptable behaviour is, or thinking about asking your partner to experiment with a particular sexual practice, it is useful to have a positive benchmark against which to test yourself. So ask yourself the following questions:

- Does this activity build self-esteem?

- Are there any negative consequences?

- Will I be hurting my partner or other people?

- What would my partner say if he or she found out?

- Taking into consideration my answers to the first four questions, what is okay sexual behaviour?

- Taking into consideration my answers to the first four questions, what is *not* acceptable sexual behaviour?

- What activities might be on slippery slope, i.e., acceptable behaviours but which might encourage me to tip over into unacceptable ones?

(When I did this exercise with Shane, he decided that *healthy* sexuality included 'sex with feelings', 'consensual sex' and 'asking for sex', but *unhealthy* sexuality included 'pestering for sex', 'paying a prostitute' and 'pornography'. For slippery-slope activity, he decided to include 'going for a massage – even if I keep my pants on' and that it would be better if he hired a man rather than a woman the next time he had back problems.)

Sexual Jeopardy

It is difficult to ask your partner's opinions about sex or to initiate a discussion about what you enjoy and how to improve your lovemaking. So I suggest my clients turn it into a game. Write all the questions below on separate pieces of paper, fold them up and put them in a hat. Toss a coin to see who goes first and picks a question to ask. After the other person has answered, the questioner gives his or her opinion too. Swap over and the other partner takes a question. For the yes/no questions, there is a supplementary question: Why? What? Tell me more.

What is the one thing you've never been able to tell me about sex?

How does your mood impact on our lovemaking?

How important is romance in lovemaking?

In your opinion, what is the difference between having sex and making love?

Do you think role playing during sex is interesting?

What are you embarrassed to ask for during sex?

What do you think of your body?

Which part of my body do you like the most?

Do you think our sex life has enough variety?

What is the most important part of lovemaking to you?

What do you think foreplay should consist of?

What do you wish I would do more of?

What do you wish I would do less of?

Why do you fall asleep/want to talk after sex?

Do you like oral sex?

Do we have sex enough?

Complete this sentence. 'I really like it when you . . .'

Do you have a fantasy you want to act on/out?

How can I show you that I want sex?

Is there anything about sex that makes you uncomfortable?

Would sex toys improve our lovemaking?

Do we need to change the places we make love [either location or the general environment]?

How can we make sex better?

Central Task for Addressing Specific Sexual Issues: The Cake of Desire

Many people think of desire as something that either they feel or they don't. If they are in the mood for sex – brilliant. If they're not – tough. However, I prefer to think of desire as like a cake. You might go to the cake tin and find it's empty, but if you have the recipe and know where to find the ingredients, you can soon bake one. While a cake needs eggs, butter, flour, sugar and water, what does desire need?

When I did this task with Rosemary, she came up with the following ingredients. I have put the most important one first:

- I'm happy with my relationship.

- I feel cared for.

- He's interested in and concerned about me.

- He finds me attractive.

- He says, 'You look beautiful' (and means it).

- Feeling appreciated.

- Time together.

- Playful touching.

- I prioritise myself and my pleasures (rather than being overrun with work).

In just the same way as there are hundreds of different types of cakes – chocolate, carrot, Victoria sponge, fruit cake, cheese cake – each with a different recipe; there are hundreds of different types of desire with a multitude of ingredients which can be combined to create a happy sex life. Draw up your list of ingredients and ask your partner to draw up his or hers. What are the differences? What are the similarities? Finally, how can you support each other's desire?

What Next for Research into Prairie Voles?

Scientists are still probing the link between bonding and oxytocin. However, the majority of the recent work has not been about promoting desire but whether oxytocin and vasopressin can combat the effects of social isolation. When it comes to translating this research from voles to humans, the focus has been on autism (a problem in the brain that makes communication and interaction more difficult). There has been some success with a nose spray (the best way of crossing the blood/brain barrier) which encouraged people to look someone in the eye, made them more likely to have positive memories of an event, and increased levels of trust in games played in the laboratory. If this work is successful, it would certainly ease the life of people with autism who find eye contact difficult (and thereby misinterpret a lot of what is being said) and make social situations easier for them.

Recently, there has been some work at Ohio State University into the impact of oxytocin and vasopressin on the quality of loving relationships. Thirty-seven heterosexual married couples were invited to discuss the history of their relationship and a particular contentious issue between them. Meanwhile, scientists monitored the amounts of oxytocin and vasopressin in their blood and discovered that those with higher levels were more likely to have positive discussions and those with lower levels to have negative ones. However, it is impossible to know whether higher amounts of these hormones lead to a better relationship or whether a good relationship raises the level of oxytocin in the blood.

In a nutshell, we are unlikely to have a pill or a spray that will make us fall in love or want sex any time soon. However, there are two simple conclusions that we can draw from all the prairie voles research. First, prairie voles spend a lot of time together – and most couples would benefit from more day-to-day contact. Second, prairie voles are incredibly tactile, forever grooming each other and huddling together, and most couples need to touch each other in a non-sexual way in order to build desire and improve their overall sexual connection.

In a Nutshell

My aim in writing this book is to give you a vocabulary and a confidence to talk about sex with your partner. At the centre, there is a ten-week programme of graduated exercises. They start by stripping your sex life back to basics, banning intercourse and then slowly reintroducing different activities and ways of looking at your partner, your body and your sexuality. Finally, I encourage you to step out of your comfort zone and explore new ideas for lovemaking.

A Month of Sensuality (see Step Two)

Each of these exercises start with fifteen minutes of touching and then swapping over for fifteen minutes of being touched and, as the weeks progress, adding extra ingredients.

Week One   *Cuddling and Sensual Touching.* Experiment with different ways of touching your partner – firm like a back rub or light and teasing – but avoid the genitals.

Week Two	*Kissing.* Stay with sensual touch but find new places to kiss your partner and different ways (butterfly, slobbering and nibbling), and still avoid the genitals. Finish with a lingering kiss on your partner's lips or mouth and keep your eyes open.
Week Three	*Advanced Sensual Touching.* Stay with sensual touch and kissing, but add in new sensations by caressing each other with different fabrics and implements. Finish off by showing each other how you like your breasts or nipples to be stimulated and guiding your partner's hand so that he or she knows how to replicate these pleasures.
Week Four	*Being Sexual Together.* Stay with sensual touch, kissing and your favourite elements of advanced sensual touch, and finish the session by masturbating yourselves in front of each other. Look at how your partner likes to be touched, so you can incorporate that knowledge into future lovemaking.

A Fortnight of Wickedness (see Step Three)

Week Five	*Show and Tell.* Take a long look at yourself in the mirror – long enough to go beyond your normal reaction to yourself naked. Say aloud or write down what you like about your body. Next examine your genitals, in detail – as if you've never seen them before. What positive

things have you discovered? Later in the week, stand naked with your partner in front of the mirror. Tell him or her what you like about your body. Show him or her your hidden or less visible parts. Look carefully at how your partner handles his or her genitals as this will provide clues for how you might touch them. Finally, give compliments to each other.

Week Six *Focus on Arousal.* After five minutes of sensual touching, the first partner begins to explore the other's genitals and then slowly mixes genital touching with whole-body touching. This exercise is not about arousing your partner, so don't worry if the penis is not erect or the vagina is not lubricated at the beginning, this is about making love to the whole person. Finish with a cuddle rather than an orgasm.

A Fortnight of Variety (see Step Four)

Week Seven *Different Strokes.* Start with the usual sensual touching and kissing to get into the mood for being sexual together. After a while, once the touchee is in the mood, he or she starts to play with his or her genitals. The toucher watches and then puts his or her hands over the touchee's and shadows the style and type of masturbation. Finally, the toucher takes over and masturbates the touchee. Afterwards, switch over roles.

Week Eight *Oral Sex.* Start this exercise by having a shower or bath together and thoroughly wash each other's genitals. The toucher builds from sensual touching to fondling genitals and graduating to using tongue, lips and mouth to give pleasure. Finally, the toucher brings the touchee to orgasm either orally or manually (or using a vibrator). Afterwards, swap over and the toucher becomes the touchee.

A Fortnight of Expansion (see Step Five)

Week Nine *Partner A Chooses.* Flip a coin and decide who goes first and takes charge of your sex life. Everything from your past styles of lovemaking is on the menu again – including intercourse – but Partner A can come up with something new that has not been done before or not for a long time. Partner B will give this idea his or her full consideration and try and find a way of incorporating it either in full or in part. It is worth noting that this is an experiment and agreeing to try something is not tantamount to signing up for this activity for life. Afterwards, discuss what you enjoyed and what elements you would like to continue using.

Week Ten *Partner B Chooses.* It is Partner B's chance to introduce something new into the relationship and for Partner A to try and embrace the idea. This is your chance to show your partner something new about your sexuality. How could you invite your partner into your journey of discovery? Finish off with another discussion and how you can use this new knowledge.

What if My Partner Will Not Cooperate?

Although there is a lot about your own sexuality to be learned from reading this book, the main benefits come from doing the programme as a couple. So if your partner has doubts, what should you do?

- Check how you have presented the programme. Is it as criticism or as an opportunity to change? Tell your partner how much you love him or her, talk about the pleasures of your current lovemaking and how you'd like to build on these achievements.

- Have you set it as a secret test? If you're angry and resentful and using your partner's reaction to this book as a way of deciding whether to stay or go, your feelings will leak out through your tone of voice and body language. Under these circumstances, your partner will be worried that trying and failing will become a stick to beat him or her.

- Instead of working on your marriage, trying working on yourself instead. The first approach risks gridlock, as it suggests that your partner needs to change before anything can improve. However, working on yourself will break the gridlock as any changes that you make will have a positive knock-on effect on your partner's behaviour.

What if We Hit a Block?

Every couple needs to find their own pace through this programme, so do not be downhearted if outside events or personal fears make progress difficult.

- I believe that ultimately every couple knows best what is right for them and their love life.

- So, although I have a general programme, it can be tailored to suit your particular needs, situation and goals. If something is not right for you, skip that part.

- However, I recommend that every couple puts a temporary ban on intercourse and follows the first four weeks of the programme. It is vital that the message that a cuddle = intercourse is broken.

- If you need longer at one particular phase than a week, that is fine. Stay with that exercise until both of you feel ready to continue. It is not a race.

- Whatever happens, keep talking. This is especially important when you feel blocked. After all, if you can talk about your problems and your fears, you are half-way to solving them.

Final Summary

- Good sex is about good communication. By learning to talk and listen better, you improve giving and receiving in the bedroom.

- Taking a break from having intercourse is often the first step to becoming more sensual and improving your love life.

- It is never too late to change and have a passionate and plentiful sex life.

- All you need is a little knowledge, patience and the belief that things will improve.

Make Love Like a Prairie Vole

Have the sex you want by recruiting your partner into Andrew's programme – even if he or she is not a keen reader – with this innovative app.

- 11 Detailed Videos — Andrew explains the key concepts in the book and takes you through his 10 Week Plan. Each week's exercise is demonstrated by a couple, so you have a clear understanding of the techniques.

- Sex Diary — Keep your own sex diary within the app to record your progress as a couple (not included in the paperback or eBook). Also featuring the fascinating results of Andrew's sex survey.

- Simmering Diary — Learn about simmering from Andrew and keep your own simmering diary within the app to record the simmering triggers you encounter.

- Interactive 'Test Your Sexual Style' quiz from the book specially designed to facilitate sharing with your partner.

- Extra articles on: 'How to Talk about Sex' and 'The Curse of the Soul Mate.'

This app is like having marital therapy but at a fraction of the cost.

andrewgmarshall.com